Cost Proxy Models and Telecommunications Policy

Regulation of Economic Activity
General Editors, Nancy L. Rose and Richard Schmalensee
MIT Sloan School of Management

Cost Proxy Models and Telecommunications Policy

A New Empirical Approach to Regulation

Farid Gasmi
D. Mark Kennet
Jean-Jacques Laffont
William W. Sharkey

The MIT Press
Cambridge, Massachusetts
London, England

This book was set in Palatino by Interactive Composition Corporation and was printed and bound in the United States of America.

Library of Congress Cataloging-in-Publication Data

Cost proxy models and telecommunications policy: a new empirical approach to regulation / Farid Gasmi . . . [et al.].
     p. cm. — (Regulation of economic activity ; 22)
   Includes bibliographical references and index.
   ISBN 0-262-07237-8 (hc : alk. paper)
   1. Telecommunication—Law and legislation—United States. 2. Telecommunication policy—United States. 3. Telecommunication—United States—Costs—Econometric models. I. Gasmi, Farid. II. Series.

KF2765 .C67 2002
384′.041—dc21   2002024611

to Aaron, Ali, Bénédicte, Benjamin, Bertrand, Cécile, Charlotte, Michael, Nadine, and Rebecca

Contents

Series Foreword

Government regulation of economic activity has undergone dramatic change during the past quarter-century. This has been marked by regulatory retrenchment in the United States, and by large-scale privatization of government-owned enterprises elsewhere. Reforms have ranged from dismantling the regulatory apparatus in sectors such as transportation and energy, to substantially relaxing regulatory restrictions in industries such as financial services, and to large-scale restructuring of markets and regulatory mechanisms as in the telecommunications and electric utility industries around the world. Economic analysis has played an important role in these initiatives. Empirical research on regulatory regimes and the performance of state-owned enterprise buttressed policy makers searching for ways to improve productivity and government budgets. Theoretical models incorporating informational asymmetries between regulated firms and oversight agencies suggested fundamental new approaches to regulatory institutions. Economists have played important advisory roles in the design of market mechanisms to replace regulatory procedures, and been active participants in the evaluation of performance in many reformed or restructured markets. There is tremendous excitement about these changes, although the implementation and performance of many of these regulatory initiatives remain controversial.

As traditional monopoly telecommunications systems have been restructured to promote competition, the regulation of remaining local monopoly segments, and the terms under which competitors can interconnect with these monopoly providers, raises a variety of new, complex issues that can be answered by neither theory nor traditional empirical analysis alone. This work by Gasmi, Kennet, Laffont, and Sharkey addresses some of the most significant challenges facing telecommunications regulators and policy makers with an innovative and provocative approach that marries an engineering cost model of local telecommunications networks to the insights of modern regulatory theory. The resulting model can be used to simulate market conditions and analyze responses to alternative regulatory rules. Moreover the authors invite the reader to explore with them. A CD-ROM included with the book contains the programs and data to reproduce the results in the book, or construct new results under alternative assumptions a reader may wish to substitute.

The Regulation of Economic Activity series is intended to inform the ongoing debate on regulatory policy by making significant and relevant research available to both scholars and policy makers. Books in this series present new insights into individual agencies, programs, and regulated sectors. They also address important economic, political, and administrative aspects of the regulatory process that cut across those boundaries. Gasmi, Kennet, Laffont, and Sharkey's work is a significant contribution in this tradition. This important book should find a broad audience among researchers and policy makers concerned with the design and operation of government regulation, the interface between competitive and regulated sectors, and especially those interested in the complex issues facing the modern telecommunications industry.

Nancy L. Rose
Richard L. Schmalensee

Preface

The research reported in this book was started during the academic year 1994–1995 when Bill Sharkey visited the Institut d'Economie Industrielle in Toulouse. The desire to bring modern industrial economics to the data was already strong for Library and Jean-Jacques Laffont. After some empirical work on oligopolistic markets (Gasmi, Laffont, and Vuong 1992), auctions (Laffont, Ossard, and Vuong 1995), and contracts (Laffont and Matoussi 1995), the challenge to confront the new economics of regulation with real world issues seemed particularly daunting. First, incentive regulation had come in place only recently. Second, the data related to these new regulatory policies were very scarce. Third, and this is particularly true for the telecommunications industry, the need to focus on current technologies that were so quickly evolving limited the power of classical econometric methods. Among us, we had only some brief experience with simulations on calibrated models (Gasmi, Ivaldi, and Laffont 1994) following Schmalensee (1989). Bill came to Toulouse with the desire to invest in empirical approaches to cost studies and industry structure. At that time the LECOM cost engineering model, developed by Gabel and Kennet (1991, 1994), had already been used to investigate economies of scale in local telecommunications. As a consequence of the debate taking place at the state level in the United States, the National Regulatory Research Institute (the research arm of state regulators) had funded the original version of LECOM through a grant to David Gabel and Mark Kennet. Bill, who was about to join the Federal Communications Commission, was further interested in using this type of instrument for enlightening debates about regulatory intervention at the national level.

The project started with the idea of using LECOM to simulate cost functions that would incorporate moral hazard and adverse selection variables. Endowed with this instrument, we could then review some of the major policy issues facing the local telecommunications industry—including the natural monopoly question, the relative performances of various regulatory mechanisms, and the effects of universal service obligations and cross-subsidies—within the intellectual framework of the new regulatory economics developed in the 1980s and the 1990s. All along, Mark Kennet was very helpful in the manipulation of the LECOM model and in its customization to our specific simulation needs.

Despite the resources put together in our team of four, this was insufficient to realize a study that could be directly policy relevant. The work presented here is largely methodological. It is aimed at showing that a combination of cost engineering models with econometrics and simulations can be applied to policy discussions of some of the major issues of regulation. Precise answers for particular industries and countries or regions would definitely require more inputs. We, however, hope to convince the reader that our approach has potential value for such further research. For the academic readers, we have provided a CDRom which will enable them to extend our modeling efforts and further develop our regulatory paradigm.

We are grateful to Nancy Rose and Richard Schmalensee for welcoming this volume in the Regulation of Economic Activity series of The MIT Press. Many thanks also go to Daniel Benitez, Srinagesh Padmanabhan, and our colleagues in Toulouse for useful comments on an earlier draft. We especially would like to thank David Gabel, who graciously allowed us to include work to which he has greatly contributed. We warmly thank Christelle Fauchié for skillfully typing the manuscript. Finally, Farid Gasmi and Jean-Jacques Laffont thank France Telecom for financial support without which the undertaking of this work would have never been possible.

Farid Gasmi, Jean-Jacques Laffont, Toulouse
Mark Kennet and Bill Sharkey
Washington, DC
August 31, 2001

**Cost Proxy Models and
Telecommunications Policy**

1   Introduction

1.1   The Need for Regulation in Telecommunications

The telecommunications industry, as every economist and industry observer knows, is an industry in transition. Once regarded as a classic example of a natural monopoly, the industry today defies easy characterization. A portion of the industry representing traditional voice communication between parties in widely separated communities—the so-called long-distance sector of the industry—has been successfully opened to competition in many countries, and few would dispute that the market for these services is highly competitive, at least for now. On the other hand, the local exchange portion of the industry, though also opened to competitive entry in recent years, has seen relatively little actual entry, except in the portion of the market serving very high volume users. Moreover the adoption of digital transmission and switching technologies has blurred the distinction between traditional voice communication and the transmission of video and data messages. The same network can carry all forms of information efficiently in a digital format, although there remain important regulatory distinctions between the packet-only networks, which include the Internet backbones, and circuit-switched networks, which continue to provide most of the voice grade services.

Technology and regulation are the defining characteristics of telecommunications. Regulation of telecommunications is generally regarded as necessary because portions of the industry have the technological characteristics of natural monopoly. In part, the definition of natural monopoly is a statement about the technology of the industry, or more precisely about the cost function. It is often said that an industry is a natural monopoly if a single firm can produce the industry output at lower cost than any alternative collection of two or more firms.[1] This definition, however, raises new questions about the meaning of cost. How are the costs of a single firm in an industry to be measured? Do these costs depend on the nature of regulation in the industry? Similarly one could ask: What are the costs of the multifirm alternative to a regulated natural monopoly? These costs will clearly depend on the nature of regulation that may continue to exist in the market as well as on the strategic behavior of the firms that seek to maximize their profits subject to regulatory constraints and the behavior of rival firms.

In the telecommunications industry, regulation has had a large impact on the costs of any firm subject to that regulation. A regulator must design and oversee the mechanism by which the regulated firm is allowed to recover its costs. A regulator may allow open entry in certain markets served by a regulated firm, while restricting entry in other markets. A regulator may impose structural or accounting constraints on a regulated firm that serves markets with differing degrees of competition. A regulator may even require a regulated firm to serve an unprofitable segment of the market in the interest of satisfying a "universal service" objective. Similarly, in a multifirm telecommunications market, both accounting or structural constraints and a universal service obligation may be imposed on one or more firms in the market. These factors clearly affect the market equilibrium and the realization of cost for each firm in the market.

An additional factor in evaluating the cost structure of a multifirm market for telecommunications services is the set of rules governing the interconnection of carriers. In the absence of any such rules, large networks may refuse to interconnect with smaller networks, and this possibility may itself create a tendency to natural monopoly, even in the absence of other cost-based factors favoring single firm production. Proper interconnections call for regulatory intervention.[2] The interconnection of networks, however, is itself costly, and the nature of the rules governing interconnection may impose additional costs on firms in the market, if they create incentives for the inefficient deployment of network facilities.[3]

Finally, an empirical evaluation of telecommunications policies must be concerned with the actual measurement of a cost function for telecommunications firms. Since it is clearly recognized that only the forward-looking costs are relevant to most policy issues in telecommunications, how can the relevant cost function be estimated? The same regulators that may impose conditions on regulated firms to advance various social objectives may also wish to evaluate alternative regulatory policies, including possibly the partial or total deregulation of the industry. In most cases historical time series data will not be adequate for an econometric investigation of cost, unless the policy change has already been implemented and the evaluation is retrospective. Cross-sectional analysis is more likely to be useful, but only if there exist other regulatory jurisdictions that have previously implemented a similar policy change.

We see little value in a pedantic reformulation of the definition of natural monopoly that incorporates the above-mentioned factors. It is sufficient to observe that both technology and market forces can lead to situations, in telecommunications and in similarly structured industries, in which regulation leads to higher social welfare than the unregulated alternative. Broadly speaking, the purpose of this book is to examine many of the issues raised above concerning natural monopoly, and the need for regulation of telecommunications, in an empirical setting. Our analysis is based on the insights of the "new theory of regulation" which we outline in section 1.3 and develop more fully in chapter 4. An important, indeed crucial, tool for this analysis is the use of a computer-based cost proxy model as a descriptor of the underlying telecommunications cost or production function. In the remainder of this introductory chapter we present the basic ingredients of what we believe to be a new and promising empirical approach to regulation.

Section 1.2 recaps the recent historical evolution of regulation in telecommunications. The so-called new theory of regulation based on a proper recognition of the regulators' information constraints is introduced in section 1.3. The difficulties faced by the econometrics of regulated industries are discussed in section 1.4. The cost proxy models, which provide an alternative to econometric approaches of costs, are described in section 1.5. Section 1.6 puts together all these elements to propose the new empirical approach to regulation which is the topic of this book.

1.2   The Historical Evolution of Practical Regulation

Alexander Graham Bell was granted patents in 1876 and 1877 for "improvements in telegraphy," which provided the basic ingredients for the new industry of voice telephone service. Regulation of telephone service began in 1879, when Connecticut and Missouri became the first states to regulate telephone companies as public utilities. By 1920 all but three states had established public utility commissions with jurisdiction over rates and practices of telephone companies.[4] After the expiration in 1894 of the basic Bell patents, there followed a period of entry by independent telephone companies and intense competition between the Bell companies and independents for local services. The Bell companies, however, maintained the only viable technology for long-distance communications between subscribers in different cities through their subsidiary, the American Telephone and Telegraph Company. In the early years of the twentieth century, many of these independent companies were forced to merge with AT&T, since that company pursued an aggressive pricing policy and generally refused to interconnect with the independent companies.

The difficulty of duplicating facilities at the local level, and the refusal of the Bell companies to interconnect, led to significant pressure to impose regulation at the federal level. Rather than opposing these calls for regulation, Theodore Vail, the president of AT&T, chose to embrace regulation. In 1913 the company voluntarily agreed to interconnect with all remaining independents and to refrain from acquiring any more independent companies. The resulting "Bell System" was initially regulated under the jurisdiction of the Interstate Commerce Commission. In 1934 the US Congress passed the Communications Act, creating the Federal Communications Commission with authority over all interstate rates and activities of the Bell System.[5]

At both the state and federal level, regulation followed traditional public utility pricing principles, based on the idea of a "fair rate of return" on the utility's rate base.[6] Under rate-of-return regulation the firm essentially reports its costs to the regulator, and subject to auditing of these reports, the regulator guarantees that the firm is fully reimbursed for its costs and is allowed to earn a normal rate of return on the firm's capital assets. It is now well known that this form of regulation leads to a number of perverse incentives for the regulated firm. The firm may have an incentive to overinvest in capital inputs relative to labor or other variable inputs as long as the allowed rate of return exceeds the firm's cost of capital.[7] Since the firm itself is likely to have more complete information about its cost function than the regulator, the firm may have weak or nonexistent incentives to engage in cost-reducing activities.[8] Finally, under rate-of-return regulation, the firm may have powerful incentives to engage in cost shifting between competitive and noncompetitive activities to the extent that these actions cannot be easily detected by the regulator.

For the reasons above, the costs of a firm operating under rate-of-return regulation are likely to be significantly different from those of a similarly situated firm operating in an unregulated market. Based on this observation, one could conclude that, at least in principle, an unregulated firm might perform better than a regulated firm in some potential natural monopoly markets. This result would occur if the various price distortions associated with the market power of the unregulated firm were judged to be less costly than the inefficiencies induced by the regulatory process. There are, however, alternative regulatory policies that should also be evaluated before assessing the proper role of regulation generally. In fact a particular alternative, known as price-cap regulation, has been widely adopted in the telecommunications industry in recent years, since it gives the regulated firm good incentives to produce outputs in a cost-minimizing manner while allowing the regulator to maintain some control over the firm's prices.

Price-cap regulation was first suggested by Littlechild (1983) in the United Kingdom and was later adopted by the FCC and many state regulatory commissions in the United States.[9] The generally favorable analysis of price-cap regulation by economists was based on a growing understanding of the role of incentives in the design of good regulatory mechanisms. Price caps are considered a good, or "high-powered," regulatory instrument because they allow the firm to capture the full benefits of any cost-reducing activities that it chooses to pursue. Since firms are generally much better informed than regulators about the nature of the cost or production function, this delegation of authority to the firm can result in significant cost savings. However, the same informational asymmetry requires that the regulator allow the firm to retain some monopoly profits in all but the most adverse circumstances. The trade-off between cost reduction and rents is fundamental to the modern approach to incentive regulation, and it will be the subject of much of this book.

The adoption of price-cap regulation occurred at approximately the same time that the so-called new theory of regulation was being developed.[10] This new approach models explicitly the informational structure of the regulator-regulated firm relationship, and solves for the optimal regulatory mechanism under a variety of constraints. This theory provides an ideal setting in which to address a broad range of policy issues in the telecommunications industry. However, while the theory is capable of offering certain qualitative conclusions of interest to telecommunications policy makers, there are many other questions that can only be resolved on the basis of quantitative results. As the discussion in section 1.4 illustrates, there are serious hurdles in conducting a traditional empirical test of the incentive approaches to regulation using econometric analysis of historical data.

Some of the problems in an econometric analysis have been alluded to above, and they are due to the inherent difficulty in estimating a forward-looking cost function for telecommunications firms. Another layer of complexity, however, is imposed by the nature of the theory itself. Optimal incentive mechanisms can be solved for mathematically, but an empirical evaluation of the resulting solution generally requires a highly detailed description of the telecommunications cost function. Hence the key factor in an empirical analysis of incentive approaches to regulation is the development of a source of data that will allow both a forward-looking representation of cost and a highly detailed analysis of the cost function.

Rather than pursuing the traditional econometric approach to estimating this cost function, we propose in the present investigation to use an engineering cost proxy model. The proxy model approach is well suited to resolve each of the difficulties noted above. With appropriate engineering assumptions and input values, the proxy model can be calibrated to give a very good approximation to the current forward-looking technologies that telecommunications firms are deploying. With alternative input assumptions, the proxy model could also be used to model past or conjectured future technologies. Since a proxy model is based on a computer-generated design of the telecommunications network, it is capable of providing almost unlimited detail about the resulting cost function. In section 1.5 we provide a brief overview of the proxy model approach. In chapter 2 we will provide a detailed description of the particular proxy model that we use for the remaining chapters in this book.[11]

1.3 The New Theory of Regulation

A major achievement of the so-called new theory of regulation has been to provide a normative framework to think about regulation.[12] This literature has put at the forefront of the analysis the decentralization of information and the strategic use of their private information by economic agents, and has borrowed its conceptual tools from the mechanism design literature.

This latter literature started with the project (Hurwicz 1960) of extending normative economics to nonconvex environments. It blossomed in 1970 with a renewal of the study of the free-rider problem.[13] The goal there was to design optimal allocation rules for public goods when the social welfare maximizer does not know the agents' willingnesses to pay for the public goods. On this occasion the revelation principle[14] was established (Gibbard 1973; Green and Laffont 1977; Myerson 1979). It made possible normative analysis in economies with decentralized information. Indeed, it showed that any allocation rule is equivalent to a truthful direct revelation mechanism. To optimize social welfare in the set of all possible allocation rules, it is then enough to characterize the set of truthful direct revelation mechanisms and maximize in this latter set. Such a characterization simply amounts to a set of inequalities, which state that faced with a direct revelation mechanism that associates allocations of goods to announcements of private information, each agent should prefer to announce the truth. The only technical difficulty is the potentially large number of such inequalities. However, under some conditions on the agent's preferences (the so-called Spence-Mirrlees conditions) this large (even infinite) number of inequalities can be synthesized by simple first-order conditions and monotonicity conditions. Normative economics can then proceed.

In the case of regulation, one can design in this way the regulatory rules that maximize expected social welfare, even though regulated firms have private information not available to the regulator despite all his efforts to acquire as much information as is reasonably possible. Indeed, one should think about the private information of the regulated firm as the private information remaining after the best use is made by the regulator of his sources of information, and in particular of the cost models of the industry he has constructed.

The new constraints due to asymmetric information (called the "incentive constraints") impose welfare losses. Intuitively it is because private information enables agents to capture information rents (as efficient agents can mimic inefficient ones without the social welfare maximizer knowing it); these information rents are costly for society either because of redistribution concerns or because there is a social cost of public funds. Consequently optimization of social welfare will in general entail efficiency distortions to mitigate those information rents. For example, lower quantities of the regulated good will be requested because it decreases the expected information rent of the regulated firm.

So it is clear that society suffers from the private information of the regulated firms. Accordingly the social welfare maximizer will attempt to bridge his informational gap, and there are various ways to do so. The traditional way is to use past information to build an approximation of the regulated firm's technology and of the demand conditions for the goods produced by that firm. Econometric techniques are by now well developed and can be used to build an estimated representation of cost and demand conditions for the regulator. In the next section we discuss this econometric approach, in particular, how the impact of regulatory rules needs to be and, in the current state of things, is taken into account in the estimation procedures.

1.4   Econometrics of Regulation

Econometrics has traditionally contributed to the debate on regulation of public utilities by producing a set of tools for evaluating economies of scale and scope. Various methodological attempts have been made to use firm-level data to estimate production and cost functions. Among the best known of these specifications is the translog cost specification popularized by Christensen et al. (1973). This translog functional form, which we use extensively in the book to summarize cost data, approximates a wide variety of cost functions and possesses some degree of flexibility that makes it one of the most favored specifications by economists.[15] The main problem faced by these early contributions was the difficulty of controlling for the effect of the technological progress when measuring economies of scale. One must recognize, however, that historically, lack of satisfactory data has been the problem for the vast majority of empirical studies of the production process.

Indeed, for our purpose here, we note that a sufficiently large number of observations is needed in order to render practical the estimation of a generally large number of structural parameters. More recently Shin and Ying (1992) have circumvented the data problem by constructing a large data set that comprises observations on a panel of 57 local exchange companies during 8 years, which they used to estimate a translog cost function of the local exchange industry. Although technically these data requirements can be met by firm-specific time series data, data on a cross section of many firms or a panel data set (e.g., Shin and Ying's), we argue that none of these data types prove to be completely suitable for proper policy analysis.

Time series data on a representative firm are inherently retrospective and typically available at best on a quarterly basis.[16] If one's goal is to analyze the data-generating process that produces significant variations in the cost figures, then one often has to examine relatively long series that correspond to different technological eras, and hence to cost structures with different technological characteristics. Clearly, even from a purely retrospective standpoint, it is crucial that the technological progress be controlled for, if the intention is to measure economies of scale for policy decisions. Furthermore, again because time series are retrospective, only limited information can be extracted from the analysis as to what type of cost structure is likely to prevail in the near or medium future.

Data on a cross section of firms raise a different type of policy problem, one that might be due to the heterogeneity of the sample.[17] Since firms may vary in their rate of implementation of technological innovations, cost parameter estimates could at best be meaningfully interpreted as those of a firm of "average efficiency." As far as policy is concerned, decisions based on industry average performance parameters may introduce unforeseen arbitrage opportunities and even some social inefficiencies.[18] Thus, although econometric studies of cost based on panel data sets may increase the statistical degrees of freedom, they present difficulties of both time series and cross-sectional data analyses.

The above-discussed pitfalls of the classical econometric approaches to the estimation of the cost structure are essentially technical, and more sophisticated instruments are now available that can alleviate them to some extent. For the ostensive purpose of our book, a more conceptual problem common to these approaches remains: that even in the most recent empirical (standard) contributions to the analysis of production processes, the effect of the regulatory environment is not explicitly accounted for. As emphasized by the new theory of regulation, however, costs are affected by regulation, and our position is that such an effect should not be ignored at both the econometric specification and the estimation levels. Such an important fact then calls for a more structural approach to the econometric modeling of production processes that focuses on the regulator-regulated firm relationship, as is analyzed at length in the book.

While such a structural approach is still at an early stage of development, some of its important underlying features and contributions have been highlighted in the literature. An extensive review of this literature that generally includes empirical work on contracts, is beyond the scope of this book, but for our purpose, it is instructive to mention the studies by Feinstein and Wolak (1992) and Wolak (1994). The first paper achieves two things. First, the authors spend a great deal of effort constructing formal econometric models that explicitly incorporate conditions that are at the heart of the new regulation modeling approach, the so-called incentive compatibility conditions (see chapter 4 of the book).

Relying on an extension of a model with adverse selection by Besanko (1985) in which the firm possesses private information on its labor costs, the authors assume a specific structure for the model disturbances and derive some estimable structural equations. Second, they investigate the possible estimation biases that can arise when one ignores the presence of asymmetric information. In particular, they reach the tentative conclusion that such an omission leads to a systematic overstatement of the scale elasticity. Wolak (1994) provides an implementation of the methodology for the case of the regulation of the class A California water utility industry and evaluates the welfare losses to consumers associated with the reduction of output due to asymmetric information.

From a methodological viewpoint it is certainly the case that the empirical strategy noted above is promising and should be pursued. However, at least for the case of the telecommunications industry, it is not so clear that the implications of such an approach can be translated into simple policy recommendations. Applied econometrics draws heavily on the past and in an industry with such a high speed of evolution of technology and industry structure as the telecommunications industry, such an approach might not be appropriate. In the sections that follow we argue that from a forward-looking perspective, cost proxy models of the type used in the book may be more suitable for policy advice and constitute a powerful tool for the empirical analysis of regulation.

1.5   Cost Proxy Models

As an alternative to standard econometric cost models, two main approaches have been developed and used by policy makers and regulators: accounting-based cost analyses and computer-based cost proxy models. Data input requirements for both accounting-based studies and proxy models vary widely. As a general rule, the proxy model approach uses more disaggregated data than the accounting approach and thus is more flexible in its application although more demanding in terms of data. The time needed for implementation may be less for accounting-based approaches, but only if good accounting systems are already in place.

As to the ability to model dynamically evolving telecommunications networks as has been alluded to in the previous section, both accounting and proxy model approaches have inherent limitations. However, a proxy model has the advantage of incorporating built-in network optimizing routines that can be used to determine an optimal static network at various points in time in order to approximate certain dynamic considerations. We should note, however, that this repeated exercise will not necessarily result in an optimal time path for the network since it always "rebuilds" the network from scratch.

Engineering process models have played a role for many years in empirical economic analysis. In many cases a detailed knowledge of cost cannot be obtained by any other method. The increasingly sophisticated computer-based cost proxy models recently developed for the telecommunications industry have provided regulators with a new source of information about the complex technologies used. A cost proxy model conceptually consists of a set of more or less detailed descriptions of the technological processes underlying the cost function of a representative firm in the industry. At the simplest level such a model might consist of a set of stylized functions that seek to approximate the costs of individual components of a firm's technology. For example, the cost of a switch might be represented by a simple linear relationship $a + bx$, where a represents the fixed cost of the switch and bx the variable cost as a function of the number of line terminations x that the switch is able to process. The cost of the distribution portion of the telecommunications network might be represented by a similar function $(a + bx)d$, where in this case a and bx represent the fixed and variable costs per unit of distance, respectively, and d represents the total length of the distribution plant. More sophisticated cost proxy models contain computer algorithms that actually design a hypothetical network based on detailed input data on the locations of customers, the range of available technologies and information on input prices.

While meeting the standards of sound engineering design for a given level of quality of service, an engineering cost model provides the user with the ability to choose a network configuration consisting of technology, routing, and capacity that minimizes the cost of providing the service. Such an approach, of course, takes us beyond the traditional realm of the economist and into areas usually explored by engineers and practitioners of operations research. However, as we will see in the next chapter, the particular cost model used for the empirical studies reported in the book keeps the fundamental features of a genuine economic model, even though, for operational reasons, it incorporates many of these "foreign" attributes.

Cost estimation methods in general, and engineering proxy models in particular, are powerful instruments with which the regulator can partially bridge the informational gap on technology discussed in the previous section. Just by how much the adverse effects due to asymmetric information can be reduced using these instruments depends to a large extent on the level of complexity of the cost models and the regulator's ability to unfold their numerous components. The situation today is that the available cost proxy models typically incorporate an exceedingly large number of technological and economic parameters that need to be specified. To be sure, while the regulator's information quality has largely improved due to the availability of such models, it is the case that asymmetric information is not completely eliminated, and thus still poses impediments to regulation. Consequently the mechanism design approach of the new theory of regulation described in section 1.3 is still relevant, and one of the goals of this book is to demonstrate that its combination with the engineering cost proxy model approach is fruitful for applied regulation. The next section describes how precisely this combination is performed.

1.6   A New Empirical Approach to Regulation

In this book we combine two of the most recent ideas of regulatory economics, namely that asymmetric information is the essence of the difficulties of regulation but that engineers can help us design fairly accurate models of the technology.

To synthesize those two elements, we need to introduce asymmetric information in a traditional engineering cost model, here the LECOM model.[19] In such a model the cost of a given quantity of traffic is the cumulated cost of the various elements of the network (distribution plant, feeder plant, switching, interoffice plant). These costs depend, in particular, on the price of labor and the price of capital. Our approach then is to simulate the cost model for various values of these prices and to interpret the results as follows: A higher cost due to a higher price of labor can also be viewed as due to a lower effort level with the same price of labor. One can then calibrate the range of variations of the price of labor to mimic a reasonable range of effort levels that can be induced by the different incentives provided by regulatory rules. Similarly a higher cost of capital can be interpreted as a less efficient technology with the same cost of capital. One can calibrate the range of variations for the cost of capital to mimic the range of the regulator's uncertainty about the firm's efficiency.

Therefore, through simulations of the basic LECOM model, we can simulate the cost function of an operator for different levels of effort and different efficiency levels. For convenience we can fit a translog or a quadratic cost function to the data so obtained. If we now think that the effort level is a moral hazard variable not observed by the regulator and the level of efficiency an adverse selection variable also private information of the regulated firm, we have generated a cost function that depends on the number of subscribers, the traffic, the geographic characteristics of the subscribers, and the level of effort of the firm as well as its efficiency.

We can complete this information with a choice for the regulator's subjective uncertainty over the firm's efficiency, a choice of the disutility of effort function for the firm, and a choice of demand characteristics, through various calibrations and estimations. We then have all the ingredients needed for an empirical approach to regulation. We can ask questions as diverse as where are the monopoly segments of the industry, what are the characteristics and properties of optimal regulatory schemes, how do well known regulatory rules compare with these schemes, what are the sizes of cross-subsidies when uniform pricing is required, what are the costs of universal service obligation with or without entry constraints, and so on.

With a rigorously constructed technological model and good demand data, one can then hope not only to reproduce the theoretical results of the regulatory literature but also to get a reasonable sense of the real trade-offs involved, of the cost of simple mechanisms, of the real cost of universal service obligation, of the real threat for entry due to cross-subsidies, and the like. In other words, one can hope to give to the regulators and to society a sense of the size of the stakes and of the most important areas of concern. One can hope to bring modern regulatory economics closer to practice and make economic theory a tool for action.

In chapter 2 we give a brief overview of what a local exchange network is, to help the reader understand the logic of the engineering LECOM model that we use in the book. The building blocks of the LECOM model are presented as well as the methodology that leads to simulated cost functions. Chapter 3 provides a first use of the LECOM model under complete information to measure economies of scope in this industry and determine if it is a natural monopoly. Chapter 4 gives a recap of regulation theory under incomplete information that we use in the book. Optimal regulation with and without cost observability is characterized as well as optimal price cap regulation and optimal cost plus regulation. Chapter 5 extends the natural monopoly test to asymmetric information both when usage and access are outputs. Indeed, under incomplete information one must take into account not only the usual costs but also the costs created by the information rents.

Chapter 6 characterizes optimal regulation under incomplete information and studies the validity of the dichotomy hypothesis. Under this hypothesis optimal regulation can be conveniently separated into cost-reimbursement rules and Ramsey pricing. More precisely, Ramsey pricing does not need to be subject to incentive corrections beyond the fact that the relevant marginal costs depend on incentives. The comparison of various regulatory rules such as cost-plus regulation or price-cap regulation with optimal regulation is carried out in chapter 7. The various redistributive consequences are assessed. They provide a useful way to understand the political economy of the choice of regulatory instruments.

The introduction of competition in some segments of the industry such as urban sectors raises new challenges for the implementation of universal service obligations (USO). We evaluate the costs of USO under various regulatory schemes and the difficulties of funding USO when tax systems are inefficient or corrupt in chapter 8. Another important question of regulation concerns the trade-off between maintaining a vertical integration of an incumbent monopolist (e.g., for the local and long-distance activities) that favors economies of scope, and maybe low transaction costs, and implementing vertical disintegration that creates scope for favoritism and preclusion. Chapter 9 evaluates the size of accounting and strategic cross-subsidies that can be associated with vertical integration to evaluate the risk of sizable unfair competition for entrants.

In the concluding chapter (chapter 10) we summarize what we consider as the main lessons we have learned from the research project that culminated into this book. We describe the most important results of our research program to date and discuss some of their implications for incentive regulation and telecommunications policy. We also discuss some useful lessons learned on the use of cost proxy models in empirical research. Finally, we draw the reader's attention to some directions for improvements in our approach and suggest some new issues that can be addressed. Appendix A provides additional information on each of the chapters, useful information on how to use LECOM to generate cost data, a guide to the Mathematica analysis, and a description of the contents of the CDRom that is included in the book. Appendix B describes a cost proxy model developed by the FCC (HCPM) and some of its international applications.

2

The Local Exchange
Cost Optimization
Model (LECOM)

2.1 Introduction

By the local exchange cost optimization model, LECOM for short, we seek to represent with reasonable accurateness the local telephone network in order to analyze its cost structure.[1] Fast technological progress characterizes the telecommunications industry. LECOM adopts, as much as possible, a flexible and forward-looking approach in the specification of technological possibilities. For a given level of demand placed on the network, the model searches for the cost-minimizing technology, number, and location of telephone switches within a city or calling area. The technology is chosen by an exhaustive search over a set of feasible alternatives. These alternative choices pertain to type (three kinds of digital and two kinds of analog) and capacity of switching equipment and type[2] (ordinary copper, subscriber line carrier on copper, and fiber), and gauge for cable if applicable.[3] The number of switches of a specified technology is determined through an exhaustive search over a range of feasible values, starting with the minimum number physically required to meet the specified demand.

Various issues pertaining to the local telecommunications market will be addressed in later chapters of the book. A necessary first step in those analyses is the derivation of a cost function. LECOM allows us to generate local exchange cost data, which are then synthesized through standard statistical estimation techniques in a smooth functional form. This procedure of examining in great detail the engineering production process in order to uncover the main properties of its cost structure has been used in other industries as well. This was the case for research that goes back to the early work by Frisch (1935) in the chocolate industry, Smith (1957) in trucking, Manne (1958) in petroleum refining, and more recently Griffin (1977) in the electric power generation industry. Chenery (1949) and Griffin (1972) discuss the general methodology, and Førsund (1995) provides a good survey of the literature. In telecommunications the Rand model developed in the late 1980s, which illustrates an incremental costing methodology, is usually considered as the starting point (see Mitchell 1990).

Although close in general spirit, the engineering optimization model discussed throughout this book is to be distinguished from the above-mentioned modeling efforts, which have been termed in the literature "process models." Typically these models do not embed a full-blown optimization of the process being studied, or, at best, employ a linear programming approximation to the optimization. LECOM attempts to optimize over *all* inputs, and is not restricted to linear objective or constraint functions.

Optimization in LECOM is performed in three steps. The switch location determination is the innermost search loop. In this search, locations for a given number of switches having given technological characteristics are sought. In the next layer, all feasible technological combinations capable of serving the (given) demand are distributed across the given number of switches. Finally, in the outermost search, the number of switches is permitted to vary.

In the subsequent chapters of the book various economic aspects of the telecommunications industry will be analyzed. This analysis will, to a large extent, be performed by means of an empirical methodology that heavily relies on LECOM. In order to evaluate the implications of the economic analyses performed, it is important to have a good understanding of the assumptions made about the network that is modeled by LECOM, the details of the basic technological assumptions, the fundamental economic trade-offs considered by LECOM, and the type of optimization algorithms used to deal with those trade-offs. The remainder of this chapter is intended to provide that background. In section 2.2 we provide a brief overview of the local exchange network and suggest working definitions for nonspecialist readers. Section 2.3 describes the LECOM technology in detail and explains how the software functions. Section 2.4 discusses the economic trade-offs modeled by the software, section 2.5 describes formally the optimization algorithm that the model performs, and section 2.6 outlines the aggregation process that leads to the local exchange cost function.

2.2   The Local Exchange Network: An Overview

The local exchange network is composed of four major components: distribution, feeder, switching, and interoffice plant. Figure 2.1 shows a stylized network incorporating the major components and subcomponents.

Working back from the telephone set in the customer's residence or business location toward the switch (also known as the central office), the customer's inside wiring connects with the company-owned network at the *network interface device* (NID). In most US jurisdictions, the NID is the point of separation between those portions of the network that are under the financial responsibility of the telephone company and those that are under the responsibility of the customer.

From the NID a *drop wire* attaches the customer to the *drop terminal*, which is in turn the point of interconnection between the drop and the rest of the network. The drop wire simply consists of one or more pairs of copper wiring indistinguishable from the rest of the copper wiring that makes up the telephone network (except perhaps by its gauge). The drop terminal is nothing more than a metal or plastic box in which the drop wire is spliced to the *distribution backbone*. Distribution backbone cables typically follow the street or road grid pattern of a local geographical area, called a *distribution area* or *serving area*, ultimately attaching to a *serving area interface* (SAI). The components described up to the SAI collectively constitute what is known as the *distribution plant*.[4]

The SAI may take one of several forms, depending on engineering considerations. For serving areas close to the central office, particularly areas with a residential customer base, the SAI is likely to be a simple *feeder-distribution interface* (FDI). Like the drop terminal but built to a larger scale, the FDI is nothing more than a box in which copper cables are spliced together.

Other serving areas may require the use of a *remote terminal* (RT) designed to work with digital technology, either some form of T1 (digital signal sent on copper plant) or fiber optics. In these cases some electronic equipment is necessary to convert to *multiplex* (multichannel) digital signals. In the case of a fiber-optic RT, additional electronics are used for conversion between optical signals and electronic impulses.

The fiber or copper (digital or analog) plant that carries telecommunications traffic between the SAI and the switch is known as the *feeder plant*. At the switch, incoming traffic is connected to the appropriate destination channel. If that channel is directly connected to the switch, such

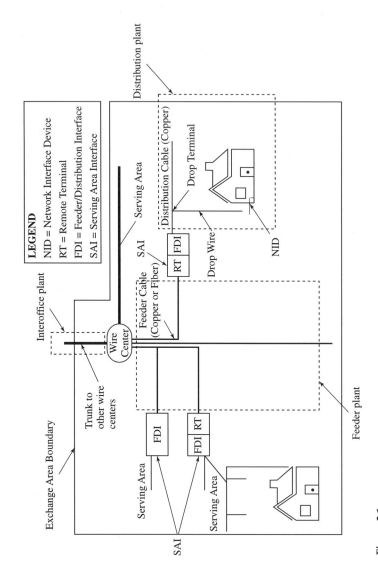

Figure 2.1
A typical wire center (adapted from *Engineering and Operations in the Bell System*, 2nd ed., 1984)

traffic is termed *intraoffice traffic*. Otherwise, it is considered as *interoffice traffic* and directed to the appropriate switch via *interoffice trunks*. Several functions besides basic switching may be performed at the switch level. First, any analog interoffice traffic must be converted to digital, since virtually all interoffice trunks are digital. Second, any advanced services (call-waiting, three-party calling, etc.) are accommodated with additional hardware and software features. Finally, signaling (e.g., the ringing of a particular telephone) may be directed to a separate signaling network.

2.3   Technological Foundations of LECOM

In this section we describe in detail the assumptions made on each type of plant modeled in LECOM. Recall from the previous section that the local exchange network is essentially viewed as the combination of, and interaction among, four elements: distribution, feeder, switching, and interoffice plant. The main design and technological aspects of these four components are examined in turn.

2.3.1   The Distribution Plant

In LECOM, customers are assumed to be distributed uniformly throughout rectangular serving areas. In principle, serving areas are intended to correspond to neighborhoods in a city or suburb, or clusters of dwellings in a rural area.[5] Figure 2.2 illustrates a prototypical city map utilized by LECOM. The number of customers in each serving area and the dimensions of the serving areas, each of which is assumed to take a rectangular shape, are set by the user of the model. Peak hour usage is assigned to each serving area, also by the user, according to whether the serving area is taken to be of business, residential, or mixed character.

The distribution plant is assumed to carry analog signals over copper pairs. The gauge of copper wire used is determined by how far the maximum-distance customer is from the switch using a lookup table that is based on engineering principles. AWG (American wire gauge) is a US standard set of nonferrous wire conductor sizes. The "gauge" means the diameter. Nonferrous includes copper and also aluminum and other materials, but it is most frequently applied to copper household electrical wiring and telephone wiring. In the United States, typical household electrical wiring is AWG number 12 or 14, while telephone wire

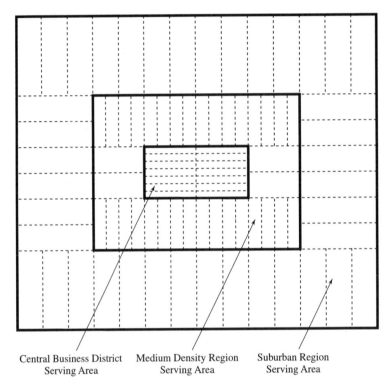

Figure 2.2
A stylized city map

is usually 22, 24, or 26. Higher-gauge numbers correspond to smaller diameters and thinner (and less costly) wires. Since thicker wire carries more current because it has less electrical resistance over a given length, thicker wire is better for longer distances (see table 2.1 for a conversion of AWG gauges into standard units and the corresponding direct current [dc] electrical resistance). For this reason, where extended distance is critical, a company installing a network uses telephone wire with lower gauge. The model lookup table implements a mix of gauges from 26 gauge to 19 gauge copper, with 26 being the smallest size and 19 the largest size.[6]

The model takes as an input the number of copper pairs per customer in the feeder and distribution plants. In the 1970s, AT&T determined that the typical outside plant design should include 1.5 pairs per customer in the feeder plant, and 2 pairs per customer in the distribution plant. Variations in peak usage of the network may cause a model user to vary these ratios.[7]

Table 2.1
Wire gauge conversions

AWG gauge (solid wire)	Wire diameter (inches)	Wire diameter (millimeters)	dc resistance (ohms/1,000 feet)
26	0.016	0.409	43.6
24	0.020	0.511	27.3
22	0.025	0.643	16.8
19	0.036	0.916	8.6

Source: Alpha Wire Company, Inc.

LECOM permits two types of structure to be deployed, *buried* and *underground*. Buried structure is cable that has been plowed under the earth after a trench has been dug. Underground cable, typically deployed in built-up areas in the center of towns and cities, is significantly more expensive: the cable must be physically drawn through conduit that has been placed in trenches that must be cut into pavement. In the real world *aerial* cable is also often deployed. The use of aerial cable can be simulated using LECOM by either substituting values of aerial cost parameters for those of buried cost parameters, or by assuming that the two "legal" structure types are actually high-cost and low-cost structure "mixes" containing percentages of each of the three structure types. The percentage of both types of structures is a user input that is permitted to vary with the location of the customers.

Since in LECOM customers are assumed to be uniformly distributed throughout each neighborhood serving area, a simplified route structure is used. The distribution routing includes a backbone running the length of the rectangle. At intervals equal to the (user input) width of a city block, distribution branch cables run from the backbone to each border and drops are added uniformly along the branch cable. Both branch cables and distribution backbones "telescope," that is, at each point of the distribution network, the size of cable used reflects only the number of pairs needed at the given point and no more.[8] All distances in the distribution module are calculated in a rectilinear fashion with axes running north–south and east–west. Figure 2.3 illustrates a prototypical distribution serving area in LECOM.

2.3.2   The Feeder Plant

Feeder plant runs from the serving area interface (SAI) to the central office.[9] In LECOM, feeder technology is chosen from three available

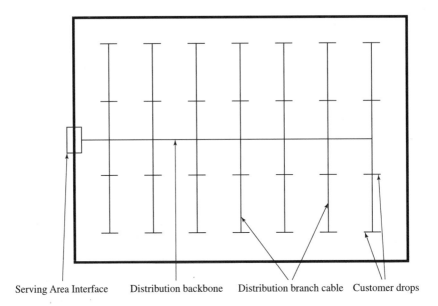

Serving Area Interface   Distribution backbone   Distribution branch cable   Customer drops

Figure 2.3
A distribution serving area

technologies: analog on copper, digital (T1) on copper, and digital on fiber.[10] The model calculates the economic crossover points, namely the route distance from the switch at which one technology is substituted for another, for these three technologies based on cost. The user can override the model's choice by specifying alternative crossover points based on other criteria such as quality of service.[11] If a digital feeder technology is chosen, the model "installs" a SLC-96 concentrator at the serving area interface.[12]

Gauge for feeder pairs carried on analog copper pairs are chosen from the same gauge-distance table used in the distribution plant. It is always assumed that T1 pairs are of 24-gauge copper. As to feeder routing, it is implemented using the relatively standard "pine tree" design. The pine tree design consists of a main backbone shared by all serving areas and each serving area connected to the backbone by means of a unique branch.[13]

As in the distribution case, feeder distances are rectilinear with axes running north–south and east–west, and feeder cables of all types are telescoped, with analog copper, digital copper, and fiber-optic cables handled separately (i.e., not carried in the same cables). Figure 2.4 illustrates the feeder plant design used in LECOM.

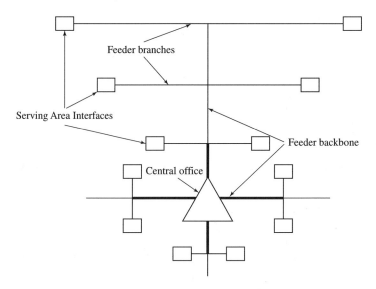

Figure 2.4
The pine tree topology

2.3.3 *Switching*

Three switch technologies are available within the LECOM model: a Northern Telecomstyle DMS-100 host switch, a DMS-10 stand-alone switch, and a DMS-100 remote switch. While the DMS-100 host and the DMS-10 can function autonomously, the DMS-100 remote requires that a DMS-100 host be present elsewhere in the network. The DMS-100 host switch has a default maximum line capacity of about 70,000 lines at average peak-hour usage. This line capacity includes that of any attached remote. The DMS-10 stand-alone switch has a default line capacity of about 20,000 lines, while the remote switch (DMS-100) has a default capacity of about 5,000 lines.[14]

The stylized model of switch cost operates as follows: For each switch, a "getting-started" or fixed cost is specified. Then, information provided by the LECOM user on the number of lines, peak-hour usage and percentages of intraoffice, interoffice, and toll traffic are used to size the components of the switch. The cost of the components is evaluated given some cost information input. Finally, software and signaling costs are added, again based on some information entered by the user, to reflect the ability of the switch to handle the so-called advanced services.

Each switch's capacity interacts critically with customer location data. First, serving areas are sorted according to their population and a

provisional cost of attachment to each switch is calculated for each serving area. Beginning with the most populated serving area, each serving
area is attached to the least costly switch that has remaining capacity.
That is, let $PC(i, j)$ be the provisional cost of attaching the serving area
indexed by i to the switch indexed by j. Let K_j be the capacity (in terms
of the number of lines) of switch j and T_j the number of lines already
served by this switch. Then serving area k will effectively be attached
to switch l if

$$l = \arg\min_j PC(k, j) \quad \text{and} \quad K_l - T_l - N_k \geq 0 \qquad (2.1)$$

where N_k is the serving area k's population.

Because of the capacity constraints imposed on each individual switch
(LECOM does not permit collocation of switches), it is possible, however, for the configuration of switches so found not to be globally optimal. In order to alleviate this shortcoming, the model permits switches
to "trade" serving areas according to the following rule. Assume that
serving areas i and j are attached to switches k and l, respectively. Then
these switches may trade the serving areas; that is, serving area i becomes attached to switch l and serving area j to switch k if

$$T_k - N_i + N_j \leq K_k, \quad T_l - N_j + N_i \leq K_l,$$
$$\text{and} \quad PC(j, k) + PC(i, l) < PC(i, k) + PC(j, l) \qquad (2.2)$$

where the T's, N's, K's, and PC's are as defined above.

Finally, as far as remote switches are concerned, each of these switches
is assigned to the most proximate host switch up to the maximum number of remote switches attachable to a host or stand-alone switch, which
is by default equal to 6.[15] Remote switches serve to transfer most of the
switching functionality of the host switch to a remote location, thereby
reducing the load on the host switch and enabling the remote traffic
to benefit from the economies associated with sharing transport plant
from the remote location to the host location. Intraoffice capability is
maintained at the remote location, but all interoffice traffic must go
through the host switch.

2.3.4 The Interoffice Plant

The cost of interoffice plant in LECOM is treated by calculating the
number of trunks required between each pair of central offices present
in the area being considered. A critical parameter used in this calculation

is, for each switch, the interoffice portion of peak-hour traffic per line (set by the LECOM user) multiplied by the number of lines served by the switch. This aggregate traffic handled by a given switch is distributed to the other switches of the network according to a formula that takes into account the distance from those switches to the original switch (the closer a switch, the more traffic it gets). The traffic so calculated is then applied to a table based on engineering principles that gives the number of interoffice trunks required to handle originating traffic from the given switch.[16] The fraction of total interoffice traffic originating from switch k that is allocated to switch j, r_{kj} is given by

$$r_{kj} = \frac{j^2}{\sum_{i \neq k} i^2} \tag{2.3}$$

where the switches $i \neq k$ are sorted by descending order of distance from switch k.[17] Figure 2.5 illustrates the interoffice design used by LECOM. In this figure the trunk to each switch's most proximate neighbor is indicated by a relatively thick link, trunks between second most proximate neighbors are denoted by a link of intermediate thickness, and the most distant neighbors are linked by the thinnest links. The figure also illustrates a host-remote link, showing how remote switches only directly communicate with the host switch to which they are attached.

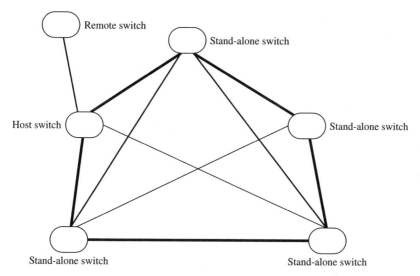

Figure 2.5
LECOM interoffice plant design

In addition to links between local switches located in the map region, LECOM also provisions a link to a toll point of presence (POP), which is assumed to be located in the center of the CBD area. The size of this link depends on the amount of switched toll traffic (TOLL CCS) and private line toll traffic (PLTOLL CCS) assumed in the system design.

2.4   Building an Optimal Network: Economic Trade-offs Modeled in LECOM

In the process of calculating the cost function, LECOM builds an optimal local exchange network. The primary type of economic decision incorporated into the LECOM model is that of substitution between various types of capital through technological choices.[18] The economic trade-offs associated with the choice of type of technology that is explicitly handled in LECOM include the substitution between stand-alone and host-remote switch configurations, substitution between analog copper, T1 on copper, fiber-optic feeder technologies, and the trade-off between added electronics in the form of more switches and building of loop plant in the form of longer loop lengths. Furthermore, in its most technologically advanced feature, LECOM takes into account trade-offs in the locations of switches between centralization of local demand and the cost of interconnection.

In effect the third trade-off described above can be thought of as a generalization of the first, since remote switches are really just extra switches being added for the purpose of reducing loop lengths and, as in the more conventional interpretation, of redistributing traffic loads to more decentralized locations. However, a distinction is made between these trade-offs in that, in the model, the host-remote system exists solely to exploit any economies of concentrated loop plant, while the trade-off between host-remote systems and stand-alones also captures the traffic redistribution effect. This is because a remote interoffice plant is assumed to connect only to hosts, while the stand-alone switches connect directly via trunks with all other switches in the network.

If the quality of service is held constant at a voice-grade level for any location within a certain distance from the central office, which is determined by line resistance and impedance, service is provided most economically, given current levels of cost of material, through analog copper pairs passing through the feeder and distribution plants directly to the customer location from the switch. As this distance increases, the voice-grade service on analog plant requires load coils, a type of amplifier, to improve signal quality as well as an increase in the gauge (thickness) of copper used. As an alternative, digital signals may be transmitted over a specially conditioned copper (T1) or fiber-optic plant, but the signals must be converted electronically at a remote location for use as voice communication, which requires a significant investment in electronic equipment at the site. The model explicitly models this trade-off by creating a set of economic crossover points that it uses to replace analog copper with digital copper, and digital copper with digital fiber.

The choice of any switch's location is sensitive to two conflicting factors: the distance of that switch from its served customers and its distance from its points of interconnection with the rest of the network. While the latter costs are relatively small, typically of the order of no more than 10 percent of total cost of the network, they can still cause changes in the number and location of central offices.

2.5 Total Cost and Optimization

Let us now express in a more compact way the total cost minimization procedure performed by LECOM. Given a specification of the (LECOM user-set) exogenous variables discussed in the previous sections (which include the city dimensions and pattern of demand), we take aggregate cost C, which is the sum of the costs attributed to each of the four fundamental components of the network (distribution, feeder, switching, and trunks), and minimize it with respect to a set of variables that characterize the technology and the spatial configuration of the network. More specifically, we undertake the following optimization process:

$$\min_{\tau_d, \tau_f, \tau_s, \tau_r, x, y, S} C = DC(\tau_d, x, y) + FC(\tau_f, x, y)$$

$$+ SC(\tau_s, x, y, S) + TC(\tau_r, x, y, S) \qquad (2.4)$$

where C is total cost composed of distribution cost (DC), feeder cost (FC), switching cost (SC), and trunk cost (TC). The set of control variables comprises $\tau_d \in T_d$, $\tau_f \in T_f$, $\tau_s \in T_s$, and $\tau_r \in T_r$ which are vectors of technologies available for, respectively, distribution, feeder, switching, and interoffice trunk, S, which is the number of switches employed, and x and y which are S-dimensional vectors representing the horizontal and vertical coordinates of the switches in the map. Note that while S does not explicitly enter as an argument into the DC and FC functions, because it corresponds to the dimension of the x and y vectors, these functions do implicitly depend on it.

The set T_d currently consists of only copper wire, with gauges determined by engineering rules. Eventually fiber technology could be added to the choice set. T_f consists of analog, digital on copper, and digital on fiber-optic technology. T_s consists of analog large switches, analog small switches, digital hosts, digital remotes, and digital stand-alone switches. Finally, T_r currently consists of only one type of digital interoffice trunk, although the user is free to specify some of its characteristics.

The search for the optimal switch location is accomplished by the derivative-free search algorithm proposed by Nelder and Mead (1965), as described in Press et al. (1986), over the x and y coordinates of a map representing in a discrete fashion the city being served by the telephone network.[19] This derivative-free algorithm suits our problem particularly well for two reasons. First, LECOM assumes that all cabling in the city follows city streets, which are set in a rectangular grid pattern, so that the L^1 norm (sum of absolute deviations) is the relevant distance measure. Second, since copper wire is only available in a finite number of gauges, the relationship between distance from wire center to customer and cabling cost is not smooth.[20]

Figure 2.6 illustrates the nested optimization process. The model takes as data the dimensions of a city, customer distribution, and usage levels. LECOM then searches for the technological mix, capacity, number, and location of switches that minimize the annual cost of production. This is equivalent to minimizing the present value of capital cost and operation, maintenance, and tax expenditures. Each of capital cost, depreciation expense, operating expense, maintenance expense, and taxes is expressed as a percentage of investment in each network component, and these percentages are summed up to form the *annual charge factor*. For example, if the cost of capital is 7 percent, depreciation is 10 percent, and the cost of operation and maintenance is 6 percent, the annual charge factor would be 0.23 (23 percent). Annual charge factors are one mechanism through which labor costs are introduced into the model. Indeed, operating and maintenance expenses are largely labor costs (as well as some material cost). Labor costs are also incorporated in the cost of installation, which is assumed to be part of the first cost, or initial investment, in each piece of equipment. The optimal locations of the switches are found by means of the nonlinear derivative-free routine mentioned earlier.

For the purpose of illustrating the inner working of the LECOM algorithms, consider the problem of simply optimizing over the number of switches. The economic trade-offs of placing an additional switch in a given network can be shown in the following simple example.[21] Suppose

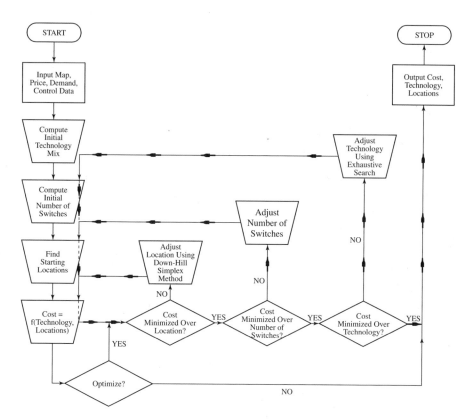

Figure 2.6
LECOM flowchart

that there is only one switch technology available, that the switches can be installed only in specific locations, and that switches come only in a single capacity. Then the only control variable left to the operating firm is S, the number of switches. The firm will choose an integer value S that minimizes total cost given by

$$C(S) = \text{Switch cost}(S) + \text{Trunk cost}(S) + \text{Feeder cost}(S)$$
$$+ \text{Distribution cost}(S)$$

$$= FC_S \cdot S + VC_S \cdot B + FC_T \cdot S + VC_T \cdot R \cdot D_T$$
$$+ FC_L + VC_L \cdot L \cdot D_L \tag{2.5}$$

where

$C(S)$ is the total cost expressed only as a function of S, the number of switches

D_T is the average distance per trunk (depends on S)

D_L is the average loop length (depends on S)

R is the number of interoffice trunks (depends on S)

FC_L is the fixed cost of loops for a given city size (exogenous cost parameter)

FC_S is the fixed cost of a switch (exogenous cost parameter)

FC_T is the fixed cost of terminating a trunk of any size at a switch (exogenous cost parameter)

VC_L is the variable cost per unit of distance of loop plant (exogenous cost parameter)

VC_S is the variable switching cost per hundred busy-hour calling seconds (exogenous cost parameter)

VC_T is the variable cost per unit of distance of trunk plant (exogenous cost parameter)

L is the number of loops (exogenous demand parameter)

B represents hundreds of busy-hour calling seconds (exogenous demand parameter)

In general, one would expect

$$\frac{\partial R}{\partial S} > 0, \quad \frac{\partial D_L}{\partial S} < 0, \quad \text{and} \quad \frac{\partial D_T}{\partial S} < 0 \tag{2.6}$$

that is, as the number of switches increases, the number of trunks increases while the average loop length and the average trunk length decrease.[22] If equation (2.5) were differentiable, the first-order condition of this optimization problem would be[23]

$$\frac{\partial C}{\partial S} = FC_S + FC_T + VC_T \left(D_T \frac{\partial R}{\partial S} + R \frac{\partial D_T}{\partial S} \right) + VC_L L \frac{\partial D_L}{\partial S} \cong 0 \tag{2.7}$$

In fact, since only integer values of S (the number of switches) are acceptable, we cannot set this equation exactly equal to zero. Hence, if the derivative $\partial C / \partial S$ is negative, namely total cost declines when an additional switch is deployed, then the switch is added. The motivation is that a switch should be added if the additional fixed cost of switching and trunks ($FC_S + FC_T$) to which we add the cost of the additional trunks $VC_T D_T (\partial R / \partial S)$ is less than the cost savings from shorter loops and trunks $VC_T R(\partial D_T / \partial S) + VC_L L(\partial D_L / \partial S)$.[24]

Table 2.2
Pseudocode for the LECOM cost function

```
Function cost (location vector, technology vector, number of switches);
BEGIN;
    IF location vector has elements outside city limits THEN
    BEGIN;
        Cost:=infinity;
        GOTO end of function;
    END;
    Attach each remote switch to nearest host;
    Adjust capacity of each host to account for remotes;
    Attach each serving area to nearest (most economical) available switch that has not yet
    been filled to capacity;
    Allows switches to trade serving areas if both switches can serve at least as cheaply;
    Calculate utilization for each switch;
    BEGIN;
        For each switch in switch type DO
        BEGIN;
            Calculate cost of pine tree feeder network for attached serving areas;
            Calculate distribution cost for attached serving areas;
            Calculate switching cost;
        END;
    END;
    Calculate cost of interoffice links;
    Cost:=feeder costs + distribution costs + switching costs + interoffice trunking costs;
END OF FUNCTION;
```

Table 2.2 gives the pseudocode for the LECOM cost function. In the pseudocode we see that equation (2.4) is integrated into the nested optimizations by declaring cost as a function of technology, number of switches, and location. Table 2.2 also gives an indication of how the switching, feeder, distribution, and trunk cost modules are integrated.

It is worthwhile to make some comments on how these modules operate. For example, the feeder module involves constructing the pine tree route design for feeder cables, which in turn involves sorting the serving areas along each feeder main by distance. The module (like the other modules computing cabling costs) exploits the economies associated with bundling cables together, which enriches the optimization procedure. Furthermore feeder (as well as distribution and trunk) cables are assumed to follow only street grids, which means that all distances are

L^1 (absolute deviation) norms rather than the more familiar Cartesian norm.

The derivative-free algorithm for the location optimization, mentioned above, is particularly useful in handling the nonlinearity of some engineering functions that are incorporated into the switching cost modules. Manufacturers of switches have developed engineering algorithms that determine the appropriate physical quantities of equipment for various levels of demand. For example, the number of multiplex loops in the DMS-10 module, the number of line group controllers in DMS-100, and the number of remote switches attached to the DMS-100 are all nonlinear functions of peak-period usage.[25]

2.6   From LECOM Simulations to a LECOM Cost Function

Recall that LECOM computes minimum cost figures as results of the optimization problem given in equation (2.4) above. This equation explicitly shows the control variables, affecting the cost of the main components of the network, over which optimization is performed.[26] However, implicit in this equation are some vectors P_d, P_f, P_s, and P_r representing prices influencing, respectively, distribution, feeder, switching, and trunking, which are exogenous to the optimization. The (total) cost function might then be represented as

$$C = DC(\tau_d, x, y; P_d) + FC(\tau_f, x, y; P_f)$$
$$+ SC(\tau_s, x, y, S; P_s) + TC(\tau_r, x, y, S; P_r) \tag{2.8}$$

Table 2.3 lists some representative values for the user adjustable pricing inputs that influence the cost of each of the four components of the network.[27]

We separate the price inputs to LECOM into three categories. At the lowest level there are factor prices for a broad range of materials and labor inputs for the telecommunications production function. These include the fixed and variable costs of deploying copper and fiber cable and structures, as well as the costs of associated circuit equipment (electronics required for digital/analog conversions) and switching equipment. Given these factor prices, and a set of additional inputs that describe user demands and the characteristics of the serving area, the LECOM optimization algorithms provide an estimate of the total network investment required to provide local exchange service.

At the next level, there are additional input variables that describe the way in which total network investment is converted to an annual (or

Table 2.3
Representative user adjustable LECOM inputs

Factor price multipliers	
0.676	Labor factor price multiplier
1.467	Capital factor price multiplier
1.000	Central office material price multiplier
1.000	Outside plant material price multiplier
Annual charge factors	
0.313	Carrying charge for land
0.326	Carrying charge for buildings
0.301	Carrying charge for circuit
0.375	Carrying charge for analog switches
0.280	Carrying charge for conduit
0.281	Carrying charge for underground cable
0.316	Carrying charge for buried cable
0.316	Carrying charge for underground fiber
0.343	Carrying charge for buried fiber
Prices for outside plant and switching equipment	
1.682	Fixed investment/foot of underground copper
2.172	Fixed investment/foot of buried copper
0.007	Marginal investment/foot of underground copper
0.009	Marginal investment/foot of buried copper
1.575	Fixed cost of underground fiber
0.187	Cost per foot of underground fiber
2.778	Fixed cost of buried fiber
0.197	Cost per foot of buried fiber
30.00	Cost per foot of conduit
0.070	Investment loading for building (circuit)
0.070	Investment loading for building (switch)
0.005	Investment loading for land (circuit)
0.005	Investment loading for land (switch)
53.00	Main distribution frame cost/customer
21.37	1990 tandem investment per CCS[a]

[a]Telecommunications traffic is measured in hundreds of busy-hour calling seconds, that is, in CCS, where the first C is the roman numeral for 100. This represents the time the average line is used per hour during the peak period.

monthly) cost per subscriber. These annual charge factors include three distinct components:

1. The cost of capital, which represents the weighted average cost of debt and equity financing for a representative firm in the industry.

2. The depreciation factor, which represents both the salvage value and the expected economic life for each category of telecommunications plant and equipment.

3. Annual operating expenses for the firm, including maintenance, network planning, and corporate overhead expenses.

At the highest level, LECOM includes input values for factor price multipliers for labor, capital, central office equipment, and outside plant. These multipliers are intended primarily to account for regional variations in the larger set of inputs that enter the firm's cost function. For example, a change in the value of the price multiplier for capital will have a significant impact on the cost of cable, circuit equipment, and switches, while a change in the labor multiplier will have the greatest impact on the cost of structure placements, maintenance activities, and other labor-intensive activities of the firm.

As is readily apparent from the foregoing discussion, a proper engineering specification of the cost of a local exchange network is significantly more complex than traditional econometric specifications. Standard economic theory shows that the programming dual to the problem of profit maximization is that of cost minimization; these problems lead to equivalent solutions in terms of the optimal choices of capital (K), labor (L), and materials (M) inputs and levels of outputs. It is easy to show that the minimization of cost given the level of output Q and input prices leads to a function

$$C(P_K, P_L, P_M, Q) \tag{2.9}$$

where the partial derivative of this function with respect to factor prices, P_K, P_L, and P_M, gives the firm's conditional factor demand for the respective inputs.[28] For the purpose of the book, this cost function may be expanded into its component-cost functions that correspond to the four fundamental modules retained in the design of the LECOM network, namely distribution, feeder, switching, and trunking.

While traditional econometric specifications assume that such a function is smooth and continuous, thereby leading to "nice" statistical specification properties, it is worth noting that a cost function does not need to be expressible in analytical form. One can simply write down a table of costs along with associated input prices and output levels.

By varying input prices and levels of output, a simulation "experiment" using LECOM can be performed leading to such a table. In a later chapter of this book, we will describe the features and details of such experiments. For our purposes we simply point out that such a table can readily be treated in a manner similar to empirical data generated in the real world. That is, the table contains independent observations on total cost, factor prices, and output levels. It is then a simple matter to apply a traditional econometric specification to these data. One must do so advisedly though, since no stochastic component in the usual sense is present.[29] This exercise is, however, worthwhile in that it is possible to summarize the properties of the cost function underlying the data (i.e., the LECOM simulation) in ways that are familiar to economists.

A full analytical representation of the aggregate cost function modeled by LECOM is not feasible as the program uses a large number of integer search algorithms and cumulates costs by summing up the costs of individual network components that connect the population of customers. Nevertheless, equations (2.4), (2.5), and (2.8) express different conceptual views of the same underlying cost function, which by the design of LECOM as an optimizing process, are fully consistent with the representation of "all of the economically relevant aspects of the technology" (Varian 1992) of the local exchange by a cost function as required by economic theory.

An overly simplified representation of this cost function might be obtained by expanding equation (2.5) as follows:

$$
\begin{aligned}
C(P_K, P_L, P_M; L, S, CCS, R) = {} & FC_S(P_K, P_L, P_M; S, CCS) \cdot S \\
& + CCS \cdot V_{CCS}(P_K, P_L, P_M; S, CCS) \\
& + FC_T(P_K, P_L, P_M; R, CCS) \cdot S \\
& + VC_T(P_K, P_L, P_M; R, CCS) \cdot R \cdot D_T \\
& + FC_L(P_K, P_L, P_M; L) \\
& + VC_L(P_K, P_L, P_M; L) \cdot L \cdot D_L \qquad (2.10)
\end{aligned}
$$

A change in any of the underlying input parameters in equation (2.4) will lead to a more or less complicated change in total cost. For example, a change in one of the "demand" parameters will directly affect one or more of the quantities L, S, CCS, and R, which will in turn lead to a direct multiplicative effect as can be seen from (2.10). In addition there will be an indirect effect to the extent that the fixed and variable cost functions depend on these quantities. Similarly a change in any of the underlying input prices P_K, P_L, and P_M will have a direct impact through the fixed and variable cost functions as well as an indirect impact to the extent that such a change in prices results in a substitution effect among the technologies that the LECOM algorithm chooses to deploy. Any change in relative price can, in principle, result in a redesigned network that will be reflected in the distance functions D_L and D_T as well as the number of switches S that LECOM selects.

3   The Use of LECOM under Complete Information

3.1 Introduction

In this chapter we develop a simple application of the LECOM cost model described in the previous chapter that demonstrates its straightforward use as a regulatory measurement aid.[1] It is well known in the now-traditional regulation literature that the presence of subadditive[2] costs in an industry is a necessary condition for natural monopoly (see Baumol et al. 1982; Sharkey 1982), leading to a justification in the eyes of most economists for government regulation of that industry. At the same time the physical conditions under which this justification exists can be difficult to establish, particularly when the industry provides products or services through joint production. As in many of the examples discussed in this book, statistical data may not be reliable for various reasons; the dynamics of technological change may render established wisdom obsolete before the regulators become aware that this is so. An optimization tool such as LECOM, then, can help to determine either the necessity for regulation or the need for its removal. In this chapter we describe the application of the software to addressing the question of whether economies of scope exist in three prototypical networks.

Beginning with the licensing of private microwave systems in the years immediately following World War II, the Federal Communications Commission (FCC) began issuing a series of decisions that have encouraged entry into the long-distance part of the telephone industry. At each stage in which a further reduction in legal barriers to entry was considered, policy makers were confronted with the welfare effect of moving from a monopoly to an oligopolistic or competitive market structure. As alluded to earlier, the contribution made by economists has been constrained by the quality of the data. Economists traditionally used Bell System data to examine the extent to which the telecommunications industry is a natural monopoly. No observations were available on the cost of having two or more firms serve the same market. Lacking observations for firms that provided only part of the industry vector of outputs, tests for subadditivity of the cost function have been constrained to the output region of the observed data (see Evans and Heckman 1984; Palmer 1992). While this approach has its appeal, in that no extrapolations are made outside the sample which is used to estimate the cost function, the methodology does not allow for the possibility that an entrant will offer service with a significantly different vector of outputs and network topology than the incumbent.

Because LECOM allows us to estimate the cost of stand-alone telecommunications networks, we are able to estimate the cost of a single network that is required to carry four distinct outputs (toll and local switched services and toll and local private line) with the costs of various combinations of networks that carry only a single output as well as the cost of networks providing only some of the services. We find that in densely populated markets, there are no economies of scope between switched and unswitched services. In all markets there are strong economies of scope between switched toll and private line services. In this chapter we first discuss in some detail data problems encountered in more traditional approaches (section 3.2) and then turn to the description of an approach that uses LECOM (section 3.3). Section 3.4 presents the results, and section 3.5 gives some concluding remarks.

3.2   Data Problems Encountered in Prior Studies

In recent years, as policy makers have considered structural and pricing changes in the telecommunications industry, parties to regulatory and judicial proceedings have presented econometric estimates of the industry's total cost curve. Researchers were initially unable to reach strong conclusions because of the poor quality of data. Working with Bell System data for the years 1947 to 1977, analysts encountered the problem of how to control for technological change (Christensen et al. 1982, p. 7). The technology during this time period varied greatly. At the end of World War II, manual switchboards constituted 50 percent of the in-service switches owned by the Bell Operating Companies. But by 1977 operators were rarely used to complete calls. Indeed, over 20 percent of the switching machines were computer controlled electronic switching (FCC 1949, 1979, tables 15 and 25). While both research and development expenditures and the number of access lines served by modern switching machines have been used as proxies for technical change, they only roughly control for shifts in the cost curve. If shifts in the cost function are not properly taken into account, biased parameter estimates may result.

Analysts have also had trouble controlling for input prices and constructing output indexes for the various categories of service. Because of these and other data problems, Evans and Heckman (1984) argued that before conclusive statements about the cost function can be made, new data would have to be located.

Somewhat more recently Shin and Ying (hereafter SY) claimed that they "solved the data problems" (1992, p. 172). Using data constructed from the Federal Communications Commission's *Statistics of Communication Common Carriers*, SY use the translog flexible functional form to estimate the local exchange carriers' cost function.[3] They conclude that the "cost function is definitely not subadditive," and therefore efficiency gains can be achieved if the local exchange carriers are broken up (1992, p. 181). There are, however, at least five flaws with their methodology that might lead to questioning these conclusions.

First, the data source used by SY classifies the firms as local exchange companies. The SY analysis suggests that the output of these firms is limited to customer access, and exchange and toll usage. Many of the firms included in the data set were simultaneously providing such vertical services as private branch exchanges and key systems. Their model specification does not control for variations in these outputs across firms.

Many of the local exchange companies were also providing interexchange services. Bell Operating Companies such as Pacific Bell Telephone, as well as many of the larger independent telephone companies, owned interexchange facilities that were used to transport calls for hundreds of miles. Other carriers, such as Cincinnati Bell and small independent companies, had few interexchange facilities. The local exchange companies that had limited ownership of interexchange facilities handed off almost all toll calls to other carriers. The larger local exchange companies, on the other hand, were actively involved in interexchange transport. Since the large firms were providing interexchange transport service while most of the small firms were not, the marginal cost of a toll call within a large firm would be significantly higher than that for a small firm. The difference in cost is attributable to the varying functions carried out within the firm rather than to the increasing marginal costs of production, all else equal. Since SY are not able to control for

variations in mode of operations between firms, their parameter estimates are likely to be biased (Mundlak 1978).

SY attempted to control for economies of density by using a proxy
variable, average loop length (1992, p. 175). SY calculated average loop
length (AL) by dividing the miles of cable by the number of telephones.
They proposed that all else equal, density decreases as AL increases.
The miles of cable listed in the *Statistics of Common Carriers* includes
the wire used for interexchange, exchange interoffice (between central
offices), building cable, as well as the variable of interest, the cable used
to connect a central office to the customer's location. For large exchange
companies, the proxy for customer density would be biased upward
because of the inclusion of building, and interoffice and interexchange
cables that are of minimal magnitude for smaller companies.

SY calculated their real capital stock measurement by dividing capital
expenditures by a single communications equipment price deflator obtained from *The National Income and Product Accounts* (1992, p. 174). This
index is based on the cost of equipment used inside buildings (Flamm
1988, p. 30).[4] It does not take into account changes in the price of outside
plant; these facilities account for approximately one-third of the local exchange companies' investment. Since the price trend for outside plant
facilities was significantly different from that for inside plant, there is
the possibility of inconsistent and biased estimates resulting from the
measurement error.[5]

Finally, many of the output values constructed by SY to test for subadditivity of the cost function were not technically feasible during the
period of the study. In their test, SY apportion market output between
two hypothetical firms A and B. They constructed hypothetical output
vectors as follows:

$$q^a = \left(q_1^a, q_2^a, q_3^a\right) = \left(\kappa q_1^m, \lambda q_2^m, \mu q_3^m\right)$$
$$q^b = \left(q_1^b, q_2^b, q_3^b\right) = \left((1-\kappa)q_1^m, (1-\lambda)q_2^m, (1-\mu)q_3^m\right)$$

$$(3.1)$$

where the scalars κ, λ, and $\mu = (0.1, 0.2, \ldots, 0.9)$ and q_i^m (for $i = 1, 2, 3$)
refer to, respectively, access, local, and toll calls of the monopoly (m)
firm (1992, pp. 1777–78). The cost function is subadditive if

$$C\left(\kappa q_1^m, \lambda q_2^m, \mu q_3^m\right) + C\left((1-\kappa)q_1^m, (1-\lambda)q_2^m, (1-\mu)q_3^m\right) > C\left(q_1^m, q_2^m, q_3^m\right)$$

$$(3.2)$$

During the peak-calling hour, the period that determines most central
office capital expenditures, usage per access line is typically in the order

of 5 minutes.[6] Assume that initially q_1, the number of customer access lines in a market, is equal to 100, and usage per subscriber during the peak calling hour is five minutes. SY allowed the value of κ to be as low as 0.1, while λ and μ can be as high as 0.9. Under these assumptions, firm A would supply 10 access lines and 450 minutes of usage. This translates to 45 minutes of usage per line. This level of usage is not observed even among the most intense users of switched services,[7] and as a result switching machines have not been designed to handle such a high load level.

3.3 Using the LECOM Model for Subadditivity Calculations

Judge Harold H. Greene, who oversaw the 1974 AT&T antitrust case, concurred with the Department of Justice that it was necessary to monitor and control the activities of the Bell Operating Companies because the local exchange market was a "natural monopoly." Judge Greene concluded that effective competition was not likely to occur in the near future because there were "very substantial economies of scale and scope" (*US* v. *Western Electric*, 673 F. Supp. 525, 538 D.D.C., 1987). Judge Greene's characterization of the cost structure of the industry critically hinges on the question of cost subadditivity. In this chapter we address the issue of economies of scope by analyzing data generated with LECOM.

Traditionally economists analyzed the cost structure of an industry using sample observations of the relationships between input prices, outputs, and the costs of production. But, to avoid the data problems encountered in earlier work (see section 3.2), we choose instead to study the cost function by working with data generated through LECOM simulations. LECOM is designed to select the combination and placement of facilities in a way that minimizes the cost of production. Since the placement and selection of the number of network nodes is endogenous, we use the simulation model to represent the long-run cost function. The simulation involves three steps. First, as explained in chapter 2, algorithms are developed that model the production function. Second, the cost–output relationship is derived from the assumed optimization behavior. Here the minimum cost of production is identified for various output levels given 1990 input prices and the production function. Finally, the information contained in the data set created by the simulation is summarized in a form familiar and useful to an economist or policy maker.

The data generated by the simulation offers some important advantages relative to the data set used in previous studies. As argued by
Griffin, "The explicit representations of the technology in the . . . process
model offers particularly important advantages for long-run analysis
in which technological and . . . policy changes lie outside the range of
historical time series experience" (1977, p. 391). The LECOM model reflects the cost of using state-of-the-art digital technology. The data set
used by SY ended in 1983, six years later than the observations used by
Christensen et al. (1983), Evans and Heckman (1983), and Charnes et al.
(1988). The use of more current cost data provides a clearer picture of
the cost structure of this rapidly changing industry.

Much of the research interest in the cost structure of the industry is tied
to a concern about the efficiency of entry and competition. In previous
econometric studies of the telephone industry, the level of observation
was the firm. The firms included in the data sets serviced small towns
and large cities. The cost data for different markets were aggregated into
a single observation. For example, the supplier, New York Telephone,
serviced cities with customer densities ranging from under 250 to over
75,000 per square mile.[8] In SY's data set, these heterogenous markets
are aggregated into one observation. Since the level of observation is
the firm, SY are unable to observe or measure competition in specific
markets.[9] In order to understand the cost structure of the markets where
competition occurs, it is necessary to have data on the cost of serving
cities or limited neighborhoods such as a city's business district.

Before examining the cost estimates from LECOM, we briefly look at
two big limitations of engineering optimization models: the estimation
of administrative costs and the matter of bounded rationality. These two
points are discussed in turn.

Optimization models are designed to identify the cost-minimizing
technical configuration that will satisfy a given level of demand. Optimization models are usually not designed to quantify the less tangible
costs of providing service. In particular, the models are intended to simulate the physical production processes, and little or no attention is paid
to measuring marketing and administrative efforts. For a number of
years the telephone companies have been submitting long-term incremental plans to state and federal commissions. In response to the charge
that their process models did not fully incorporate overhead costs, the
telephone companies have developed loading factors that take into account administrative and marketing expenses. Those loading factors
have been included in our model.[10]

The analytical properties of the LECOM cost function are difficult to determine outside of a direct experimental context. That is, it is not possible to know whether the cost function is globally concave, which means that we do not know if the solution found by our optimization model is a local or global minimum. Since there are an infinite number of possible configurations to be considered, and each proposed solution is costly to evaluate, we limit our research to a reasonable number of possibilities. For each economically and technically feasible combination of switches, we allow for up to 1,000 possible iterations. An iteration involves the calculation of the cost of service at one or more alternative locations for the switches. For each market, and a given level of demand, LECOM evaluates a number of different switch combinations. This further increases the number of solutions that are evaluated. Therefore, while this search process is not exhaustive, the model considers a wide range of feasible solutions.

3.4   Empirical Results

3.4.1   *Measuring Economies of Scope*

An industry is considered to be a natural monopoly if and only if a single firm can produce the desired output at lower cost than any combination of two or more firms. This property, known as the subadditivity of the cost function, holds if for any set of goods $N = \{1, \ldots, n\}$ and for any m output vectors $Q_1, \ldots, Q_m$ of goods in N: $C(Q_1) + C(Q_2) + \cdots + C(Q_m) > C(Q_1 + Q_2 + \cdots + Q_m)$ (Baumol 1977, p. 810). A necessary but not sufficient condition for a natural monopoly is the presence of economies of scope. Economies of scope exist if there is some exhaustive partitioning of the output space into nonintersecting subsets and the cost of separately producing each subset exceeds the cost of producing all outputs jointly (Panzar 1989, pp. 15–16).[11]

Let us assume that the firm produces four outputs measured in terms of the standard North American unit of hundred call seconds (CCS): switched toll and exchange services, and toll and exchange private line services.[12] Let X_1, X_2, X_3, and X_4 represent exchange switched service, toll switched service, local private line service, and toll private line services, respectively. We have estimated the annual cost (in 1990 $US) of producing these services in common (i.e., if all four services are provided through one network), as well as the cost of producing only subsets of these services. These computations were made by entering the desired value for each X for each subset of services and setting remaining

Table 3.1
Cost of stand-alone networks

	Cost
Outputs	
X_1, X_2, X_3, X_4	25,549,965
X_1	20,367,226
X_2	18,793,975
X_3	2,313,658
X_4	1,882,234
X_1, X_2	21,553,947
X_3, X_4	3,544,048
X_1, X_3	22,694,392
X_2, X_3	21,467,396
X_2, X_4	19,928,418
X_1, X_3, X_4	24,152,641
X_1, X_2, X_4	23,028,627
X_1, X_2, X_3	24,355,382
X_2, X_3, X_4	22,018,534
Volume	
X_1 Busy-hour exchange CCS	402,530
X_2 Busy-hour toll CCS	55,932
X_3 Local private lines	17,308
X_4 Toll private lines	4,685
Access lines	157,007

inputs to zero. The results for a city with 179,000 customers spread over 8.12 square miles are reported in table 3.1.[13]

In order to determine the extent to which there are economies of scope, in table 3.2, we compare the cost of providing all four services on one network ($C(X_1, X_2, X_3, X_4) = 25,549,965$), with the cost of providing the four services on two or more networks (see column b).

The first row of table 3.2 shows that the total cost of providing exchange service on one network $C(X_1)$ and switched toll and private line services on a second network $C(X_2, X_3, X_4)$ is 42,385,760, which by table 3.1 is equal to (20,367,226 + 22,018,534). The cost of providing the four services on one network is 25,549,965. Consequently the ratio appearing in column d is greater than zero. When this ratio is greater than zero, economies of scope are present. This indicates that it is more expensive to construct two networks than to provide all four services on one network.

Table 3.2
Economies of scope

Multinetwork offering* (a)	Stand-alone cost (b)	Degree of scope economies** (d)
$C(X_1) + C(X_2, X_3, X_4)$	42,385,760	0.658936
$C(X_2) + C(X_1, X_3, X_4)$	42,946,616	0.680887
$C(X_3) + C(X_1, X_2, X_4)$	25,342,285	−0.008130
$C(X_4) + C(X_1, X_2, X_3)$	26,237,616	0.026914
$C(X_1) + C(X_2) + C(X_3) + C(X_4)$	43,357,093	0.696953
$C(X_1, X_2) + C(X_3, X_4)$	25,097,995	−0.017690
$C(X_1, X_4) + C(X_2, X_4)$	42,165,522	0.650316
$C(X_1, X_2) + C(X_3) + C(X_4)$	25,749,839	0.007823
$C(X_1, X_3) + C(X_2) + C(X_4)$	43,370,601	0.697482
$C(X_1, X_4) + C(X_2) + C(X_3)$	42,575,029	0.666344
$C(X_2, X_3) + C(X_1) + C(X_4)$	42,947,586	0.680925
$C(X_2, X_4) + C(X_1) + C(X_3)$	42,609,303	0.667685
$C(X_3, X_4) + C(X_1) + C(X_2)$	42,705,249	0.671441

*The volumes X_1, X_2, X_3, and X_4 are given in the lower panel of table 3.1.
**In this column, values greater than zero indicate economies of scope and values less than zero indicate diseconomies of scope. This column d is computed according to the formula $(d) = (b - c)/c$, where b refers to the column b containing the cost of stand-alone networks and c is the cost of providing all services jointly, which is 25,549,965 from table 3.1.

In two of the combinations appearing in table 3.2, the value in column d is less than zero and therefore there are diseconomies of scope. The absence of economies of scope is due to the trade-off between longer loops and interoffice trunks. When switched exchange or toll service is offered, costs are minimized by housing switch functions at more than one location. While this increases the cost of interoffice trunking, it provides significant savings in loop costs.[14]

The model determined that if all services were offered on one network, cost would be minimized by providing service through four different offices. For a stand-alone private line system, LECOM determined that cost would be minimized by having all loops terminate at one wire center.[15] For the stand-alone private line systems, the additional trunking costs made it inefficient to establish more than one office.

When private line services are offered on a common network with switched services, extra trunk costs are incurred (because of the need to use interoffice trunks to connect local private line customers who are served by more than one central office). This additional cost is the primary source of diseconomies of scope.

Table 3.3
Customer density

Type of neighborhood	Density (customers per square mile)
Single-family	2,560–3,840
High-density residential (high-rise apartments)	20,480–49,960
Office park	7,680–10,240
Industial park	1,280–11,536
Medium-density business	5,120–7,680
High-density business	153,600–179,200
Commercial strip (linear mile)	614

Source: Gabel and Kennet (1991).

Table 3.4
Economies of scope

Customers per square mile* (a)	Degree of economies of scope: minimum/ maximum (b)	Exchange CCS (c)	Toll CCS (d)	Local private lines (e)	Toll private lines (f)	Access lines (g)
2,772	0.09/0.81	266,924	62,367	13,611	7,169	101,437
3,419	0.06/0.82	502,434	110,141	21,337	7,265	183,438
4,052	0.08/0.82	411,750	68,817	15,395	8,289	154,348
4,889	0.07/0.94	415,645	57,216	5,392	2,596	146,984
5,994	0.08/0.81	938,338	204,583	27,250	7,375	309,371
8,199	0.01/0.74	402,354	55,908	17,308	4,685	157,007
22,037	−0.02/0.70	402,530**	55,932	17,308	4,685	157,007
25,323	0.01/0.74	411,750	68,817	15,395	8,289	154,348
170,060	−0.20/0.70	402,530	55,932	17,308	4,685	157,007

*[Local private lines + Toll private lines + Access lines]/Square mile.
**Data also appear in table 3.1.

For the data reported in table 3.2 there were 22,037 customers per square mile. As indicated in table 3.3, this is in the range of customer density found in high-density residential neighborhoods in the United States. This density is, however, considerably lower than the number of customers per square mile found in high-density business districts.

Table 3.4 provides summary information for a range of city sizes and usage levels. In column *a* we report customer density per square mile. In column *b* we report the degree of economies of scope. Columns *c* through *g* identify the level of output. In column *b*, values greater than zero indicate the presence of economies of scope, whereas values less than zero indicate the presence of diseconomies of scope. The reported values are the minimum and maximum values of the different output combinations identified in table 3.2.

Cost savings are achieved in low-density markets by everyone sharing a fixed cost of production. Economies of scope are present in these markets, and therefore the necessary condition for a natural monopoly is satisfied.[16] These economies dissipate as the number of customers per square mile increases to the level associated with high-density residential communities (more than 20,000 customers per square mile). In two of the three densely populated markets that we studied, the degree of economies of scope is less than zero. The results from the optimization model indicate that if the stylized city were serviced by separate networks for switched and unswitched services, costs would be lower relative to the case where one network provided both types of services. The separate networks for switched and private line services could be run by either an existing local exchange carrier or an entrant.

The results reported in table 3.4 suggest that the likelihood of entry increases with customer density. This is consistent with recent trends in the industry; entry has indeed largely occurred in high-density nonresidential markets. Entry could be the result of one or both of the following factors. First, in high-density markets the distance between the customer and the telephone company's office is relatively short compared to less dense markets (New England Telephone 1986, b1). The cost of connecting a customer to the office increases with the distance of that customer from the nearest facility shared with other customers. If the lower cost of providing connections on short routes is not reflected in the rates, subscribers in densely populated markets may be charged a rate that exceeds the cost of service. The supracompetitive price would attract entry.

Second, an entrant may also be attracted to a densely populated market because of the diseconomies of scope of the type of those that have been identified by LECOM. The number of nodes on a network is determined by the number of customers served and the size of the service territory. In densely populated markets the incumbent telephone companies provide service through multiple locations.

Entrants have found that because they serve a smaller number of customers than the incumbent, and provide almost exclusively unswitched services (X_3 and X_4), production costs are minimized by constructing a network with fewer nodes. For example, while New York Telephone serves the area of Manhattan south of 96th Street with switching machines at over 15 locations, an entrant, Teleport, serves the same territory with just one node.[17] We note that the incremental cost estimates we show here are similar to those of Mitchell (1990) and those made by at least one industry participant (New England Telephone 1986). For example, for a roughly similar experiment involving a city of about 40,000 lines, LECOM gives a loop cost estimate of about $113 per year (Gabel and Kennet 1991), while Mitchell shows about $104 and NET shows a range from $69 to $156.

3.4.2 Economies of Scope in Switched Services

The data reported in table 3.5 indicate that the degree of scope economies between toll and exchange service is in the order of 0.8 for a large range of customer densities. These economies of scope mostly arise from the public input nature of the local loop. Panzar defines joint goods as inputs that "once acquired for use in producing one good, they are costlessly available for use in the production of others" (1989, p. 17). Local and toll usage on an access line during the peak hour is in the order of five minutes (Rey 1983, p. 125). Once the loop is installed for a given service, the additional cost of providing another service over the same facility is nil.[18] If, on the other hand, local and toll services are provided on

Table 3.5
Economies of scope for switched services

Customers per square mile*	Degree of economies of scope**	Exchange CCS	Toll CCS	Access lines
2,301	0.74	266,924	62,367	101,437
2,958	0.81	502,434	110,141	183,438
3,513	0.82	411,750	68,817	154,348
4,637	0.78	415,645	57,216	146,984
5,390	0.81	938,338	204,583	309,371
7,191	0.81	402,354	55,908	157,007
19,322	0.82	402,530***	55,932	157,007
21,954	0.78	411,750	68,817	154,348
149,165	0.82	402,530	55,932	157,007

*Access lines per square mile.
**Values greater than zero indicate economies of scope, and values less than zero indicate diseconomies of scope.
***Data also appear in table 3.1.

separate networks, the nontrivial cost of the loop is duplicated. In light of these intuitively clear strong economies of scope that derive from the shared use of the local loop, there are reasons to be skeptical about SY's finding that for the products access lines and toll and exchange calls, the cost function is superadditive.

It should be noted that a potential shortcoming of the bottom-up modeling approach is the failure to account for managerial economies and diseconomies. The bottom-up method used here necessarily investigates costs at the level of the service area, while managerial economies and diseconomies would occur at a super-regional level. One can argue, however, that the evidence in the industry suggests that, if anything, there are managerial economies of scale rather than diseconomies. For example, the number of regional Bell Operating Companies has dropped from seven after the breakup in 1984 to four today. Several of these four, in turn, have either absorbed, or been absorbed by, non-Bell companies. In 1985, according to the FCC, there were 1,518 study areas in the United States. A study area represents the service area of a unique company operating within a state. By 1999 this number had fallen to 1,426. While both numbers actually represent overestimates of the number of telephone companies operating within the United States, the change together with anecdotal evidence clearly indicates that the total number of companies has declined significantly in recent years. This fact suggests that management believes it can operate most efficiently when the scale of operations is larger rather than smaller. Thus it would appear that if anything, the bottom-up approach underestimates rather than overestimates the degree of economies of scope, since it fails to capture the managerial effect.

3.5 Conclusion

The main results from LECOM derived in this chapter appear to be consistent with the evolution of the industry. Prior to 1980, local and toll calls were completed through separate exchange networks. AT&T found that there were strong economies of scope from combining these two services in one exchange network.[19] More recently the local exchange companies have faced their strongest competition in the private line market. There has been little entry into the switched exchange market. This is consistent with the economies of scope for switched services identified in this chapter, although one should mention the effect of higher regulatory barriers to entry in the switched market (NTIA 1988).

One policy implication of the study described in this chapter is that regulatory oversight of the incumbents' pricing of local network access in the presence of private line service may be problematic. The question of a proper allocation of cost between these two services which share a large portion of the network infrastructure can be addressed using LECOM, but regulators must be aware of the appropriate methodology for such an allocation (see Sharkey 1982). At times when faced with entry, the local exchange companies have adopted rates that were based on the cost structure of their competitors (Temin 1990, p. 353). If the incumbents continue to use one network for both switched and unswitched services, efficient production could be achieved provided that regulatory authorities allow incumbents to set rates for private line services based on the marginal cost of production of the existing network architecture.

While there are diseconomies of scope in part of the local exchange market, the LECOM calculation approach departs from Shin and Ying in the measurement of their magnitude. This approach does not yield "considerable" (Shin and Ying 1992, p. 181) diseconomies of scope. Consequently the larger gains expected from competition are most likely to arise from the dynamic incentives of rivalry rather than static diseconomies of scope.

4

Regulation under
Incomplete Information

4.1 Introduction

The literature on the new economics of regulation has stressed the role of asymmetric information between regulators and regulated firms, in particular, asymmetric information about cost functions.[1] Before explaining in chapter 5 how asymmetric information is introduced in the engineering model described in chapter 2, we present in this chapter a canonical model of regulation that will constitute the central theoretical basis of the empirical analyses conducted in this book.

In section 4.2 we describe the basic theoretical model we will be using throughout the remaining chapter. This regulation model of a telecommunications monopoly is borrowed from Laffont and Tirole (1986). The production cost of the regulated good depends on an efficiency characteristic that is private information of the regulated firm and on a level of effort that decreases cost but creates a disutility for the firm's managers. The complete information benchmark is also derived in this section. In this complete information scheme, the marginal disutility of effort equates the marginal cost saving, the price of the regulated good equates the social marginal cost, and no rent is left to the firm.

Optimal regulation under incomplete information when cost is observable ex post is characterized in section 4.3. Asymmetric information obliges the regulator to give up an information rent to efficient firms. This rent is socially costly because it must be financed with distortive taxes and the regulator wishes to decrease it. To do so, the regulator accepts some distortions. First, it offers a menu of cost-reimbursement rules among which firms self-select themselves according to their type. These rules induce underprovisions of effort relative to the complete information allocations. Second, pricing is made according to the Ramsey rule with two corrections: an incentive correction may be added to the Ramsey pricing formula (under some conditions on the cost function this correction is not needed) and the marginal cost in the Ramsey rule is evaluated at the effort level induced by the cost-reimbursement rule and not the complete information effort level. The ex post observability of cost requires proper auditing, which may not be available or which may be too costly, and regulation must then be designed in the absence of cost observability. Section 4.4 derives optimal regulation in the absence of cost observability. In addition to transfers, regulation has then only one instrument, namely pricing, to decrease the socially costly information rents that must be given up to the efficient types. Distortion of pricing, and therefore of the production level, with respect to Ramsey pricing is then always needed.

The two types of regulation characterized in sections 4.3 and 4.4 use transfers from the regulator to the firm. These transfers could alternatively come from consumers in the form of the fixed fees of two-part tariffs; then the social distortions would not arise from the distortive financing of the transfers but from the costly disconnections of those who would not find it worthwhile to pay the fixed fees. We do not derive this type of regulation for it requires a delicate modeling of consumers' behavior; instead, we characterize in section 4.5 several variants of price-cap regulation which is a regulation without transfers and without cost observability. A simple cap on prices makes the firm residual claimant for its cost saving and induces an effort level that is efficient conditionally on the quantity produced. However, it yields high rents to the efficient types. This very common regulatory rule is sometimes complemented by taxation of the firm's profit (in which case cost observability is again assumed). This approach decreases profits, and therefore incentives for cost minimization, but enables the regulator to decrease the information rents.

Finally, in section 4.6 the traditional cost-plus regulation is characterized. Under this scheme the firm that is fully reimbursed for its costs has no incentive to minimize them. Effort is minimal and efficiency low. However, the regulator is then able to eliminate information rents. To mitigate the distortions due to the balanced budget condition implicit in cost-plus regulation, the regulator may complement the revenues of the firm with costly transfers. This cost-plus regulation with transfers is also considered in this section.

4.2   The Model

We consider a single-product regulated firm with aggregate cost function

$$C = C(\beta, e, q) \tag{4.1}$$

where β is a technological parameter or firm's type, with $C_\beta > 0$, e is its managers' cost-reducing effort, with $C_e < 0$, q is the firm's output level, with $C_q > 0$ and $C_{qq} < 0$.

We denote $E(\beta, C, q)$ the effort required for a firm of type β to produce q at cost C. By definition,

$$C = C(\beta, E(\beta, C, q), q) \tag{4.2}$$

First, we assume that cost is ex post observable, and we make the accounting convention that cost is reimbursed by the regulator to the firm and that the revenue $R(q)$ generated by the sale of outputs is received by the regulator.

Letting t denote the net monetary transfer[2] from the regulator to the firm and ψ the disutility of effort for the firm's managers (with $\psi(0) = 0$, $\psi' > 0$, $\psi'' < 0$), the objective function of the firm is

$$U = t - \psi(e) \tag{4.3}$$

The firm is willing to participate in the regulatory process if and only if its participation constraint is satisfied; here

$$U \geq 0 \tag{4.4}$$

Let $1 + \lambda$ (> 1) denote the social value of public funds. If $S(q)$ is the gross consumer surplus attached to the consumption of telecommunications goods q, the social value of q, denoted $V(q)$, is equal to the sum of the net consumer surplus, $S(q) - R(q)$, and of the social value from the sales of the goods, $(1 + \lambda)R(q)$. That is,

$$V(q) = S(q) + \lambda R(q) \tag{4.5}$$

This social value of production is composed of the utility of the good supplemented by the fiscal value of revenues, namely the decrease of tax distortions allowed by these revenues. In particular, for linear prices such that $R(q) = P(q)q$, where $P(\cdot)$ is the inverse demand function,

$$V(q) = S(q) + \lambda P(q)q \tag{4.6}$$

Consumers' welfare (CW) equals the utility of the good minus the costs, which include the real cost C and the transfer to the firm t evaluated at the social value of public funds:

$$CW = V(q) - (1 + \lambda)(t + C(\beta, e, q)) \tag{4.7}$$

The utilitarian social welfare function is the sum of the consumers' welfare and the firm's welfare:

$$W = [V(q) - (1 + \lambda)(t + C(\beta, e, q))] + U \tag{4.8}$$

$$= V(q) - (1 + \lambda)(C(\beta, e, q) + \psi(e)) - \lambda U \tag{4.9}$$

From expression (4.9) of the social welfare function we see that it is costly to give up rents ($U > 0$) to the firm. Under complete information this does not happen. Then maximizing social welfare under the firm's participation constraint (4.4) yields

$$\psi'(e) = -C_e(\beta, e, q) \tag{4.10}$$

$$V'(q) = (1 + \lambda)C_q(\beta, e, q) \tag{4.11}$$

$$t = \psi(e) \quad \text{or} \quad U = 0 \tag{4.12}$$

The marginal disutility of effort is equated to the marginal cost saving of effort, (4.10). The marginal social valuation of production is equated to the marginal social cost of production, (4.11). As the regulator is fully informed, he leaves no rent to the firm in order to save on the tax distortions, (4.12).

Under complete information this optimal allocation can be implemented in various ways with cost-plus schemes, price-caps, or more general cost-sharing rules.

4.3 Optimal Regulation under Incomplete Information with Cost Observability

Regulation takes place now under incomplete information. The regulator observes neither β nor e, which are known by the firm. The regulator must design regulation without knowing the cost characteristic β. He is modeled as a Bayesian statistician who has a prior probability distribution on β and who maximizes expected social welfare. We assume thus that it is common knowledge that β is drawn from a cumulative distribution function[3] $F(\cdot)$ on $[\underline{\beta}, \bar{\beta}]$ with a density function $f(\beta) > 0$ for any β.

For simplicity of exposition we assume that no type is ever shut down in the solutions of the various programs below. In other words, the social value of production is so high that the firm must be active whatever its cost characteristics.

We model regulation as a revelation mechanism[4]

$$q(\tilde{\beta}), C(\tilde{\beta}), t(\tilde{\beta}) \tag{4.13}$$

which specifies, for each announcement $\tilde{\beta}$, a production level to realize, a cost target to meet, and a net transfer from the regulator.

The utility level of a β-firm claiming that it is of type $\tilde{\beta}$ is

$$\hat{U}(\beta, \tilde{\beta}) = t(\tilde{\beta}) - \psi(E(\beta, C(\tilde{\beta}), q(\tilde{\beta}))) \tag{4.14}$$

Truthful revelation of the cost characteristic β or incentive compatibility amounts to

$$t(\beta) - \psi(E(\beta, C(\beta), q(\beta))) \geq t(\tilde{\beta}) - \psi(E(\beta, C(\tilde{\beta}), q(\tilde{\beta}))) \tag{4.15}$$

for all $(\beta, \tilde{\beta})$. In other words, $\tilde{\beta} = \beta$ must maximize $\hat{U}(\beta, \tilde{\beta})$ and for a differentiable mechanism,[5]

$$\dot{t}(\beta) = \psi'(e)(E_C \dot{C}(\beta) + E_q \dot{q}(\beta)) \tag{4.16}$$

Let $U(\beta)$ denote firm β's utility level when it tells the truth, $U(\beta) = \hat{U}(\beta, \beta)$. From the envelope theorem[6] the first-order incentive compatibility condition is[7]

$$\dot{U}(\beta) = -\psi'(e)E_\beta(\beta, C(\beta, e, q), q) \tag{4.17}$$

So incentive theory characterizes, through (4.17), the additional constraints put by asymmetric information on the allocation of resources. The regulator who does not know β behaves as a Bayesian statistician and maximizes expected social welfare under the participation constraints (4.4) and the new incentive constraints (4.17). That is, he solves

$$\max_{\{q(\cdot), e(\cdot), U(\cdot)\}} E_\beta W = \int_{\underline{\beta}}^{\bar{\beta}} [V(q(\beta)) - (1 + \lambda)(C(\beta, e(\beta), q(\beta)) + \psi(e(\beta))$$

$$- \lambda U(\beta)]f(\beta) d\beta \tag{4.18}$$

subject to conditions (4.4) and (4.17). The first-order conditions of this program[8] are

$$\psi'(e) = -C_e - \frac{\lambda}{1+\lambda} \frac{F(\beta)}{f(\beta)} \frac{d}{de}(\psi'(e)E_\beta) \tag{4.19}$$

$$V'(q) = (1+\lambda)C_q + \lambda \frac{F(\beta)}{f(\beta)} \psi'(e) \frac{d}{dq} E_\beta \tag{4.20}$$

Equation (4.19) refers to the cost-reimbursement rule embedded in the optimal regulation. Let us see why. When the firm is a residual claimant for its cost savings due to effort, the firm equates the marginal disutility of effort, $\psi'(e)$, to marginal cost saving, $-C_e$. If a share α of its cost is reimbursed, the firm solves

$$\min_e [\psi(e) + (1-\alpha)C(\beta, e, q)] \tag{4.21}$$

hence

$$\psi'(e) = -(1-\alpha)C_e \tag{4.22}$$

Therefore, in (4.19),

$$\frac{\lambda}{1+\lambda} \frac{F(\beta)}{f(\beta)} \frac{d(\psi'(e)E_\beta)/de}{(-C_e)} \tag{4.23}$$

can be interpreted as the share α of costs reimbursed to the type β firm.

The share $1-\alpha$ represents the power of the incentive scheme. Indeed, if $\alpha = 0$, the firm is residual claimant of its cost savings and chooses the level of effort that is first best conditionally on the level of output. This is a high-powered incentive scheme. If $\alpha = 1$, the whole monetary cost is reimbursed to the firm and there is no incentive for effort. This is a low-powered incentive scheme.

Equation (4.20) describes optimal pricing. For linear pricing $R(q) = P(q)q$ and

$$V'(q) = S'(q) + \lambda[P'(q)q + P(q)] \tag{4.24}$$

Noting that $S'(q) = p$, from (4.20) we have the Lerner index formula:

$$\frac{p - C_q}{p} = \frac{\lambda}{1+\lambda} \frac{1}{\eta} + \frac{\lambda}{1+\lambda} \frac{F(\beta)}{f(\beta)} \frac{\psi'(e)}{p} \frac{d}{dq} E_\beta \tag{4.25}$$

or

$$L = R + I \tag{4.26}$$

where η is the price elasticity of demand. We thus obtain a modified Ramsey pricing rule in which the Lerner index, $L = (p - C_q)/p$, equals the inverse price elasticity of demand times $\lambda/(1 + \lambda)$, $R = (\lambda/(1 + \lambda))(1/\eta)$, to which an incentive correction I given by

$$I = \frac{\lambda}{1 + \lambda} \frac{F(\beta)}{f(\beta)} \cdot \frac{\psi'(e)}{p} \cdot \frac{d}{dq} E_\beta \tag{4.27}$$

is added.

In general, incentive considerations affect pricing. Let us see why. We can integrate equation (4.17) to obtain the information rent of a type β form (using the fact that $U(\bar{\beta}) = 0$, since rents are costly to the regulator)

$$U(\beta) = \int_\beta^{\bar{\beta}} \psi'(e(b)) E_\beta(b, C(b, e(b), q(b)), q(b)) \, db \tag{4.28}$$

Contrary to the situation of complete information, the regulator is now obliged to give up this rent which is socially costly.[9] He will then want to decrease it. From (4.28) this is possible by decreasing $e(\beta)$ to decrease $\psi'(e(\beta))$ and also by more sophisticated distortions involving also $q(\beta)$ and therefore pricing when E_β is a function of $q(\cdot)$.

A dichotomy between pricing and incentives occurs when the incentive correction vanishes, that is, when

$$\frac{d}{dq} E_\beta \equiv 0 \tag{4.29}$$

which holds if and only if

$$C = C(\Phi(\beta, e), q) \tag{4.30}$$

by the Leontief theorem.[10] When the rate E_β at which the firm can substitute a decrease of effort to an increase of β—which affects how the information rent must decrease with β for incentive reasons; see (4.28)—is independent of the production level, it is useless to distort the production level to decrease the information rent. This benchmark case of dichotomy is interesting for its simplicity, and we will investigate empirically whether it can be viewed as a reasonable approximation for the true cost function.[11]

Optimal regulation with cost observability will be referred to as LT regulation from Laffont and Tirole (1986).

4.4   Optimal Regulation without Cost Observability

When cost is not observable and therefore cannot be reimbursed, the firm has always the incentive to choose the optimal effort level given its type and production level,

$$\psi'(e) = -C_e(\beta, e, q) \tag{4.31}$$

Letting $e^*(\beta, q)$ denote the solution of (4.31), the firm's objective function is now

$$U(\beta) = t(\beta) - C(\beta, e^*(\beta, q(\beta)), q(\beta)) - \psi(e^*(\beta, q(\beta))) \tag{4.32}$$

Following the same steps as in the previous section, we can derive the incentive constraint which, from the envelope theorem, writes now as

$$\dot{U}(\beta) = -C_\beta(\beta, e^*(\beta, q(\beta)), q(\beta)) \tag{4.33}$$

The regulator's program becomes

$$\max_{q(\cdot), U(\cdot)} \int_{\underline{\beta}}^{\bar{\beta}} [V(q(\beta)) - (1 + \lambda)(C(\beta, e^*(\beta, q(\beta)), q(\beta))$$
$$+ \psi(e^*(\beta, q(\beta))) - \lambda U(\beta)] f(\beta) \, d\beta \tag{4.34}$$

subject to (4.33) and $U(\beta) \geq 0$ for any β. The first-order condition of this program is

$$V'(q) = (1 + \lambda)C_q + \lambda \frac{F(\beta)}{f(\beta)} C_{\beta q} \tag{4.35}$$

or for linear pricing,

$$\frac{p - C_q}{p} = \frac{\lambda}{1 + \lambda} \frac{1}{\eta} + \frac{\lambda}{1 + \lambda} \frac{F(\beta)}{f(\beta)} \frac{C_{\beta q}}{p} \tag{4.36}$$

Without cost observability we have lost one instrument and the distortion of the pricing rule away from Ramsey pricing is now the only way to decrease the information rent. Indeed, from (4.33) the information rent is

$$U(\beta) = \int_\beta^{\bar{\beta}} C_\beta(b, e^*(b, q(b)), q(b)) \, db \tag{4.37}$$

and only a distortion of $q(\cdot)$ can affect it.

The optimal regulation without cost observability will be referred to as BM regulation from Baron and Myerson (1982).

4.5 Price-Cap Regulation

Price-cap regulation is a regulation without cost observability and without transfer. Let $q(p)$ be the demand function. Let us denote by $p^M(\beta)$ the profit-maximizing price associated with the optimal effort level, that is, the solution in p of

$$\max_{e,p} pq(p) - C(\beta, e, q(p)) - \psi(e) \tag{4.38}$$

The first-order conditions of (4.38) can readily be seen to be[12]

$$\psi'(e) = -C_e(\beta, e, q(p)) \tag{4.39}$$

and

$$p - C_q(\beta, e, q(p)) = -\frac{q(p)}{dq(p)/dp} \quad \text{or} \quad \frac{p - C_q}{p} = \frac{1}{\eta} \tag{4.40}$$

the latter being the classical monopoly pricing formula. Under appropriate assumptions on the aggregate cost function ($C_{ee} > 0$, $C_{\beta e} > 0$, $C_{eq} < 0$, and $C_{\beta q} > 0$), it can be shown, by using a standard revealed-preference argument, that the monopoly price is nondecreasing in β. A regulatory solution with a price-cap $\bar{p}$ gives the monopoly price $p^M(\beta)$ for β less than or equal to some β^* and $\bar{p}$ for $\beta > \beta^*$ (see figure 4.1).[13]

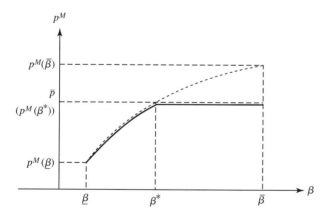

Figure 4.1
Price-cap with downward price flexibility

So the optimal price-cap regulation in this simple example with a single price is obtained by finding the optimal value β^* or the optimal $\bar{p}$ under the condition that the least efficient firm (type $\bar{\beta}$) does not make negative profit; that is, the optimal price-cap regulation solves

$$\max_{\bar{p}} \left(\int_{\underline{\beta}}^{\beta^*} [S(q(p^M(\beta))) - C(\beta, e^*(\beta, q(p^M(\beta))), q(p^M(\beta)))\right.$$

$$- \psi(e^*(\beta, q(p^M(\beta))))] f(\beta) \, d\beta$$

$$+ \int_{\beta^*}^{\bar{\beta}} [S(q(\bar{p})) - C(\beta, e^*(\beta, q(\bar{p})), q(\bar{p}))$$

$$\left. - \psi(e^*(\beta, q(\bar{p})))] f(\beta) \, d\beta \right) \tag{4.41}$$

under the participation constraint of the least efficient firm,

$$\bar{p} q(\bar{p}) - C(\bar{\beta}, e^*(\bar{\beta}, q(\bar{p})), q(\bar{p})) - \psi(e^*(\bar{\beta}, q(\bar{p}))) \geq 0 \tag{4.42}$$

Two regimes are possible a priori, according to whether or not the constraint (4.42) is binding. With $C_{qq} < 0$, this constraint is binding. Suppose that it is not. Then $q(\bar{p})$ maximizes (4.41) without constraint. Using (4.39), the first-order condition is

$$\int_{\beta^*}^{\bar{\beta}} [S'(q(\bar{p})) - C_q(\beta, e^*(\beta, q(\bar{p})), q(\bar{p}))] f(\beta) \, d\beta = 0 \tag{4.43}$$

or using $\bar{p} = S'(q(\bar{p}))$,

$$\bar{p} = \frac{\displaystyle\int_{\beta^*}^{\bar{\beta}} C_q(\beta, e^*(\beta, q(\bar{p})), q(\bar{p})) f(\beta) \, d\beta}{1 - F(\beta^*)} \tag{4.44}$$

Since $C_{q\beta} > 0$, $C_{qe} < 0$ and $\partial e^*/\partial \beta > 0$, (4.44) implies that $\bar{p} \leq C_q(\bar{\beta}, e^*(\bar{\beta}, q(\bar{p})), q(\bar{p}))$ which gives a contradiction of (4.42) since $C_{qq} < 0$.[14] We will therefore solve for $\bar{p}$ from (4.42) above to obtain the optimal price-cap regulation in which β^* is defined by $p^M(\beta^*) = \bar{p}$, when the regulator wants the firm to be active whatever its type in $[\underline{\beta}, \bar{\beta}]$. This mechanism corresponds to an optimal price-cap regulation without transfers and without cost observability. It is designated by PC in the book.

The excessive profits associated with (pure) price-cap regulation have sometimes led regulators to append to it a profit-sharing rule.[15] The firm's financial profit net of taxes (at a rate τ) is then given by[16]

$$(1 - \tau)[pq(p) - C(\beta, e^*(\beta, q(p)), q(p))] \qquad (4.45)$$

The price-cap $\bar{p}$ is again determined by the individual rationality constraint of the least efficient firm $\bar{\beta}$,

$$(1 - \tau)[\bar{p}q(\bar{p}) - C(\bar{\beta}, \hat{e}(\bar{\beta}, q(\bar{p}), \tau), q(\bar{p}))] - \psi(\hat{e}(\bar{\beta}, q(\bar{p}), \tau)) = 0 \qquad (4.46)$$

where $\hat{e}(\beta, q(\bar{p}), \tau)$ is defined as the solution to

$$\psi'(\hat{e}) = (1 - \tau)C_e(\beta, \hat{e}, q(\bar{p})) \qquad (4.47)$$

Let $\bar{p}(\tau)$ be the solution obtained from (4.46) and (4.47), and let $p^M(\beta, \tau)$ be the monopoly price under profit sharing. Note that if the revenue from taxing the firm is used to decrease taxes elsewhere in the economy,[17] then it has net social value

$$\lambda\tau \left(\int_{\underline{\beta}}^{\beta^*} [p^M(\beta, \tau)q(p^M(\beta, \tau)) - C(\beta, \hat{e}(p^M(\beta, \tau)), q(p^M(\beta, \tau)))]f(\beta)\,d\beta \right.$$

$$\left. + \int_{\beta^*}^{\bar{\beta}} [\bar{p}(\tau)q(\bar{p}(\tau)) - C(\beta, \hat{e}(\beta, q(\bar{p}(\tau))), q(\bar{p}(\tau)))]f(\beta)\,d\beta \right) \qquad (4.48)$$

The optimal sharing rule then solves

$$\max_{\tau} \left(\int_{\underline{\beta}}^{\beta^*} [S(q(p^M(\beta, \tau))) - (1 + \lambda\tau)C(\beta, \hat{e}(\beta, q(p^M(\beta, \tau))), q(p^M(\beta, \tau))) \right.$$

$$+ \lambda\tau p^M(\beta, \tau)q(p^M(\beta, \tau)) - \psi(\hat{e}(\beta, q(p^M(\beta, \tau))))]f(\beta)\,d\beta$$

$$+ \int_{\beta^*}^{\bar{\beta}} [S(q(\bar{p}(\tau))) - (1 + \lambda\tau)C(\beta, \hat{e}(\beta, q(\bar{p}(\tau))), q(\bar{p}(\tau)))$$

$$\left. + \lambda\tau \bar{p}(\tau)q(\bar{p}(\tau)) - \psi(\hat{e}(\beta, q(\bar{p}(\tau))))]f(\beta)\,d\beta \right) \qquad (4.49)$$

where β^* is defined by $p^M(\beta^*, \tau) = \bar{p}(\tau)$.

The particularly interesting feature of price-cap regulation with taxation of earnings (called PCT) is the simplicity and practicability of the mechanism. However, it presumes the observability of profits, which is equivalent to the observability of costs if revenues are observable as we have assumed so far, and uses one-way transfers, that is, taxes but not subsidies. Conditionally on these informational or institutional constraints, it is not an optimal mechanism, because expected social welfare could be improved by using a menu of price-cap/tax rates or by making a better use of cost observability.

It is worthwhile to note that the quality of price-cap mechanisms, which is a mechanism without transfers contrary to LT and BM, is related to the size of the fixed costs. As fixed costs increase, pricing is more and more distorted away from optimal Ramsey pricing to cover costs and disutility of effort.

4.6   Cost-Plus Regulation

Under cost-plus regulation the regulator is again assumed to observe costs ex post and to fully reimburse the firm for them. We will first consider the case where no additional transfers to the firm are made, namely where a balanced-budget constraint is imposed. This regulatory scheme, called $C+$, will be thought of as a formal representation of standard cost-plus regulation. Since the firm's utility is then given by $-\psi(e)$, the profit-maximizing firm can be assumed to choose the minimum level of effort ($e_{\min} = 0$), which gives zero disutility. In this case the regulator imposes a production level $q(\beta)$ that solves

$$P(q(\beta))q(\beta) - C(\beta, 0, q(\beta)) = 0 \tag{4.50}$$

leading to expected social welfare given by

$$\int_{\underline{\beta}}^{\bar{\beta}} [S(q(\beta)) - C(\beta, 0, q(\beta))] f(\beta)\, d\beta \tag{4.51}$$

Alternatively, one could consider the case where, after collecting revenues, the regulator gives to the firm a net transfer $T = C(\beta, 0, q(\beta)) - P(q(\beta))q(\beta)$, which can be used to ensure that the firm's budget is balanced ex post. Since the firm has its cost reimbursed, it is indifferent to the level of output. Under this scheme, called $C + T$, the regulator can therefore instruct the firm to produce the level $q(\beta)$ that maximizes expected social welfare given by

$$\int_{\underline{\beta}}^{\bar{\beta}} [S(q(\beta)) - P(q(\beta))q(\beta) - (1+\lambda)T] f(\beta)\, d\beta$$

$$= \int_{\underline{\beta}}^{\bar{\beta}} [V(q(\beta)) - (1+\lambda)C(\beta, 0, q(\beta))] f(\beta)\, d\beta \tag{4.52}$$

4.7 Remark

In the Laffont and Tirole (1986) model described above, the disutility of effort which decreases the monetary cost has the nature of a fixed cost. One might want to extend the model to cases where the disutility of effort depends on the level of production, namely when it can be written as $\psi(e, q)$.

Following the same steps as above, we have now

$$U = t - \psi(e, q) \tag{4.53}$$

$$W = V(q) - (1 + \lambda)(C(\beta, e, q) + \psi(e, q)) - \lambda U \tag{4.54}$$

Under the assumption that $C(\beta, e, q) + \psi(e, q)$ is convex in (e, q), optimal regulation is characterized by the first-order conditions

$$\psi'(e) = -C_e - \frac{\lambda}{1 + \lambda} \frac{F}{f} \frac{d}{de} (\psi_e E_\beta) \tag{4.55}$$

$$V'(q) = (1 + \lambda)(C_q + \psi_q) + \lambda \frac{F}{f} \frac{d}{dq} (\psi_e E_\beta) \tag{4.56}$$

A noticeable difference with the analysis above is that the condition for the incentives-pricing dichotomy to hold is now expressed as

$$\frac{d}{dq}[\psi_e E_\beta] = 0 \tag{4.57}$$

It is natural to look for independent conditions on the cost function and on the disutility of effort function to obtain (4.57). We need the same condition on the cost function as before (i.e. when ψ is independent of q), which ensures that $dE_\beta/dq = 0$, and then we must have $\psi_{eq} = 0$. With the normalization $\psi(0, q) = 0$ for all q, we are back to the original Laffont-Tirole formulation. So we cannot expect the incentives-pricing dichotomy to hold when the disutility of effort depends on the production level unless the terms in q of ψ_e and E_β cancel out which is, in general, very unlikely to occur.

Pursuing this latter strategy is not very attractive since we do not have enough prior information on $\psi(e, q)$ in order to make interesting the characterization of cost functions such that (4.57) holds for particular specifications of $\psi(e, q)$. Nevertheless, in chapter 6 we will test the robustness of the other features of optimal regulation for the case $\psi(e, q) = \varphi(e)q$ by leaving out the dichotomy property.

5   The Natural Monopoly Test

5.1 Introduction

While in chapter 3 we illustrated the use of the forward-looking cost model LECOM (described in full detail in chapter 2) in a complete information context, in this chapter we further consider its usefulness within an incomplete information framework as described in chapter 4. The specific issue addressed here is that of assessing the relative merits of policies that promote entry into the local exchange market versus maintaining a regulated monopoly. This issue has traditionally been addressed both at a theoretical and empirical level by the literature concerned with the concept of natural monopoly. In this chapter we argue that the new economics of regulation, whose fundamentals were outlined in chapter 4, offers some interesting opportunities for enlarging the empirical testing of this concept.

It is by now widely recognized that asymmetric information is a fundamental feature of the relationship between public utilities and regulatory and/or competition (antitrust) authorities. Instances where the regulated firm (the agent) has information not available to the regulator (the principal) constitute the rule rather than the exception. This is most certainly the case in telecommunications where the provision of increasingly sophisticated services is made possible by rapid technological progress. Moreover, and to some extent as a consequence of this progress, it is becoming increasingly difficult for regulators to obtain information on the cost of input factors used in increasingly complex production processes.[1]

The availability of advanced technology allows incumbent firms to engage in vast programs of upgrading and modernization of their existing networks, but it also allows entrants to invest in new facilities that offer superior service quality or lower marginal cost than that of the incumbent. In the investigation of precisely how the introduction of these new technologies affects costs, firms have a clear advantage. Hence, under regulation, incumbent firms should be able to extract information rents on the basis of this advantage. In face of these dynamics, a regulator who is chiefly concerned with the best possible allocation of resources should carefully account for these information asymmetries while regulating the activities of incumbent firms, and should simultaneously consider policies that foster (efficient) entry and prepare for deregulation.

Competition policy that promotes entry when it is technically feasible can be a useful policy instrument, since it can simultaneously encourage technological innovation and limit socially costly rents to incumbent firms. Entry may not always be desirable, or even possible, however. If the market is a natural monopoly, successful entry may result in duplication of facilities and higher costs than a monopoly provider would incur. These costs need to be weighted against the benefits of competition in an evaluation of any deregulation or active promotion of competitive entry.

While the technical definition of natural monopoly in terms of subadditivity of the cost function has been given a precise foundation in the literature (see Sharkey 1982), the term itself has been used more broadly. On the one hand, *natural monopoly* has been used to designate a market equilibrium condition in which only a single firm can survive. On the other hand, the concept has been used in a normative context in order to suggest that a monopoly can, in some circumstances, be a socially desirable outcome. While we believe that both interpretations can be valid and useful, this chapter will strictly adhere to the second interpretation.[2]

Early empirical investigations of telecommunications technology tested for natural monopoly by estimating the degree of economies of scale. As already described in chapter 3, the work by Shin and Ying (1992) attempts to directly test the subadditivity of the industry cost function. These authors estimated a translog cost function for the US local exchange market, using a pooled cross-sectional time series data set composed of observations on 58 local exchange carriers over 8 years, 1976 to 1984.[3] Based on simulations of a very large number of hypothetical postentry configurations of output, they concluded that "the cost function is definitely not subadditive" and that their results "also support permitting entry into local exchange markets." While the authors point out the importance of controlling for the impact of technological change on the costs in their estimations, one wonders whether some other important factors related to market structure should also be taken into account in the comparison of the pre-entry and postentry industry configurations.

Given the new issues raised by the evolution of the industry, at both a practical and a theoretical level, we believe that the methodology of testing for the existence of natural monopoly characteristics needs to be reconsidered. On the one hand, since output does not need to remain constant after entry occurs, a broader test of its costs and benefits should account for changes in consumer welfare associated with entry. Such a test should incorporate the benefit of entry coming from the reduction or, in the most favorable case, the elimination of information rents to a monopoly firm. On the other hand, entry may generate a duplication of fixed costs and some interconnection costs as the entrant's network needs to provide communication with the incumbent's subscribers. At a more conceptual level, the cost structure that summarizes the essential features of the technology does not need to be independent of the market structure and market conduct of the firms after entry occurs as is assumed in the traditional approach.[4] In this chapter we explore some ways to extend the traditional empirical natural monopoly test by incorporating each of these factors in a comparison of the monopoly and the duopoly market structures.[5]

To extend this test, we propose in this chapter an approach that combines the forward-looking engineering process model of the costs of the local exchange telecommunications network (LECOM) with economic modeling. This engineering model is flexible enough to allow us to specify some internal parameters for a given market structure. Hence we use this model as a process by which we generate, through simulations, cost data summarized in market structure-specific cost functions that depend on the actual entry strategies used. These cost functions together with the appropriate economic model describing the market structure are used to calculate a market equilibrium. In place of, or rather in addition to, a strictly cost-based test for natural monopoly, our approach allows us to compare a regulated monopoly to both regulated and unregulated duopoly outcomes in terms of the aggregate social welfare achieved under each of these outcomes.

The use of an engineering process approach in an empirical analysis of the telecommunications market is a departure from the traditional econometric approach, and this may require further explanation. Our simulation approach is not intended to model the costs of a particular company providing a service in an actual geographic area; if a detailed map of subscriber locations and a set of price and technology inputs specific to that company were available, this would be feasible. Since our objective is rather to model the cost structure of a representative company serving a representative area, on this account the simulation approach is entirely satisfactory. As explained in chapter 2 and in section 5.3 below, the proxy model we use has been designed with flexible data structures that can be customized to describe specific company locations, and in our approach we simply use a generic set of inputs for the model. Moreover the proxy model approach has a significant advantage over a typical econometric approach in terms of its ability to accurately model the forward-looking cost of providing service. Historical data are limited in both the quality and quantity that would be needed to model a cost function at the level of technical detail that we require for the present analysis. An important capability of the proxy model that we use is that it locates switching centers according to forward-looking cost minimization criteria. This provides us with a representation of the long-run cost function that would not be obtainable by any other empirical methodology. The long-run cost function is appropriate for the empirical issues that we address in this and other chapters of the book.

The next section describes the theory underlying the empirical tests of natural monopoly that we perform. In chapter 4 we have already described the essential features of this theory; here we content ourselves with recalling only the components that are necessary for the purpose at hand. Section 5.3 describes our empirical methodology based on the LECOM model and introduces some variables that serve as proxies for the asymmetric information on the local exchange cost function. Section 5.4 presents and discusses the results of empirical tests. The final section summarizes the main implications of our approach to the empirical evaluation of deregulatory policies.

5.2 Theoretical Framework

This section presents the structural equations that will be used in our empirical comparison of monopoly and duopoly in local telecommunications markets. These equations, which determine the endogenous variables of interest, are derived from the model of regulation presented in the previous chapter. Here we briefly recall the main determinants of this theoretical framework and put together the structural equations we will use for the implementation of the empirical tests of natural monopoly.

The new view of regulation stresses the role of asymmetric informa-tion in the analysis of the regulator–regulated firm relationship. In a framework where the regulator designs the regulatory contract, an im-portant consequence of this asymmetry is that he must recognize the need to give up a rent to the firm (which has superior information) in order to provide that firm with (social welfare enhancing) incentives to minimize costs. This is the fundamental rent–efficiency trade-off that regulators need to deal with when regulating public utilities.[6]

The canonical model of the regulator–monopoly relationship may be reviewed as follows: Supply is characterized by a regulated firm pro-ducing various levels of output q according to a cost function C. As is usual in telecommunications studies, output is treated as either usage or as the number of access lines. This technology is better known to the firm than to the regulating authority. First, the regulated firm pos-sesses knowledge of a technological parameter β that is unavailable to the regulator. Second, the firm may invest in some cost-reducing ac-tivity, e (effort), that the regulator does not observe. In the former case the information problem concerns an exogenous variable (this leads to a so-called adverse selection situation), whereas in the latter case the information problem concerns an endogenous variable (this is a moral hazard situation). Total cost of production is a function of these two variables, $C = C(\beta, e, q)$.[7] Cost-reducing effort generates disutility to the firm according to an increasing convex function $\psi(e)$. We assume an in-verse demand function $P(q)$ for the monopoly good, yielding a gross consumer surplus $S(q)$.

Say that the firm's cost is observable ex post; then, without loss of gen-erality, we can use the convention that the regulator (the government) collects the firm's revenue, reimburses its production cost, and gives it a (net) transfer t. If the firm is assumed to value income and effort only, its utility, which is commonly referred to as the firm's "rent," is expressed as $U = t - \psi(e)$. The revenue from the firm diminishes the need for the government to rely on distortionary taxes and hence should be evalu-ated at the shadow price of public funds. Consequently social surplus (net consumer surplus plus revenue for the government) brought about by the production of the good is given by $V(q) = S(q) + \lambda P(q)q$, where λ is the shadow cost of public funds.[8] Social welfare, the objective func-tion of the regulator who is assumed to weigh equally the consumers' and the firm's welfare, is given by (see section 4.2)

$$W = V(q) - (1 + \lambda)[C(\beta, e, q) + \psi(e)] - \lambda U \qquad (5.1)$$

The right-hand side of equation (5.1) clearly indicates that leaving rent to the firm is socially costly. A properly designed incentive regulatory contract, however, allows the firm to retain some rents in return for exerting a higher level of effort than the firm would choose to provide under a cost-based regulatory contract.

If we assume that the regulator's beliefs about the firm's technology can be described by a cumulative distribution F with support $[\underline{\beta}, \bar{\beta}]$ and density f, then the regulator's (optimal) policy can be made contingent on these beliefs. The greater the efficiency gains that accrue to the firm, the greater become its incentives to produce efficiently, but also the greater becomes the (socially costly) information rent that the regulator must leave to the firm. Characterizing optimally this trade-off is the fundamental objective of optimal regulation. The optimal regulatory contract with ex post cost observability, labeled LT, was previously characterized in section 4.3 by its first-order conditions (4.16) and (4.17) and its qualitative properties. Here we seek to express concisely the optimization program associated with such a regulatory contract.

Recall the firm's rent given by (4.28), which we repeat here as

$$U(\beta) = \int_{\beta}^{\bar{\beta}} \psi'(e(b)) E_{\beta}(b, C(b, e(b), q(b)), q(b)) \, db \tag{5.2}$$

where the function $E(\beta, C, q)$ is the effort required from a firm of type β to produce output q at cost C.[9] Integrating by parts, we have the expected value of this rent:

$$\int_{\underline{\beta}}^{\bar{\beta}} U(\beta) f(\beta) \, d\beta = \int_{\underline{\beta}}^{\bar{\beta}} \frac{F(\beta)}{f(\beta)} \psi'(e(\beta)) E_{\beta}(\beta, C(\beta, e(\beta), q(\beta)), q(\beta)) f(\beta) \, d\beta$$

$$\tag{5.3}$$

We differentiate the function E to obtain an expression for E_{β} and substitute back into the regulatory program of equation (4.15) to obtain the following program for the optimal regulatory mechanism LT:

$$\max_{q(\cdot), e(\cdot)} \int_{\underline{\beta}}^{\bar{\beta}} \left\{ V(q(\beta)) - (1 + \lambda) \left[C(\beta, e(\beta), q(\beta)) + \psi(e(\beta)) \right] \right.$$

$$\left. + \lambda \frac{F(\beta)}{f(\beta)} \psi'(e(\beta)) \frac{C_{\beta}(\beta, e(\beta), q(\beta))}{C_{e}(\beta, e(\beta), q(\beta))} \right\} f(\beta) \, d\beta \tag{5.4}$$

While optimal regulation can sometimes be implemented by a menu of relatively simple linear contracts, here we consider two simpler forms of regulation that are widely observed in practice—price-cap regulation and cost-plus regulation. Under price-cap regulation the price (output) decision is decentralized. The main objective of the regulator in this case is to ensure productive efficiency, which is a consequence of the fact that the firm is the residual claimant of any cost reductions. The firm therefore chooses the optimal level of effort e^* conditionally on the level of production.[10] To prevent the firm from exercising monopoly power, the regulator sets a price ceiling $\bar{p}$. The firm may, however, choose a monopoly price p^M if the ceiling turns out to be nonbinding. The regulatory mechanism determines the level of this cap that maximizes expected social welfare. This price-cap mechanism, labeled PC, was discussed earlier in section 4.5, where we saw that the participation constraint is

$$\bar{p}q(\bar{p}) - C(\bar{\beta}, e^*(\bar{\beta}, q(\bar{p})), q(\bar{p})) - \psi(e^*(\bar{\beta}, q(\bar{p}))) \geq 0 \qquad (5.5)$$

which is binding.

Under cost-plus regulation the regulator is assumed to observe ex post costs and to fully reimburse the firm for them. Clearly, the firm has no incentive to minimize its production cost, so it can be expected to choose its minimum level of effort $\underline{e}$ (normalized to zero). The regulator does not make any additional transfers to the firm (besides reimbursing its production cost) and imposes the output level that balances the firm's budget. Hence, as seen in section 4.6, cost-plus regulation, labeled $C+$, is characterized by the equation

$$P(q(\beta))q(\beta) - C(\beta, \underline{e}, q(\beta)) = 0 \qquad (5.6)$$

As a benchmark, we consider the case of an unregulated monopoly (labeled UM) whereby the firm selects the price that maximizes its utility given by

$$\tilde{\pi} = pq(p) - C(\beta, e^*(\beta, q(p)), q(p)) - \psi(e^*(\beta, q(p))) \qquad (5.7)$$

To compare social welfare under regulated (or unregulated) monopoly and duopoly, we require a formal model of equilibrium behavior of the competing firms in the case of regulated duopoly. First, we consider a model of regulated duopoly, labeled YS, in which yardstick competition allows the regulator to uncover the technological parameter, which is assumed to be the same for both firms, and the regulator infers effort from the cost function $C = C(\beta, e_i, q_i)$, using the observation of cost and output.[11] The regulator then solves for output and effort, maximizing

$$V(q_1 + q_2) - (1 + \lambda)[C(\beta, e_1, q_1) + C(\beta, e_2, q_2) + \psi(e_1) + \psi(e_2)] \quad (5.8)$$

Next we consider three models of an unregulated (symmetric) duopoly. The first model, referred to as *CD*, is a Cournot-type of model in which firm i selects a quantity q_i and a level of effort e_i in order to maximize its utility given by

$$P(q_1 + q_2)q_i - C(\beta, e_i, q_i) - \psi(e_i) \quad (5.9)$$

In a second model, labeled *AC*, average-cost pricing, we assume that Bertrand competition drives the utility of each firm to zero. Hence this model is characterized by

$$P(q_1 + q_2)q_i - C(\beta, e_i^*(\beta, q_i), q_i) - \psi(e_i^*(\beta, q_i)) = 0 \quad (5.10)$$

Finally, in a third model, labeled *MC*, firms are assumed to apply marginal-cost pricing and to use the fixed part of a two-part tariff to recover the associated losses. In this model

$$P(q_1 + q_2) = \frac{\partial C(\beta, e_i^*(\beta, q_i), q_i)}{\partial q_i} \quad (5.11)$$

These equations are solved to yield equilibrium output, effort, and social welfare given in each case by[12]

$$W^*(\beta) = S(2q_i^*(\beta)) - 2[C(\beta, e_i^*(\beta, q_i^*(\beta)), q_i^*(\beta)) + \psi(e_i^*(\beta, q_i^*(\beta)))]$$
$$(5.12)$$

5.3 Empirical Methodology

Our empirical approach to the analysis of the relative (social welfare) performance of monopoly versus duopoly will be illustrated by two exercises where we use LECOM quite differently. In the first analysis, usage is the output, so we assume that the number of subscribers is the same under both monopoly and duopoly. Under duopoly each subscriber obtains access to both networks but divides usage between them based on prevailing prices.[13]

In the second analysis, we explicitly develop a model in which firms compete in the provision of telephone access lines. Telephone service is assumed, in this model, to be a homogeneous commodity, so that each potential subscriber will wish to obtain service from at most one company. Furthermore, whenever two or more companies succeed in attracting subscribers, the costs of interconnecting networks must be accounted for, since we assume that access to the network includes the ability to communicate with the subscribers of rival networks.

It should be clear from the theoretical exposition of the previous section that an evaluation of monopoly versus duopoly outcomes will depend on the properties of the cost and demand functions that characterize the market. In the following subsections we describe the steps that we have followed in order to calibrate these functions. First, we present the simulations of LECOM that generate the cost data we used in the analyses mentioned above. Second, we present the empirical cost functions corresponding to different market structure scenarios that we compare. Third, we discuss the method used to measure interconnection costs in a duopoly. Finally, we show how we calibrate the demand and disutility of effort functions.

5.3.1 Simulations of the Engineering Process Cost Model LECOM

To define a cost function for both monopoly and duopoly providers, we use the cost proxy model LECOM. Since this model was fully described in chapter 2, here we will only recall some of its critical features as we model the variables introduced in section 5.2 over which the regulator has incomplete information.

LECOM combines an engineering process model, which computes the cost of a local exchange network for a given configuration of switch locations, with an optimization algorithm, which solves for the optimal number and location of switches. It allows the user to specify a local exchange territory that consists of three areas, namely a central business district, an area of mixed residential and commercial demand, and a residential area. Both the size and the population density of each area are specified by the user, as are more detailed data on calling patterns. In addition the user is able to specify a set of technological inputs and a detailed set of input prices in order to calibrate the model to the specific characteristics of a given exchange area.

In our empirical analysis of monopoly and duopoly performances, we use LECOM to generate, through appropriate simulations, the cost data in order for us to estimate a cost function. We use the properties of this cost function to calibrate the demand and disutility of the effort functions. A theoretical cost function expresses cost as a function of output and input prices. In addition to a large number of engineering and technical parameters, LECOM allows the user to specify multipliers for the prices of labor and capital. We use the multiplier for the price of capital (PK) as a proxy for the level of technological uncertainty, β, which enters the firm's cost function. We believe that this multiplier represents a plausible one-dimensional measure of uncertainty as it has a direct impact on all of the technological variables embedded in the engineering model.[14] Equivalently, if we had access to the internal structure of LECOM, we could have modeled the technological uncertainty by the variation of a large number of technological parameters, all of which would be constrained to vary proportionately.

Similarly we use the multiplier for the price of labor (PL) as a proxy for the cost-reducing effort, e. Since our analysis focuses on managerial effort, we assume that labor is measured in efficiency units; an increase in effort leads to an increase in the number of efficiency units associated with a given size of workforce and hence a decrease in the unit price of labor.[15] Again, the underlying assumption is that effort is primarily directed toward efficiently utilizing labor inputs. We believe that this is a plausible assumption because it accounts for dramatic reductions in the workforce that often come with industry reforms (e.g., with privatization of state-owned firms). This assumption is also useful in calibrating the firm's disutility of effort function.

In our first approach to the issue studied in this chapter, we apply LECOM to obtain an empirical cost function for a firm operating a generic local exchange network of 108,000 subscribers in an area of approximately 57 square miles. This represents a large local exchange area with a medium population density of approximately 1895 subscribers per square mile.[16] Since our measures of technological uncertainty and effort are multipliers for the price of capital and labor, respectively, where the average price for each input is equal to one, we have chosen to simulate local exchange costs in the range 0.5 to 1.5 for both parameters.[17] In this first approach, our measure of output consists of telephone usage of a representative subscriber measured in CCS. We let this usage output vary within the (0.5, 5.5) range, which includes the range of 1 to 4 CCS reported in standard engineering data. The result of the simulation allows us to obtain a generic cost function of the form $C(PK, PL, CCS)$, which is the empirical counterpart of the theoretical cost function $C(\beta, e, q)$ used in the models of regulation presented in section 5.2.[18] We will devote more attention to this empirical cost function in the next chapter.

In the second approach, we estimate a cost function in which output is measured in number of access lines. Several new issues arise when cost is expressed as a function of the number of access lines.[19] First, the cost of a telecommunications network depends largely on the subscriber density of the territory served. Thus the cost function for a provider must account for not only the number of access lines but also the size of the area in which those access lines are located. Second, in a duopoly (and more generally in any model of multifirm competition) there will be interconnection costs incurred in transferring calls between the two separate networks. As was noted at the beginning of this chapter, these costs must be accounted for when assessing the relative performance of monopoly and duopoly.

To address the economies of density, we use LECOM to simulate the cost of providing service as a function of both the number of access lines (subscribers) N and the size of the area served A. In addition, as discussed above, we use appropriate LECOM inputs to model the technology type of the firm β and the level of hidden managerial effort used by the firm e, which are arguments of the cost function. This results in a generic cost function $C(\beta, e, N, A)$ that can be used to model both monopoly and duopoly regimes. We estimated this cost function using "pseudodata" obtained from running LECOM for 900 combinations of values of these four parameters. These 900 LECOM simulations were performed as follows: Area varied from 5.7 to 57 square miles with increments of 5.7, while the number of access lines varied from 20,000 to 100,000 with increments of 10,000. For each value of N and A we ran nine simulations for values of PL and PK equal to 0.6, 1.0, and 1.4. Another special feature of this approach is that it allows us to customize the empirical cost function to the specific market structure under which the firm operates. Let us describe the way we generate the various cost functions.

5.3.2 Market Structure–Specific Cost Functions

When access rather than usage is the output, we use a generic cost function C to generate cost functions for three distinct market structure scenarios. In a regulated monopoly whereby a single firm serves an entire territory, the cost function is

$$C^M(\beta, e, N) = C(\beta, e, N, \bar{A}) \tag{5.13}$$

Furthermore we assume that as the number of subscribers varies, the population of subscribers remains uniformly distributed over each of the respective density zones. Together, these zones comprise an area of $\bar{A} = 57$ square miles.

For the case of a duopoly we consider two entry scenarios. In the first scenario *uniform entry* occurs as each duopolist serves subscribers distributed over the serving area. Strictly speaking, each duopolist does not serve a uniform distribution of subscribers, since we have used a feature of LECOM that allows us to define a stylized local exchange area as one consisting of three separate regions (a central business, a mixed commercial and residential, and a residential district) of varying subscriber density. Under the uniform entry scenario, we assume that an entering firm that gains a certain share of access lines serves exactly the same share of business, mixed, and residential sectors.[20] In visualizing the impact of the uniform entry assumption, the reader may find figure 5.1 helpful. In the figure the local exchange territory consists of a set of three nested rectangles corresponding to the three density zones served by a representative firm. If the firm serves 25 percent of the residential market, it is assumed that these residential subscribers are uniformly

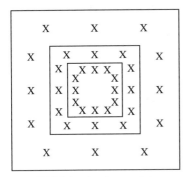

Initial situation (monopoly)

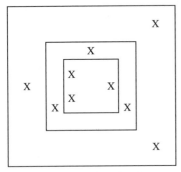

Entrant with 25% market share

Figure 5.1
Uniform entry

distributed over the entire residential service area. Similar assumptions apply to the mixed and business markets. The cost function for a duopolist under the uniform entry scenario is the same (before we account for interconnection costs) as that of the monopolist and is given by

$$C_U^D(\beta, e, N_i) = C(\beta, e, N_i, \bar{A}) \tag{5.14}$$

The second entry scenario that we consider is *targeted entry*. Under targeted entry, we assume that an entrant can select its customer locations. Since the cost of serving a given number of subscribers is a strictly increasing function of area served, the cost-minimizing entrant would like to serve 100 percent of the subscribers in its chosen service area. In the targeted entry scenario, we assume that this entry strategy is successful. Note that under targeted entry, subscriber density is the same for each duopolist; it is equal to the subscriber density of a monopoly provider. The targeted entry scenario is illustrated in figure 5.2. The cost

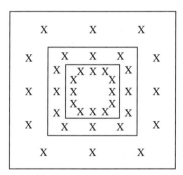

Initial situation (monopoly)

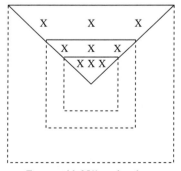

Entrant with 25% market share

Figure 5.2
Targeted entry

function for a duopolist in this case is

$$C_T^D(\beta, e, N_i) = C\left(\beta, e, N_i, \bar{A} \times \frac{N_i}{N_1 + N_2}\right) \tag{5.15}$$

5.3.3 Interconnection Costs

In the case of duopoly with access lines as output, we take into account the cost of traffic that originates on one network and terminates on a different network. LECOM was originally conceived for a monopoly environment. It accounts for the cost of providing switching and inter-office transmission capacity to handle toll traffic, which is carried outside of the local network to a toll provider's point of presence (a user input sets the amount of toll traffic as a percentage of total traffic). There is no comparable method of accounting for the cost of interconnecting with an alternative local access provider. We believe that it is important to account for these costs in any analysis that attempts to evaluate the performance of duopoly versus monopoly.

In the case of a duopoly equilibrium where each firm supplies exactly one half of the market, we are able to estimate the costs of such a firm for both uniform and targeted entries. Figure 5.3a gives a stylized representation of a LECOM simulation for a targeted duopolist serving 50 percent of the market. The relevant costs include the cost of access lines that connect each subscriber to a local switch, and the cost of the switching and interoffice transport capacity that accords with the level of usage demand among all subscribers in the duopolist's network. In figure 5.3b is depicted the network that both duopolists would construct assuming that each duopolist carried only the traffic that both originates and terminates on its own network. In order to measure the increase in switching and interoffice transport capacity that would be required to carry internetwork traffic, we treat the combined network as if it were a monopoly, and run a constrained LECOM simulation of the resulting costs. That is, we take the exact set of switch locations and levels of network investment that LECOM calculates for the two duopoly firms in isolation, and perform a new simulation to compute total network costs, assuming that the monopoly network is constrained to use the duopoly investments. The resulting network is illustrated in figure 5.3c.

In the final step of the analysis, we compute the ratio of switching and interoffice transport traffic costs in the constrained monopoly over the costs in the duopoly without interconnection. This way we obtain a

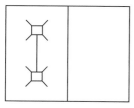

(a) Optimal network for one firm assuming
targeted entry

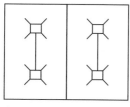

(b) Optimal network for both firms ignoring
interconnection costs

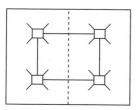

(c) A monopoly network (based on duopolists' switch locations) that includes
all appropriate switching and transport costs

Figure 5.3
Interconnection costs

multiplier for both switching and transport that can be used as a proxy
for the true costs of interconnection.[21] In the case of targeted entry we
find that switching costs are approximately 10 percent higher and transport costs are approximately 44 percent higher under the constrained
monopoly scenario than under the duopoly without the interconnection.[22] We then adjust the data from LECOM for the case of targeted
entry by multiplying switching costs by 1.1 and transport costs by 1.44
for each simulation. With these data we proceed to obtain a translog representation of the duopoly cost function for that scenario. For the case of
uniform entry, a similar exercise found that switching costs increased by
0.56 percent and transport costs increased by 5.6 percent in comparing

the constrained monopoly to the unconstrained duopoly outcomes. We used these values to adjust the raw LECOM data, which then were used to estimate a translog cost function.[23]

5.3.4 Calibration of Demand and Disutility

We have described above how, in our two approaches and for each scenario, we have defined a cost function in terms of three independent variables—technology, effort, and output. The next step is to specify the market demand function and the cost of public funds in order to obtain some measure of social surplus. Since public funds are obtained through taxation, their cost depends on the efficiency of the tax collection system. In our analysis we use the value of 0.3 as a benchmark, suggesting that each dollar transferred to the firm costs 1.3 dollars to society.[24] As for demand, we use an exponential function.[25] The two parameters of the exponential demand function were determined through calibration by relying on two assumptions. First, we assume that the elasticity of demand is equal to −0.2 and −0.05 when, respectively, output is usage and access. Second, we assume that revenue collected from the representative customer covers the cost of serving this customer, which by using LECOM amounts to approximately $240.[26] These two assumptions yield two independent equations that we solve to obtain the (inverse) demand functions used in our two approaches. When usage is taken as the output, we obtain

$$P(q) = -421 \log[0.204683q] \tag{5.16}$$

when access is the output, we obtain

$$P(q) = -4800 \log[0.951229q] \tag{5.17}$$

Clearly, much less is known about the disutility of effort function than about market demand because the variables of this function are, by definition, unobservable. Nevertheless, any increasing convex function would be consistent with theory. We have specified a polynomial form of degree 2 when usage is the output and of degree 4 when access is the output. In order to calibrate these functions, we use the facts that under cost-plus regulation the marginal disutility of effort should be equal to zero and that after deregulation it should be equal to marginal cost saving. We also make the assumption that labor force gets reduced by 40 percent after deregulation.[27] This yields disutility of effort functions of the form

$$\psi(e) = (1.04397 \times 10^7)e^2 \qquad (5.18)$$

and

$$\psi(e) = (1.20928 \times 10^7)e^4 \qquad (5.19)$$

in, respectively, the first (usage as output) and the second (access as output) cases. Since we do not have all the information on the regulatory environment, we have assumed a uniform probability distribution in order to model the regulator's uncertainty about the technology. The support of this distribution has been assumed to be (0.5, 1.5), which includes the values for which the LECOM cost functions have been defined in our simulations. When usage is the output, we also show how sensitive the results of the natural monopoly test may be to the demand elasticity used in the calibration, the distribution of the technological parameter β, and the cost of public funds λ.

5.4 Empirical Results

We have argued above that any criterion used in a comparison of monopoly and duopoly should account for the differences in not only technological efficiency but also consumer and producer surpluses. Aggregate social welfare therefore appears as the appropriate measure of performance because it encompasses both of these factors. We have calculated social welfare in each of the market structure scenarios discussed above, which we summarize in table 5.1. In the following subsections we analyze the results in two cases: in case I usage is assumed to be the output, and in case II access is the output.

Table 5.1
Market structure scenarios

Type	Description
LT	Optimally regulated monopoly
PC	Price cap regulated monopoly
C+	Cost plus regulated monopoly
UM	Unregulated monopoly
CD	Cournot duopoly
AC	Average cost pricing duopoly
MC	Marginal cost pricing duopoly
YS	Yardstick competition duopoly

82

5.4.1 Case I: Usage as Output

Results

Table 5.2 reports effort e and total industry output Q, for different values of the firm's type β, under the market structures optimally regulated monopoly (*LT*), yardstick competition regulated duopoly (*YS*), unregulated Cournot duopoly (*CD*), and unregulated monopoly (*UM*) as was discussed in section 5.2. Table 5.3 presents the social welfare corresponding to these alternative scenarios. A casual look at the data in

Table 5.2
Effort and output levels

β	e^{LT}	e^{YS}	e^{CD}	e^{UM}	Q^{LT}	Q^{YS}	Q^{CD}	Q^{UM}
0.50	0.64	0.55	0.52	0.54	3.78	3.72	2.82	1.72
0.60	0.61	0.55	0.52	0.54	3.77	3.71	2.81	1.72
0.70	0.59	0.55	0.52	0.54	3.77	3.71	2.81	1.71
0.80	0.57	0.55	0.52	0.54	3.76	3.70	2.80	1.71
0.90	0.54	0.55	0.52	0.54	3.75	3.69	2.79	1.71
1.00	0.52	0.55	0.52	0.54	3.75	3.68	2.79	1.70
1.10	0.50	0.55	0.52	0.54	3.74	3.67	2.78	1.70
1.20	0.48	0.55	0.52	0.54	3.73	3.67	2.77	1.69
1.30	0.47	0.55	0.52	0.54	3.73	3.67	2.77	1.69
1.40	0.45	0.55	0.52	0.54	3.72	3.65	2.76	1.69
1.50	0.43	0.55	0.52	0.54	3.72	3.64	2.75	1.68

Table 5.3
Social welfare (10^6 annualized US\$)

β	LT	YS	CD	UM
0.50	192.91	170.04	155.14	137.47
0.60	191.63	167.13	152.83	136.18
0.70	190.32	164.20	150.51	134.90
0.80	188.98	161.28	148.19	133.61
0.90	187.63	158.38	145.89	132.33
1.00	186.26	155.49	143.60	131.06
1.10	184.88	152.61	141.32	129.80
1.20	183.48	149.75	139.05	128.54
1.30	182.06	146.89	136.79	127.29
1.40	180.62	144.06	134.54	126.04
1.50	179.17	141.23	132.29	124.79

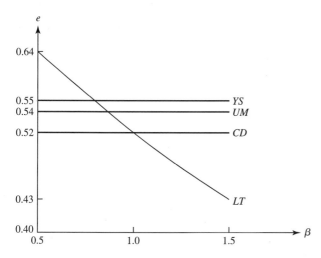

Figure 5.4
Effort

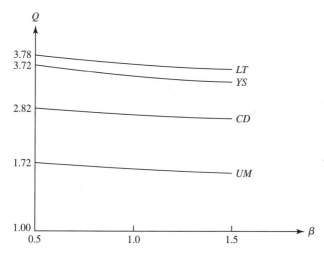

Figure 5.5
Output

these tables shows that except for *LT*, effort is not sensitive to the technological efficiency parameter β. Output and social welfare are moderately
sensitive to β. Figures 5.4, 5.5, and 5.6 illustrate these results.

From figure 5.4 we see that in terms of level of effort achieved, for
any value of the technological efficiency parameter β in our grid, *YS*
dominates *UM*, which in turn dominates *CD*. Optimal regulation (*LT*)

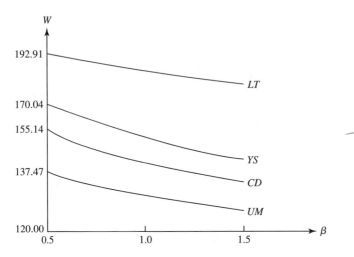

Figure 5.6
Social welfare

yields higher effort than all of these scenarios for the more efficient firms and lower effort for the less efficient ones. As to output (see figure 5.5) the ranking is unambiguously $Q^{LT} > Q^{YS} > Q^{CD} > Q^{UM}$, and the same ranking holds when it comes to aggregate social welfare (see figure 5.6). This says that from an ex ante standpoint (which is the most relevant for public policy purposes), regulation of either monopoly or duopoly dominates a situation with no regulation, and the benefit from economies of scale in the monopoly structure dominates the cost of the information rent it is associated with.

Sensitivity Analysis
Since we were able to evaluate social welfare only after providing a value for the elasticity used to calibrate demand, a distribution for the technological parameter, and a value for the cost of public funds, we ask whether the outcome of our comparison above of market structures is sensitive to the specific assumptions we made. We duplicated the test based on table 5.3 for two values of demand elasticity higher than -0.2 (in absolute value), which is the value we used in the base case. These higher values are -0.4 and -0.6. Although the relative welfare rankings were slightly different, the policy of regulating optimally the monopoly remained unambiguously a dominant policy.

We tried an alternative distribution for the technological parameter β, namely a truncated normal (instead of a uniform) distribution, and also alternative values for the shadow cost of public funds λ, namely 0, 1, and 10. The relative welfare rankings were unaffected; the normal distribution had the effect of increasing expected output and effort and social welfare for the optimal regulatory mechanism.[28] As to the effect of varying the cost of public funds, at $\lambda = 0$ the optimal regulation coincided with the first best, and at $\lambda = 1$ and $\lambda = 10$ the output and effort (and social welfare) were diminished for all the market structures that we considered while the relative rankings remained the same.

5.4.2   Case II: Access as Output

Social Welfare Comparisons
Table 5.4 gives the expected values of social welfare achieved by monopoly with regulation (*LT*, *PC*, and *C*+) and without regulation (*UM*). Table 5.5 gives the expected social welfare for duopoly with regulation (*YS*) and without regulation (*CD*, *AC*, and *MC*) under both uniform and targeted entry, and with and without taking account interconnection costs (IC).[29]

Observe that if there is no regulation and competition is at least as intense as in a Cournot duopoly, the duopoly is always desirable because *CD*, *AC*, and *MC* always achieve a higher level of expected social welfare than *UM*. This indicates that the inconvenience of duplicating fixed costs is more than offset by the benefits of competition. We therefore turn to the more interesting situation in which both monopoly and duopoly can be regulated. We first consider the case of uniform

Table 5.4
Monopoly: Expected social welfare (in 100M)

LT	PC	C+	UM
4.93	4.80	4.75	3.52

Table 5.5
Duopoly: Expected social welfare (in 100M)

Entry	CD	AC	MC	YS
Uniform without IC	4.32	4.76	4.76	4.90
Uniform with IC	4.32	4.76	4.76	4.89
Targeted without IC	4.36	4.81	4.81	4.95
Targeted with IC	4.34	4.79	4.79	4.93

entry. Uniform entry imposes a large penalty on the entrant and the incumbent firms by requiring that they both serve lower density markets. Under uniform entry a regulated duopoly (*YS*) outperforms traditional nonincentive regulation (*C*+) and a monopoly regulated by a price-cap. It achieves, however, lower aggregate welfare than optimal incentive regulation (*LT*). Moreover the unregulated but highly competitive Bertrand scenarios (*AC* and *MC*) dominate cost-plus regulation.

The case for deregulation is stronger when one considers targeted entry. Indeed, as tables 5.4 and 5.5 demonstrate, when interconnection costs are neglected, both average-cost and marginal-cost pricing under duopoly dominate the two widely observed forms of regulated monopoly, namely price-cap regulation and cost-plus regulation. In addition yardstick competition achieves higher social welfare than optimal regulation. These results no longer hold when the interconnection costs are accounted for. Then yardstick competition dominates any price cap but is slightly dominated by the optimal regulation.

Because transfers are allowed for in the (monopoly) optimal regulation *LT* and the (duopoly) yardstick competition *YS*, we have also investigated their relative performance as a function of the cost of public funds λ. Setting λ equal to 1.0 and 2.0, respectively, yields the values of social welfare given in tables 5.6 and 5.7.[30]

As these tables show, at higher values of the cost of public funds, duopoly under yardstick competition becomes as attractive as monopoly under optimal regulation for targeted entry with interconnection costs. Since the cost of public funds depends on the level of efficiency of

Table 5.6
Optimal regulation (*LT*): Expected social welfare (in 100M)

$\lambda = 1.0$	$\lambda = 2.0$
5.77	7.31

Table 5.7
Yardstick competition (*YS*): Expected social welfare (in 100M)

Entry	$\lambda = 1.0$	$\lambda = 2.0$
Uniform without IC	5.72	7.23
Uniform with IC	5.72	7.23
Targeted without IC	5.80	7.34
Targeted with IC	5.78	7.31

the taxation system in the economy, or equivalently, the extent of the deadweight losses associated with distortionary taxes necessary to fund transfers, this result suggests that deregulation may be more appropriate for developing economies than for developed economies with efficient taxation systems.[31]

Given the well-known trade-off between consumer surplus and firm's rent inherent in all of these second-best schemes of resources allocation, one might want to examine more carefully how the regulatory choices and the market structures affect the redistributional consequences of deregulation. Tables 5.8 and 5.9 disaggregate the social welfare results into consumer surplus and firm's utility.[32]

The disaggregation reveals a strong conflict between the consumer and the firm. Under targeted entry the regulated duopoly YS dominates any form of regulated monopoly from the perspective of the consumer.[33] In the case of a price-cap regulated monopoly (PC), the highest information rent is left to the firm, and therefore this is the preferred alternative for the firm but not for the consumer.[34]

Reconsidering the Standard Natural Monopoly Test

It is instructive to examine the outcome of a traditional natural monopoly test of the type used by Shin and Ying (1992).[35] In addition to being based solely on costs, such a classical test uses the same cost function for both the monopoly and the duopoly market structures and hence neglects interconnection costs in the case of duopoly. Plotted in figure 5.7 are the total average cost functions for a monopoly and for two firms that equally split the market using the monopolist's cost function.[36] The

Table 5.8
Optimal regulation (LT): Expected consumer surplus and the firm's utility (in 100M)

Welfare of	$\lambda = 0.3$	$\lambda = 1.0$	$\lambda = 2.0$
Consumer	4.91	5.76	7.30
Firm	0.02	0.01	0.01

Table 5.9
Monopoly: Expected consumer surplus and the firm's utility (in 100M)

Welfare of	PC	UM
Consumer	4.75	1.78
Firm	0.05	1.74

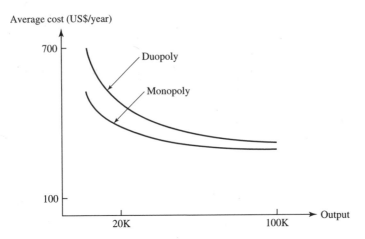

Figure 5.7
Traditional cost-based natural monopoly test: Uniform entry without IC

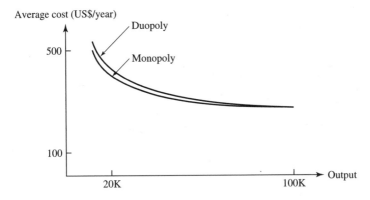

Figure 5.8
Cost-based natural monopoly test: Targeted entry with IC

multifirm cost function displayed in figure 5.7 is equivalent to our duopoly cost function in the uniform entry scenario before accounting for interconnection costs. By the standard definition, the market is unambiguously a natural monopoly, since the multifirm average cost function lies everywhere above the monopoly average cost function.

Most of the cost advantage, however, disappears when we consider the cost functions appropriate to a duopoly with targeted entry. The corresponding average cost curves, which are displayed in figure 5.8, illustrate that while average costs continue to decline at all output levels, the average costs of a duopoly are only slightly higher than the average costs of a monopoly. As demonstrated in the previous subsection, such a residual cost advantage of a monopoly over a duopoly may be more than offset by the benefits, in terms of social welfare, of higher output and stronger incentives for efficiency in a duopoly. As we have argued in this chapter, these effects should be accounted for in a broader evaluation of both monopoly and duopoly market structures.

5.5 Conclusion

The telecommunications industry worldwide is, beyond any doubt, one of the most interesting recent examples of successful introduction of technological progress coupled with the implementation of deregulatory policies. For example, in the United States, since the breakup of the Bell system in the early 1980s, a wave of deregulatory reforms has successively swept the long-distance and the local exchange markets. The evolution toward a generalized deregulation of the industry is a reality which is beyond any dispute. However, some observers have come to question the rhythm of arrival of new competitors in the local markets, and, in some instances, have expressed reservations about the deregulatory trend itself.

Given the fast evolution of technology and the questions raised by the economics of regulations on the one hand, and the dearth of econometric data, on the other hand, in this chapter we have presented an empirical methodology for evaluating the relative merits of policies that promote entry into the local exchange market as opposed to those that maintain a regulated monopoly. Our methodology employs a flexible state-of-the-art technological process model, following an old tradition pioneered by Frisch (1935) that involves generating pseudodata on costs within a reasonable range of output. We then calibrate various models of monopoly and duopoly markets in order to assess their relative performances on the basis of aggregate social welfare. An attractive feature of this methodology is that it allows us to empirically model incomplete information, a cornerstone of the new economics of regulation.

The social welfare comparisons of monopoly and duopoly are made under various assumptions on firms' behavior, the regulatory context, and the nature of output. In our first exercise, in which usage is considered as the output and the serving territory area, and the number of subscribers is held constant, we find a cost elasticity of 0.3 indicating that when output increases by 1 percent, cost increases only by

0.3 percent. These quite strong economies of scale allow local exchange telecommunications to retain monopoly characteristics even when information costs of regulation, due to a cost uncertainty of the order of 20 to 30 percent in our case, are properly taken into account. This exercise shows that even total expropriation of firms' rents by means of effective yardstick competition is not enough, in this case, to offset the cost of duplicating fixed costs.

Our second exercise, in which access is considered as the output and average usage is held constant, develops a richer model of competitive entry, and a broader comparison of regulated and competitive scenarios. A methodological point made by this latter exercise is that using a strictly cost-based test of natural monopoly, as is traditionally done, may be misleading when it comes to evaluating the relative performance of monopoly and duopoly in a broader sense. Our empirical results strongly demonstrate that deregulatory policies can enhance social welfare in a variety of situations. The performance of a deregulated market clearly depends on the assumptions made about the way firms compete. Under either regulated (YS) competition or highly competitive unregulated competition (AC or MC), we have found that duopoly outperforms traditional cost plus ($C+$) regulated monopoly. In the most favorable targeted entry scenario, yardstick competition outperforms incentive regulation under price-cap regulation (PC), while competitive unregulated duopoly achieves slightly lower aggregate social welfare. When only consumer welfare is used as the criterion, regulated competition is unambiguously preferred to regulated monopoly, while unregulated competition leads to outcomes that are superior to price-cap regulated monopoly as long as competition is sufficiently intense.

While from the perspective of theory we do not regard our conclusions as surprising, we should note that the process model approach, on which our empirical methodology rests, is the best-suited approach for a full exploration of the question of natural monopoly from a forward-looking point of view. By necessity, the econometric approach must rely on historical data in which the industry structure and regulatory environment are fixed or rather retrospective. In order to provide a quantitative estimate of the costs and benefits of deregulatory policies in the telecommunications arena, it is necessary to model as carefully as possible the actual technologies that are most likely to be used by future entrants and incumbent firms. This chapter is an example of a research approach that can be used with success in future analyses of telecommunications and other rapidly evolving industries.

6

Optimal Regulation
of a Natural Monopoly

6.1 Introduction

By now the reader should be familiar with the methodology suggested in this book for jointly applying engineering and economic models to the empirical analysis of telecommunications markets. In the previous chapter we showed how the LECOM engineering model can be used to generate a cost function that incorporates some elements of incomplete information as has been emphasized in the new economics of regulation. Furthermore we suggested a technique for obtaining an empirical cost function that makes an explicit account of the relationship between the cost function and the market structure under which firms operate. Using the same methodology, in this chapter we consider a local exchange telecommunications industry that possesses the features of a natural monopoly and investigate in some detail the economic properties and the implementation of the optimal incentive regulation of a firm that serves the market.

Recall from the previous two chapters that in models of incentive regulation the solutions typically depend on detailed information about the cost function (both observable cost and unobservable disutility of effort) and about the form of the regulator's beliefs regarding the uncertain technological parameters. Applying these models therefore requires a careful specification of the relevant cost functions and probability distributions. Schmalensee (1989) presented some simulation results in which cost and disutility of effort functions are given specific functional forms. His objective was not to model actual cost structures but rather to compare analytically the performance of linear regulatory mechanisms, which include cost-plus and price-cap regulation as extreme cases, without attempting to solve for the optimal mechanism. Gasmi et al. (1994) used the Schmalensee model in order to measure the trade-off between rent extraction and efficiency in various incentive regulation mechanisms including optimal regulation under asymmetric information. These authors did not attempt to evaluate empirically costs or beliefs but rather relied on sensitivity analyses for a range of plausible values for these unknown terms. Wunsch (1994) applied the Laffont-Tirole model to the regulation of European urban mass transit firms. The focus of his work was the empirical estimation of the parameters of the regulator's beliefs about technological uncertainty, with which he calibrated the firm's disutility of effort function.

This chapter attempts to carry this line of research a step further by incorporating into the analysis a detailed model of the firm's cost. Rather than using field data and econometric techniques to model costs, we make use of the engineering simulation model of the costs of local exchange telecommunications networks LECOM, described in chapter 2, which generates the cost data. In section 6.2 we recall the optimal regulatory mechanism under asymmetric information and the various functions necessary to analyze the efficiency and welfare properties of this mechanism.[1] In section 6.3 we describe the way the LECOM model is used to estimate the cost function and show how the various functions entering the expressions can be parameterized to characterize the optimal regulatory mechanism, namely the consumer surplus function, the disutility of effort function, and the density function representing regulatory uncertainty. Section 6.4 presents the empirical results related to the endogenous variables of the mechanism, the implied values of some welfare measures, and the outcome of a sensitivity analysis of the results to some factors used in the calibration.

A couple of implications of these results are discussed in section 6.5. First, we evaluate the extent of the incentive correction, which expresses the divergence of pricing under the optimal mechanism from optimal pricing under complete information. Second, we ask whether the optimal regulatory mechanism can be implemented through a menu of linear contracts. We find that the incentive correction term is small in magnitude and that optimal regulation can be well approximated by a menu of simple linear contracts. Section 6.6 investigates the stability of the optimal regulatory scheme by using an alternative disutility of effort function to that used above. We summarize our approach and empirical findings in a concluding section.

6.2   The Optimal Regulatory Mechanism: Theory

We briefly recap in this section the main features of the optimal regulatory mechanism with ex post cost observability.[2] Recall from chapter 4 that $P(q)$ denotes the inverse demand function for a private good produced by a regulated firm, $S(q)$ represents gross consumer surplus, and $V(q) = S(q) + \lambda P(q)q$ represents the social value associated with production of the good, where λ is the shadow cost of public funds.

The firm has private information about (knows) its technological parameter β, which we refer to as the type of the firm. In addition the firm exerts an unobservable level of "effort" e, which reduces costs, according to $C = C(\beta, e, q)$ for a production level q but which also generates a disutility to the firm of $\psi(e)$ with $\psi' > 0$ and $\psi'' > 0$. The utility of the firm, which chooses effort level e, is given by $U = t - \psi(e)$, where t is the net transfer to the firm determined by the regulatory mechanism. The regulator is assumed to have beliefs about the uncertain technological parameter given by a cumulative distribution $F(\beta)$ on the interval $[\underline{\beta}, \bar{\beta}]$ with density $f(\beta)$.

Recall that the utilitarian social welfare function (the sum of the consumers' and firm's welfare) is given by

$$W = V(q) - (1 + \lambda)[C(\beta, e, q) + \psi(e)] - \lambda U \tag{6.1}$$

The regulator is assumed to have complete information about this objective function, except for the values of β and e. (That is to say, the regulator knows the functions $P(\cdot)$, $C(\cdot)$ and $\psi(\cdot)$.)

As seen in chapter 4, a regulatory mechanism is equivalent to a truthful revelation mechanism $\{q(\beta), C(\beta), t(\beta)\}$. Cost observation allows the regulator to invert $C = C(\beta, e, q)$ to obtain the effort function $E(\beta, C, q)$. The regulatory mechanism can therefore be rewritten as $\{q(\beta), e(\beta), U(\beta)\}$, where $e(\beta) = E(\beta, C(\beta), q(\beta))$ and $U(\beta) = t(\beta) - \psi(e(\beta))$. The regulatory program is thus given by

$$\max_{q(\cdot), e(\cdot), U(\cdot)} \int_{\underline{\beta}}^{\bar{\beta}} \{V(q(\beta)) - (1 + \lambda)[C(\beta, e(\beta), q(\beta)) + \psi(e(\beta))]$$

$$- \lambda U(\beta)\} f(\beta) \, d\beta \tag{6.2}$$

under the participation, and incentive compatibility constraints given by

$$U(\beta) \geq 0 \qquad \text{for all } \beta \text{ in } [\underline{\beta}, \bar{\beta}] \tag{6.3}$$

and

$$\dot{U}(\beta) = -\psi'(e(\beta))E_\beta(\beta, C(\beta, e(\beta), q(\beta)), q(\beta)) \tag{6.4}$$

Integrating (6.4), using (6.3)[3] and substituting for $U(\beta)$ in (6.2) yields the regulatory program

$$\max_{q(\cdot),e(\cdot)} \int_{\underline{\beta}}^{\bar{\beta}} \left\{ V(q(\beta)) - (1+\lambda)\left[C(\beta, e(\beta), q(\beta)) + \psi(e(\beta))\right] \right.$$
$$\left. + \lambda \frac{F(\beta)}{f(\beta)} \psi'(e(\beta)) \frac{C_\beta(\beta, e(\beta), q(\beta))}{C_e(\beta, e(\beta), q(\beta))} \right\} f(\beta) \, d\beta \tag{6.5}$$

We proceed to quantify the variables that are endogenous to this optimal regulatory mechanism for the case of local exchange telecommunications markets by developing appropriate measures for each term that enters the regulator's objective function (6.5).

6.3 The Local Exchange Cost Function, Welfare, and Regulatory Uncertainty: Estimation and Calibration

In section 5.1 we provided some justifications of the way we use some input parameters of the LECOM engineering cost computation software to model elements of incomplete information that affect the cost function. More specifically, those LECOM input parameters were used to model an adverse selection parameter representing some uncertainty that the regulator has on the firm's production technology and a moral hazard variable that measures the intensity of the firm's (unobservable) investment in a cost-reducing activity. Here we devote more attention to the procedure for constructing this cost function which, as can be seen from the previous section, is a critical component of the optimal regulatory mechanism.

We recall from chapter 5 that we use the ranges of values [0.5, 1.5] and [0.5, 5.5] for, respectively, the capital and labor price multipliers (PK and PL) and the level of telephone usage measured in CCS (output Q) to run LECOM and generate cost data for a firm covering an area of about 57 square miles and serving 108,000 subscribers. These data are then fitted to a cost function of a translog form. However, we have to take care of two minor difficulties. First, increasing the level of effort reduces cost, whereas an increase in the multiplier of the price of labor PL increases cost. Second, since these data are to be used to fit a translog functional form for the cost function, it is necessary that the values of all independent variables be bounded away from zero.

Let $PL_0 = 1.50$ be the maximal value of the price of labor in the grid that we consider. It corresponds to the minimum level of effort equal to an arbitrary small number ϵ. Effort e decreases the price of labor PL according to $PL = PL_0 + \epsilon - e$, that is, $e = PL_0 + \epsilon - PL$. Then we can define the empirical cost function $\tilde{C}$ from the theoretical cost function C according to

$$\tilde{C}(PK, PL, Q) = C(PK, PL_0 + \epsilon - PL, Q) \tag{6.6}$$

Through simulations of LECOM we calculate the values of this cost function for $Q = 0.50, 1.00, \ldots, 5.00, 5.50$ and $PK, PL = 0.50, 0.60, \ldots, 1.40, 1.50$. Hence we obtain a data set of 1331 points.[4] Since our analysis requires detailed information about the derivatives of the cost function, we use, as mentioned above, these data to fit a smooth translog functional form to the underlying data. In the translog functional form we estimate the quadratic relationship between the natural logarithm of the dependent variable $\tilde{C}$ and the logarithm of independent variables PK, PL, and Q, respectively, the multiplier of price of capital, the multiplier of price of labor, and usage output.[5] This translog function is given by

$$\log \tilde{C}(PK, PL, Q) = 16.96 + 0.44 \log PK + 0.44 \log PL + 0.15 \log Q$$
$$+ 0.11(\log PK)^2 + 0.12(\log PL)^2 + 0.02(\log Q)^2$$
$$- 0.18 \log PK \log PL + 0.007 \log Q \log PL$$
$$- 0.007 \log PK \log Q \tag{6.7}$$

Table 6.1 presents the standard regression results that lead to such a cost function.[6]

At this stage it is worthwhile to examine some economic properties exhibited by this empirical cost function and to compare these properties with what has been reported in the literature. Shin and Ying (1992) estimated a translog cost function using data on 58 local exchange (Baby Bell and independent) carriers from 1976 to 1983. Despite our smaller number of explanatory variables, we obtained comparable results in terms of the parameter estimates.[7] Our parameter estimates could be used to investigate returns to scale in the local exchange technology. Shin and Ying found a scale elasticity, evaluated at the sample mean for all variables, equal to 0.958, "indicating mild scale economies." When

Table 6.1
Parameter estimates of the translog cost function: Dependent variable = $\log \tilde{C}$

Independent variable (log)	Coefficient	t-measure
Constant	16.96	12752.40
PK	0.44	139.00
PL	0.44	140.04
Q	0.15	92.47
PK × PK	0.11	20.26
PL × PL	0.12	21.22
Q × Q	0.02	18.57
PK × PL	−0.18	−35.78
PK × Q	−0.007	−2.80
PL × Q	0.007	2.71

Note: Number of observations: 1331; corrected R-squared: 0.9918.

they considered the averages of variables associated only with Bell Operating Companies, they found more pronounced economies of scale. While they do not report the range of this scale elasticity, it is reasonable to assume that it lies within [0.8, 0.9] based on their aggregate scale elasticity. That is, an increase of 1 percent in output leads to an increase of cost in the [0.8, 0.9] percent range.

In our simulation, we found a considerably higher scale elasticity of the order of 0.30, indicating very strong economies of scale. This result is largely due to the fact that our data correspond to a local exchange network in which the serving area and the number of subscribers are held constant and only the usage per subscriber varies.[8] Our cost function also shows some substitutability between capital and labor. The Hicks-Allen partial elasticities of substitution between capital and labor are given by $\sigma_{PK,PL} = \sigma_{PL,PK} = 0.7$. The conventional prices elasticities are given by $\epsilon_{PK,PL} = 0.029$ and $\epsilon_{PL,PK} = 0.031$.[9]

To evaluate the social value of production $V(q) = S(q) + \lambda P(q)q$, we have to specify both the inverse demand function P and the cost of public funds λ. For our base case we use the value of 0.3 for λ. We assume an exponential demand function $q(p) = ae^{bp}$, a form that has been widely used in empirical studies of local telecommunications demand. To determine the parameters a and b, we make two assumptions. First, we assume that the price elasticity of demand is equal to -0.2.[10] Second, we assume that the revenue collected from the representative customer corresponds to the annual cost of serving this customer, which by using

LECOM amounts to $246.68.[11] These two assumptions yield two independent equations that we solve to obtain the individual (inverse) demand function

$$P(q) = -421 \log[0.204683q] \tag{6.8}$$

leading to a social value of production function given by

$$V(q) = 5.91084 \times 10^7 q \, [2.35552 - \log q] \tag{6.9}$$

We now discuss the way we calibrate the disutility of effort function $\psi(\cdot)$ which, in contrast to consumer demand, is unobservable by definition. Our approach is then to assume a functional form consistent with theory, namely a function that is increasing and convex in effort, and to rely on information obtained from LECOM and other sources to determine the precise values of its parameters. The following procedure is applied.

We assume that $PL_0 = 1.5$ is the multiplier associated with a minimum level of effort (corresponding to a cost-plus regulatory environment). We compute the multiplier corresponding to the first-best level of effort as $PL^* = PL_0(L^*/L_0)$, where L_0 and L^* are, respectively, the number of employees prior and posterior to regulation in markets where telecommunications markets have been deregulated or privatized. Using the ratio $(L^*/L_0) = 0.6$, which corresponds to an assumption that deregulation leads to a 40 percent reduction in labor force, yields $PL^* = 0.9.[12]$

Next we calibrate the disutility of effort function $\psi(\cdot)$ by assuming the quadratic form $\psi(e) = ce + de^2$. We determine the parameters c and d by solving

$$\psi'(0) = 0 \tag{6.10}$$

and

$$\psi'(e^*) = -C_e \tag{6.11}$$

where $e^*(= 1.5 - 0.9)$ is the optimal level of effort corresponding to PL^* when ϵ, the constant defined in equation (6.6), is equal to zero. Equation (6.10) says that under cost-plus regulation the marginal disutility of effort is equal to zero.[13] After deregulation a cost-minimizing firm sets effort such that marginal disutility equals marginal cost saving as is shown in equation (6.11).[14] Solving these equations yields parameter values $c = 0$ and $d = 1.04397 \times 10^7$. The calibrated disutility of effort function is then

$$\psi(e) = (1.04397 \times 10^7)e^2 \tag{6.12}$$

Finally, concerning the regulatory environment, we assume that the regulator's uncertainty about the technological parameter β is captured by a uniform distribution of this parameter over the range $[0.5, 1.5]$, which is the range of values for which the cost function has been simulated. We nevertheless examine how sensitive our results are to changes in the support of this uniform distribution.

6.4   The Optimal Regulatory Mechanism: Empirical Evaluation

We now use the empirical cost function given by equation (6.7), the social valuation of production given by equation (6.9), and the uniform distribution with support $[0.5, 1.5]$ of the parameter β to solve the regulator's program given in (6.5) above. Table 6.2 presents the optimal levels of output Q and effort e as a function of firm type β.[15] We see that output as well as effort decline as β increases, namely as the firm's efficiency decreases. The result is striking: while the effort of the least efficient firm is about 30 percent lower than that of the most efficient firm, production drops only by about 2 percent.

Given the output and effort levels, we compute the firm's information rent U as a function of its type. These results are presented in

Table 6.2
Optimal levels of output and effort

β	Q	e
0.50	3.78	0.64
0.60	3.77	0.61
0.70	3.77	0.59
0.80	3.76	0.57
0.90	3.75	0.54
1.00	3.75	0.52
1.10	3.74	0.50
1.20	3.73	0.48
1.30	3.73	0.47
1.40	3.72	0.45
1.50	3.72	0.43

Note: We proxy effort (e) by the derivation of the labor cost multiplier from the multiplier associated with the minimum level of effort ($e = PL_0 - PL$).

Table 6.3
Firm's information rent, cost, and consumers' gains from efficiency (10^6 annualized US$)

β	U	$\tilde{C}$	ψ	CG
0.50	10.44	21.26	4.24	2.96
0.60	9.20	22.87	3.90	2.65
0.70	7.99	24.44	3.60	2.35
0.80	6.83	25.99	3.34	2.05
0.90	5.72	27.52	3.09	1.75
1.00	4.66	29.04	2.87	1.46
1.10	3.64	30.54	2.65	1.16
1.20	2.66	32.03	2.45	0.87
1.30	1.73	33.52	2.26	0.58
1.40	0.85	35.00	2.08	0.29
1.50	0.00	36.47	1.91	0.00

table 6.3, which shows that rent is declining in β and that the least efficient firm receives no rent. In table 6.3 we also report the firm's production cost $\tilde{C}$, disutility of effort ψ, and the gains to consumers associated with various levels of technological efficiency of the firm β, CG where $CG(\beta) = CS(\beta) - CS(\bar{\beta})$ and CS is net consumer surplus.[16] We note the increasing gains to consumers generated by efficient firms which, however, obtain higher rents. Calculating the expected ratio of rents to total cost yields an expected rate of return to the firm of about 16.5 percent.

Let us examine further the impact of the efficiency parameter β on welfare. For this purpose we rewrite aggregate social welfare W given in (6.1) as

$$W = \{S(q) - P(q)q\} + \{-(1 + \lambda)(t + C(\beta, e, q) - P(q)q)\} + \{t - \psi(e)\}$$

$$(6.13)$$

that is, as the sum of net consumer surplus $CS = S(q) - P(q)q$, taxpayers' gain $\hat{T} = -(1 + \lambda)(t + C(\beta, e, q) - P(q)q)$, evaluated at the cost of public funds λ, and firm's rent $U = t - \psi(e)$. Increasing efficiency generates gains in aggregate welfare W. However, we seek to examine more closely the behavior of its three components CS, $\hat{T}$, and U. Table 6.4 shows that while the consumer surplus and the firm's rent increase monotonically with efficiency (decreasing β), the taxpayers' gain experiences an increase for the less efficient firms and a decrease for the more efficient ones.[17] Figure 6.1 displays the behavior of these three components of social welfare.[18]

Table 6.4
Decomposition of social welfare into consumer surplus, taxpayers' gain, and firm's rent
(10^6 annualized US$)

β	CS	$\hat{T}$	U	W
0.50	171.88	10.56	10.44	192.91
0.60	171.58	10.86	9.20	191.64
0.70	171.27	11.05	7.99	190.31
0.80	170.98	11.18	6.83	188.99
0.90	170.68	11.23	5.72	187.63
1.00	170.38	11.22	4.66	186.26
1.10	170.09	11.15	3.64	184.88
1.20	169.80	11.01	2.66	183.47
1.30	169.51	10.82	1.73	182.06
1.40	169.22	10.56	0.85	180.63
1.50	168.93	10.24	0.00	179.17

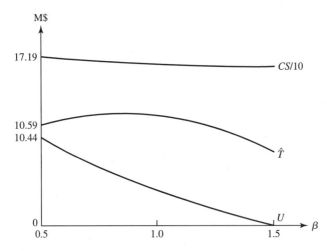

Figure 6.1
Impact of efficiency gains on consumer welfare, taxpayers' gain, and firm's rent

Since our results depend on the calibration of the consumer demand function, we conducted a sensitivity analysis of these results with respect to the demand elasticity. Table 6.5 summarizes these results. Each of the entries of the last three columns of the table exhibits the range of optimal output, effort, and rent, respectively, for three levels of the demand elasticity, low (−0.2), medium (−0.4), and high (−0.6). We report in parentheses the standard deviations of these three variables for the three

Table 6.5
Sensitivity of output, effort, and rent to demand elasticity (10^6 annualized US$)

Elasticity	$[Q(\bar{\beta}), Q(\underline{\beta})]$	$[e(\bar{\beta}), e(\underline{\beta})]$	$[U(\bar{\beta}), U(\underline{\beta})]$
Low	[3.72, 3.78]	[0.43, 0.64]	[0.00, 10.44]
(−0.2)	(0.021)	(0.065)	(3.307)
Medium	[4.39, 4.53]	[0.45, 0.66]	[0.00, 10.89]
(−0.4)	(0.045)	(0.066)	(3.447)
High	[5.21, 5.45]	[0.48, 0.69]	[0.00, 11.38]
(−0.6)	(0.074)	(0.067)	(3.602)

values of demand elasticity. We note that higher elasticity leads to both a higher level of output and higher variance.

In the case of linear pricing, the first-order condition of optimal regulation with respect to price (see chapter 4) is given by

$$\frac{p - C_q}{p} = \frac{\lambda}{1 + \lambda}\frac{1}{\eta} + \text{incentive correction term} \qquad (6.14)$$

According to this formula, and in the absence of any strong countervailing effect of the marginal cost or of the incentive correction term, the price decreases with elasticity, and hence production increases. As production increases, a first effect is to increase the effort level, which applies now to more units. However, as the rent increases with the production level, the regulator is more eager to reduce the power of incentives (i.e., effort) in order to decrease the information rent. Table 6.5 shows that the first effect dominates but effort, marginal cost, quantity, and rent are all more spread out when the price elasticity increases.

We also conducted a sensitivity analysis with respect to the support of the distribution of the regulator's prior beliefs about the technological uncertainty parameter β. When we varied the support of the uniform distribution of β, we found that a tighter support, which can be interpreted as an improvement of information, leads to lower rent for every firm and higher expected social welfare.[19]

6.5 Implications

6.5.1 Incentives and Pricing

In our model of optimal regulation described in section 6.2, asymmetric information requires that the regulator leave a rent to the firm for inducing efficient production. A regulator with complete information would set production at the socially efficient level by equating the marginal social value of production with its social marginal cost,[20] that is,

$$V'(q) = (1 + \lambda)C_q \qquad (6.15)$$

In addition a regulator with complete information would ensure that effort is set at its cost-minimizing level so that

$$\psi'(e) = -C_e \qquad (6.16)$$

Under asymmetric information, however, the regulator's desire to minimize the transfer to the firm is in conflict with his desire to minimize cost. This conflict may give rise to an incentive distortion as can be seen from the first-order condition of the regulator's program (6.5)

$$V'(q) = (1 + \lambda)C_q + \left[\lambda \frac{F(\beta)}{f(\beta)} \psi'(e) \frac{d}{dq} \left(\frac{\partial E}{\partial \beta} \right) \right] \qquad (6.17)$$

In this equation, $\psi'(e) \cdot d(\partial E/\partial \beta)/dq$ measures the impact of a unit increase in output on the firm's rent, $d(\partial U/\partial \beta)/dq$ (see chapter 4). The total derivative $d(\partial E/\partial \beta)/dq$ provides a measure of how output effects the potential effort savings associated with an increase in efficiency. The ratio $F(\beta)/f(\beta)$ expresses the fact that the gain in reducing $|\partial U/\partial \beta|$ is proportional to the probability, $F(\beta)$, that the firm is more efficient than a type β firm. The relative cost (with respect to the complete information case) of the distortion is proportional to the probability ($f(\beta)$) of its occurrence.

In equation (6.17) the term in brackets is an incentive correction that we designate by $I(\beta)$. The incentive correction I is a complex function involving the effort function E and the marginal disutility of effort. Hence an analytical evaluation of its magnitude and sign is far from straightforward. However, we can use (6.17) which tells us that

$$I = V'(q) - (1 + \lambda)C_q \qquad (6.18)$$

showing that the distortion term depends only on the known functions V and C and the value of λ. In table 6.6 we express this distortion as a percentage of social marginal cost, namely

$$\tilde{I} = \frac{I}{(1 + \lambda)\tilde{C}_q} \times 100 \qquad (6.19)$$

The empirical results presented in table 6.6 reveal that the incentive correction term is consistently negative but also very small. For all firm

Table 6.6
Distortion as a percentage of social marginal cost

β	$\bar{I}$
0.50	0.00
0.60	−0.20
0.70	−0.35
0.80	−0.47
0.90	−0.56
1.00	−0.63
1.10	−0.68
1.20	−0.72
1.30	−0.76
1.40	−0.78
1.50	−0.79

types it is less than 0.8 percent in absolute value.[21] Whenever the incentive correction is identically zero, in which case the "incentive-pricing" dichotomy is said to hold, a regulator uses the two policy instruments, the transfer t and the regulated price p, for separate ends. Prices can be set to maximize social welfare so that (6.15) is satisfied, while the transfer is used to optimally determine the trade-off between leaving rent to the firm and giving the firm an incentive to minimize cost.[22] In fact a necessary and sufficient condition for the incentive-pricing dichotomy to hold is that efficiency and effort can be aggregated in the cost function, that is, that there exists a function such that $C(\beta, e, q) = C(H(\beta, e), q)$.[23] The preceding results suggest that our simulated cost function approximately satisfies this condition.

To provide an additional empirical confirmation of this result, we fit the LECOM data to an incomplete translog functional form which has the same structure as the one presented in equation (6.7) and table 6.1, but with the cross-effects between β and q and between e and q omitted. Table 6.7 shows the results of this new approximation of the cost function. As shown by the corrected R-squared, which remains practically unchanged and by the high indicative t-measures, neglecting the two cross-effect terms did not deteriorate our approximation of the cost function. This is further evidence that our simulated cost function approximately satisfies the above-noted efficiency and effort aggregation condition.[24]

Table 6.7
Parameter estimates of an incomplete translog cost function: Dependent variable $= \log \tilde{C}$

Independent variable (log)	Coefficient	t-measure
Constant	16.96	12,796.00
PK	0.43	190.79
PL	0.45	197.57
Q	0.15	92.70
PK × PK	0.11	20.16
PL × PL	0.12	21.11
Q × Q	0.02	18.48
PK × PL	−0.18	−35.60

Note: Number of observations: 1331; corrected R-squared: 0.9917.

6.5.2 Implementation of Optimal Regulation

We now consider the implementation of the optimal incentive regulation program. In the previous section we found that our empirical cost function satisfies the incentive-pricing dichotomy so that optimal prices are set according to a Ramsey rule and optimal effort levels are determined by the transfer from the regulator to the firm. In some cases the optimal transfer can be implemented by a menu of linear cost-sharing rules, and we examine this issue next.

An attractive feature of linear cost-sharing rules, besides the fact that they are "easy" to implement, is that they are robust. Under risk neutrality of the agents, these rules are unaffected by the presence of an additive accounting or forecasting error in the cost function and changes in the distribution of this noise does not affect their optimality. Linear implementation of the regulatory transfer function is possible when some functions G and F exist such that[25]

$$C(\beta, e, q) = G(\beta - e)F(q) \tag{6.20}$$

Condition (6.20) is clearly stronger than the separability property that we found to hold in the previous section. We now seek to find a reasonable empirical approximation to the cost function that would satisfy (6.20). Consider the following specification:

$$\tilde{C}(PK, PL, Q) = \exp\{\alpha_0 + \alpha_1 \log(PK + PL) + \alpha_2[\log(PK + PL)]^2 + \alpha_3 \log(Q) + \alpha_4[\log(Q)]^2\} \tag{6.21}$$

Table 6.8
Parameter estimates of a reduced translog cost function with aggregation of labor and capital and their separability with output: Dependent variable $= \log \check{C}$

Independent variable (log)	Coefficient	t-measure
Constant	16.38	4876.77
$(PK + PL)$	0.80	73.43
Q	0.15	91.64
$(PK + PL) \times (PK + PL)$	0.05	5.99
$Q \times Q$	0.02	18.27

Note: Number of observations: 1331; corrected R-squared: 0.9915.

Observing that $PK + PL = \beta + 1.5 - e$ (see section 6.3), we see that such an empirical cost function would indeed verify the sufficient condition. Fitting our data to such a specification yields the results in table 6.8. As can be seen from the high level of both the corrected R-squared and the indicative t-measures, table 6.8 shows that this specification fits the data quite well.[26]

Using this approximation of the cost function, we now construct the way in which the optimal regulatory mechanism can be implemented through a menu of linear contracts. We write the (approximated) cost function given in table 6.8 as

$$\tilde{C}(PK, PL, Q) = \exp\{16.38 + 0.80 \log(PK + PL) + 0.15 \log(Q)$$
$$+ 0.05[\log(PK + PL)]^2 + 0.02[\log(Q)]^2\} \qquad (6.22)$$

The empirical counterparts of the functions G and F in equation (6.20) are given, respectively, by

$$\tilde{G}(PK, PL) = \exp\{16.38 + 0.80 \log(PK + PL) + 0.05[\log(PK + PL)]^2\}$$
$$(6.23)$$

and

$$\tilde{F}(Q) = \exp\{0.15 \log(Q) + 0.02[\log(Q)]^2\} \qquad (6.24)$$

Using these functions, we define a measure of performance of the firm $\bar{C}$ as[27]

$$\bar{C}(PK, PL, Q) = \frac{\tilde{C}(PK, PL, Q)}{\tilde{F}(Q)} \qquad (6.25)$$

Table 6.9 describes, for every firm's type considered in the grid, the optimal transfer as a function of the generalized average cost $\bar{C}$ using the cost function defined in equation (6.20). This table also gives a discrete approximation, $\bar{s}$, of the slope of this transfer function. This table demonstrates that the transfer function is convex (figure 6.2 illustrates this function). Therefore the transfer function can be approximated arbitrarily closely by a menu of linear cost reimbursement rules that

Table 6.9
Performance, transfer (10^6 annualized US$), and slope of the transfer function

β	Performance, $\bar{C}$	Transfer, t	Slope, $\bar{s}$
0.50	16.75	14.68	-1.24
0.60	18.05	13.09	-1.20
0.70	19.32	11.59	-1.16
0.80	20.56	10.17	-1.12
0.90	21.80	8.82	-1.07
1.00	23.02	7.52	-1.03
1.10	24.25	6.29	-0.98
1.20	25.46	5.12	-0.94
1.30	26.68	3.99	-0.90
1.40	27.90	2.92	-0.86
1.50	29.11	1.91	-0.82

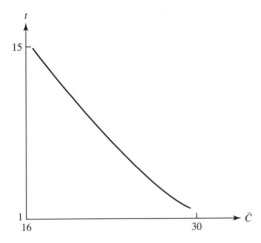

Figure 6.2
Transfer function

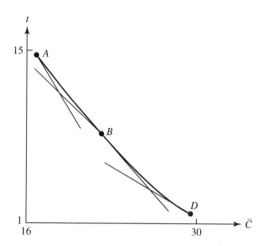

Figure 6.3
Approximation of optimal regulation with linear reimbursement rules

specifies a fixed payment to the firm and a share of cost overruns that the firm will have to bear. Indeed, the convexity of this function ensures that it can be replaced by the family of its tangents and accordingly implemented by a menu of linear (generalized average) cost-reimbursement rules.

It has been argued in the literature (Wilson 1989) that in practice, a few elements are needed in the menu of linear reimbursement rules for approximating quite closely the optimal regulation mechanism.[28] Below we consider a menu with three elements and compute the associated welfare loss. We consider the tangents associated with the transfer-performance pairs[29] denoted A, B, and D in figure 6.3.

Point A in figure 6.3 corresponds to $\beta = 0.50$, and the equation of the tangent at A is given by

$$t = 14.68 - 1.24(\bar{C} - 16.75) \tag{6.26}$$

Similarly point B corresponds to $\beta = 1$ with

$$t = 7.52 - 1.03(\bar{C} - 23.02) \tag{6.27}$$

and point D corresponds to $\beta = 1.50$ with

$$t = 1.91 - 0.82(\bar{C} - 29.11) \tag{6.28}$$

For each tangent we can compute the optimal effort level chosen by a type-β firm by solving

$$\max_e U = t - \psi(e) \tag{6.29}$$

or

$$\max a - b(G(\beta - e) - c) - \psi(e) \tag{6.30}$$

where a, b, and c are the parameters of the appropriate tangent, $G(\beta - e)$ is the estimated function[30]

$$G(\beta - e) = \exp\{16.38 + 0.80\log(1.5 + \beta - e) + 0.05[\log(1.5 + \beta - e)]^2\} \tag{6.31}$$

and $\psi(e)$ is the calibrated function

$$\psi(e) = (1.04395 \times 10^7)e^2 \tag{6.32}$$

We obtain in this way three effort functions $e_A(\beta)$, $e_B(\beta)$, and $e_D(\beta)$.

Next we determine the cutoff points β_1 and β_2 such that

- For $\beta \in [\underline{\beta}_1, \beta_1]$, type β prefers the tangent to A than the tangent to B or D.
- For $\beta \in [\beta_1, \beta_2]$, type β prefers the tangent to B than the tangent to A or D.
- For $\beta \in [\beta_2, \bar{\beta}]$, type β prefers the tangent to D than the tangent to A or B.

The associated information rents are[31]

$$
\begin{aligned}
U(\beta) &= \int_\beta^{\bar{\beta}} \psi'(e_D^*(b))\, db \qquad \text{for } \beta \in [\beta_2, \bar{\beta}] \\
&= \int_\beta^{\beta_2} \psi'(e_B^*(b))\, db + \int_{\beta_2}^{\bar{\beta}} \psi'(e_D^*(b))\, db \qquad \text{for } \beta \in [\beta_1, \beta_2] \\
&= \int_\beta^{\beta_1} \psi'(e_A^*(b))\, db + \int_{\beta_1}^{\beta_2} \psi'(e_B^*(b))\, db \\
&\quad + \int_{\beta_2}^{\bar{\beta}} \psi'(e_D^*(b))\, db \qquad \text{for } \beta \in [\underline{\beta}, \beta_1]
\end{aligned}
\tag{6.33}
$$

We can then compute the associated best welfare for the regulation by solving

$$\max_{q(\cdot)} \int_{\underline{\beta}}^{\bar{\beta}} [V(q(\beta)) - (1 + \lambda)(C(\beta, e(\beta), q(\beta)) + \psi(e(\beta))) - \lambda U(\beta)] f(\beta) \, d\beta$$

$$(6.34)$$

with

$$e(\beta) = e_A(\beta) \quad \text{for } \beta \in [\underline{\beta}, \beta_1]$$
$$= e_B(\beta) \quad \text{for } \beta \in [\beta_1, \beta_2]$$
$$= e_D(\beta) \quad \text{for } \beta \in [\beta_2, \bar{\beta}] \qquad (6.35)$$

and compare it with the optimal social welfare. We obtain a loss of 0.054 percent.[32]

6.6 Using an Alternative Disutility of Effort Function

This and the other empirical chapters of the book are based on a theoretical framework in which effort is viewed as the investment that the firm's manager makes in order to reduce costs. An assumption appended to this interpretation is that the firm's disutility of effort has the nature of a fixed cost, namely that it is independent of the level of output. However, if effort is of a more disaggregated nature, such as if it affects cost at the level of each piece of capital, then it is reasonable to assume that the disutility it creates depends on the level of output. In this section we present the results of a computation of the optimal regulatory mechanism using a disutility of effort of the form $\psi(e, q) = \varphi(e)q$.

The first-order conditions that define the optimal regulatory mechanism in the general case $\psi(e, q)$ were derived in section 4.7. In the special case where $\psi(e, q) = \varphi(e)q$, the regulatory program that we solve takes the following compact form:

$$\max_{q(\cdot), e(\cdot)} \int_{\underline{\beta}}^{\bar{\beta}} \left\{ V(q(\beta)) - (1 + \lambda)[C(\beta, e(\beta), q(\beta)) + \varphi(e(\beta))q(\beta)] \right.$$

$$\left. + \lambda \frac{F(\beta)}{f(\beta)} \varphi'(e(\beta))q(\beta) \frac{C_\beta(\beta, e(\beta), q(\beta))}{C_e(\beta, e(\beta), q(\beta))} \right\} f(\beta) \, d\beta \quad (6.36)$$

Using the same calibration techniques as when the disutility of effort function is $\psi(e)$, we solve the program (6.36). Tables 6.10, 6.11, and 6.12

Table 6.10
Optimal levels of output and effort with disutility, $\psi(e, q) = \varphi(e)q$

β	Q	e
0.50	3.68	0.65
0.60	3.68	0.62
0.70	3.67	0.60
0.80	3.67	0.58
0.90	3.66	0.56
1.00	3.65	0.54
1.10	3.65	0.52
1.20	3.64	0.50
1.30	3.64	0.48
1.40	3.63	0.46
1.50	3.63	0.45

Table 6.11
Firm's information rent, cost, and consumers' gains from efficiency with disutility, $\psi(e, q) = \varphi(e)q$ (10^6 annualized US$)

β	U	$\tilde{C}$	ψ	CG
0.50	10.44	21.04	4.27	2.61
0.60	9.20	22.63	3.94	2.35
0.70	8.00	24.18	3.65	2.08
0.80	6.84	25.71	3.39	1.79
0.90	5.73	27.22	3.16	1.51
1.00	4.67	28.71	2.94	1.24
1.10	3.65	30.19	2.73	0.97
1.20	2.68	31.67	2.54	0.71
1.30	1.74	33.14	2.35	0.47
1.40	0.85	34.60	2.17	0.23
1.50	0.00	36.05	2.00	0.00

duplicate tables 6.2, 6.3, and 6.4 for this case where $\psi(e, q) = \varphi(e)q$. We also have evaluated the incentive distortion as a percentage of social marginal cost (see section 6.5.1) and found it to be on average close to 81 percent. This confirms our expectation that the incentive-pricing dichotomy does not hold. Besides this expected result these new figures show that the main qualitative features of the optimal regulatory mechanism are robust to this change in the disutility technology.

Table 6.12
Decomposition of social welfare into consumer surplus, taxpayers' gain, and firm's rent with disutility, $\psi(e, q) = \varphi(e)q$ (10^6 annualized US$)

β	CS	$\hat{T}$	U	W
0.50	167.52	14.99	10.44	192.95
0.60	167.26	15.20	9.20	191.66
0.70	166.98	15.38	8.00	190.36
0.80	166.70	15.49	6.84	189.03
0.90	166.42	15.54	5.73	187.69
1.00	166.15	15.51	4.67	186.33
1.10	165.88	15.42	3.65	184.95
1.20	165.62	15.27	2.68	183.57
1.30	165.38	15.04	1.74	182.16
1.40	165.14	14.75	0.85	180.74
1.50	164.91	14.39	0.00	179.30

6.7 Conclusion

In this chapter we have used a detailed engineering optimization model of local exchange telecommunications to investigate the properties of optimal incentive regulation of telecommunications firms. This model has allowed us to approximate by a translog function the forward-looking costs for a chosen output range. In addition the cost model has proved useful in calibrating consumer demand and an unobservable disutility of effort. We were able to explicitly solve for the optimal regulatory contract concerning the output of the firm and the monetary transfer to the firm by the regulator.

Next we characterized optimal regulation of a monopoly under asymmetric information and we addressed the issue of its implementation. Using our cost function and our demand and disutility of effort functions, we found that optimal regulation takes a relatively simple form. Prices can be set according to the Ramsey rule, and a monetary transfer to the firm determines the firm's optimal level of rent (and simultaneously the firm's optimal deviation from cost-minimizing behavior). Moreover an optimal transfer can be implemented by a menu of contracts that are linear in performance and whose designs we have discussed at length.

7

Comparison of Performance of Incentive and Traditional Regulatory Schemes

7.1 Introduction

In chapter 6 we provided a detailed empirical analysis of the optimal regulation of a natural monopoly under asymmetric information when cost observations are available for the regulator. More specifically, we attempted to evaluate the extent of the incentive distortion associated with this optimal regulatory mechanism and due to incomplete information, and we addressed the issue of its implementation. In this chapter we take the more systematic approach of making an inventory of regulatory mechanisms, of both the incentive and the more traditional types, that are discussed in the literature and implemented in various industries and compare them along some dimensions of interest.

The new regulatory economics of the 1980s and 1990s has supplied us with a host of models that handle many of the critical issues at stake in the regulation of public utilities. Incentive regulatory mechanisms were proposed that account for the asymmetric information present between regulators and regulated firms and thus explicitly recognize the need to give up rent to the firm (which has superior information about its technology) in order to provide incentives for production efficiency. In a typical incentive regulation model, it is assumed that a regulated firm possesses knowledge about technological parameters that is unavailable to the regulator and, in some approaches, that the firm can choose levels of (cost-reducing) effort that are not observable to the regulator. The regulator is assumed to maximize a social welfare function subject to incentive compatibility and individual rationality constraints.[1]

Optimal solutions were derived by Baron and Myerson (1982) for the case where aggregate costs of the regulated firm are not observable ex post, and by Laffont and Tirole (1986) for the case where cost observations can be used to improve the performance of the regulatory mechanism. Mechanisms that do not allow for transfers between the regulator and firms have also been introduced, with cost observability (rate-of-return regulation) or without cost observability (price-cap regulation). While the solutions obtained allow one to analyze many of the essential qualitative aspects of regulation, when it comes to implementation they typically require detailed information about costs (both observable technological cost and unobservable disutility of effort) and about the form of the regulator's beliefs regarding the uncertain technological parameters.

In chapters 5 and 6 we carried the empirical analysis of incentive regulation a step further. In both chapters we used a stylized engineering model of local exchange telecommunications networks, LECOM, to derive the cost function that we use to analyze incentive regulation. In this chapter we apply this approach to a family of regulatory mechanisms implemented both with traditional regulation (cost plus) and new regulatory reforms (price cap), and compare the results with various optimal regulatory schemes. In section 7.2 we briefly review the various types of regulatory mechanisms, most of which were already formally presented in chapter 4. These mechanisms are differentiated according to whether they give the regulated firm incentives for cost minimization, whether ex post costs are observable, and whether the regulator can use transfers.

The various functions entering the expression that determines the optimal levels of the endogenous variables of the regulatory mechanisms are calibrated as in chapter 6 and they therefore are not recalled in this chapter. In section 7.3 we present the empirical results and discuss their main features. The comparisons of the alternative regulatory regimes (presented in section 7.4) are organized in three steps. In section 7.4.1 we assess their relative performance in terms of expected social welfare. In section 7.4.2 we analyze the redistributive consequences of the various forms of regulation. In section 7.4.3 we discuss the results and implications of a sensitivity analysis of the performance of the mechanisms with respect to the cost of public funds. We summarize our findings in a concluding section (section 7.5).

7.2 Alternative Regulatory Regimes

The regulatory regimes analyzed in this chapter are described by some basic theoretical ingredients as were presented in previous chapters. For the purpose of evaluating the performance of regulation, it is worth recalling that within our framework, the basic objective function of the

regulator is a utilitarian social welfare function (the sum of the consumers' and the firm's welfare). This social welfare function can be
written as

$$W = V(q) - (1 + \lambda)[C(\beta, e, q) + \psi(e)] - \lambda U \qquad (7.1)$$

where $V(q)$ is social value of the production q, C is the firm's cost function, β is a technological parameter, e is effort, ψ is the firm's disutility
of effort function, U is the firm's utility level, and λ is the cost of public
funds. The regulator is assumed to have complete information about
this objective function (i.e., the regulator knows the demand, cost, and
disutility functions) except for values of β, on which he has some beliefs,
and e, which he cannot observe.[2]

The incomplete information regulatory mechanisms considered in
this chapter are characterized by various institutional assumptions that
constrain their performance relative to a complete information situation.
So it is useful to derive a complete information regulation to use as a
benchmark in the comparisons. This regulatory solution, which we call
CI, is found by solving for output, effort, and utility levels q, e, and
U that maximize social welfare given in (7.1) under the participation
constraint that all types of firms achieve nonnegative utility. Clearly, the
participation constraint is binding, and the problem reduces to finding
q and e that maximize

$$W^{CI} = V(q) - (1 + \lambda)[C(\beta, e, q) + \psi(e)] \qquad (7.2)$$

The formal presentation of the regulatory mechanisms we consider
is given in chapter 4 where we also give some of their important qualitative properties.[3] Table 7.1 provides a brief description of these regulatory schemes. These schemes are subject to constraints of three types.
Mechanisms differ in the (ex post) observability of costs, in the feasibility of lump-sum transfers to the firm, and in the degree of bounded
rationality of the regulator (in addressing incentive issues). Conceptually the mechanisms can be visualized as a pair of two-dimensional
transfer-observability diagrams as shown in figure 7.1. Along the transfer axis there are three possibilities: no transfers, one-way transfers,
and two-way transfers. Along the observability axis there is (ex post)
cost observability and effort observability (which applies only to the
complete-information benchmark).

The upper panel of figure 7.1 shows the schemes falling under incentive regulation. At the origin is the (pure) price-cap mechanism *PC* with
no observability of cost or effort and no possibility of transfer. The *BM*

Table 7.1
Description of the regulatory mechanisms

Description	Shorthand code
Complete information benchmark	CI
Incomplete information optimal regulation with cost observability and transfers	LT
Incomplete information optimal regulation without cost observability and with transfers	BM
Price-cap regulation with no cost observability and no transfers	PC
Price-cap regulation with sharing of earnings with cost observability and one-way transfers	PCT
Cost-plus regulation with reimbursement of observable costs and no additional transfers (balanced budget)	C+
Cost-plus regulation with transfers used to balance the firm's budget	C + T

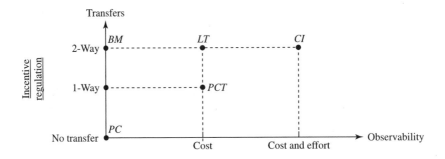

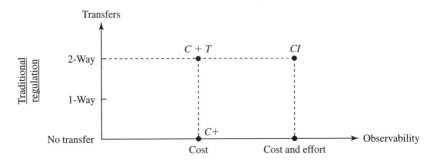

Figure 7.1
Summary of the regulatory mechanisms

scheme is located two steps up along the transfer axis, and it reflects the possibility of two-way transfers. The PCT scheme is obtained by moving, from the origin, one step to the right because of cost observability and one step up because of one-way transfers. The LT mechanism is located one step to the right from BM along the observability axis, to allow for ex post cost observability. One step further to the right along this same axis is located the CI scheme, in which managerial effort is also observable.

The lower diagram represents the schemes falling under traditional regulation. For both $C+$ and $C + T$, cost observability is assumed, and these schemes are differentiated only by whether or not transfers are allowed. Again, the CI benchmark can be reached from $C + T$ by introducing observability of effort.

7.3 Overview of the Results

We now make use of the LECOM cost model, as summarized by the estimated translog cost function, and the subsidiary functions that we calibrated (see chapter 6) to solve for the regulatory schemes presented in table 7.1. Tables 7.2 through 7.6 present output (Q), effort (e), consumers' welfare (CW), rent (U), and the associated rate of return (RoR), respectively, achieved by each of the regulatory schemes in our base case.[4] The results contained in these tables are derived with a low price elasticity of demand (η) of -0.2. Tables 7.7 through 7.11 present the results, which will appear in some of our later discussions, obtained with a higher

Table 7.2
Output, $\eta = -0.2$

β	Q^{CI}	Q^{LT}	Q^{BM}	Q^{PCT}	Q^{PC}	Q^{C+}	Q^{C+T}
0.50	3.78	3.78	3.78	3.92	3.95	4.16	3.74
0.60	3.77	3.77	3.77	3.92	3.95	4.13	3.73
0.70	3.77	3.77	3.77	3.92	3.95	4.10	3.73
0.80	3.76	3.76	3.76	3.92	3.95	4.07	3.72
0.90	3.76	3.75	3.75	3.92	3.95	4.03	3.72
1.00	3.75	3.75	3.75	3.92	3.95	4.00	3.71
1.10	3.75	3.74	3.74	3.92	3.95	3.97	3.71
1.20	3.74	3.73	3.73	3.92	3.95	3.93	3.70
1.30	3.74	3.73	3.73	3.92	3.95	3.90	3.70
1.40	3.73	3.72	3.72	3.92	3.95	3.86	3.69
1.50	3.73	3.72	3.72	3.92	3.95	3.83	3.69

Table 7.3
Effort, $\eta = -0.2$

β	e^{CI}	e^{LT}	e^{BM}	e^{PCT}	e^{PC}	e^{C+}	e^{C+T}
0.50	0.64	0.64	0.64	0.52	0.64	0.00	0.00
0.60	0.63	0.61	0.63	0.51	0.64	0.00	0.00
0.70	0.63	0.59	0.63	0.51	0.64	0.00	0.00
0.80	0.63	0.57	0.63	0.51	0.64	0.00	0.00
0.90	0.63	0.54	0.63	0.51	0.64	0.00	0.00
1.00	0.63	0.52	0.63	0.51	0.64	0.00	0.00
1.10	0.63	0.50	0.63	0.51	0.64	0.00	0.00
1.20	0.63	0.48	0.64	0.52	0.64	0.00	0.00
1.30	0.64	0.47	0.64	0.52	0.64	0.00	0.00
1.40	0.64	0.45	0.64	0.52	0.64	0.00	0.00
1.50	0.64	0.43	0.64	0.52	0.64	0.00	0.00

Table 7.4
Consumers' welfare, $\eta = -0.2$ (10^6 annualized US\$)

β	CW^{CI}	CW^{LT}	CW^{BM}	CW^{PCT}	CW^{PC}	CW^{C+}	CW^{C+T}
0.50	196.05	182.47	179.78	182.45	179.41	189.24	190.58
0.60	194.40	182.43	179.77	182.12	179.41	187.84	189.02
0.70	192.74	182.33	179.77	181.79	179.41	186.38	187.41
0.80	191.09	182.33	179.77	181.47	179.41	184.88	185.77
0.90	189.45	182.15	179.77	181.15	179.41	183.37	184.12
1.00	187.82	181.91	179.77	180.83	179.41	181.85	182.47
1.10	186.20	181.61	179.77	180.52	179.41	180.32	180.82
1.20	184.58	181.24	179.77	180.20	179.41	178.78	179.18
1.30	182.97	180.81	179.77	179.89	179.41	177.23	177.54
1.40	181.37	179.78	179.77	179.58	179.41	175.68	175.91
1.50	179.77	179.17	179.77	179.29	179.41	174.12	174.28

elasticity of -0.6. In this section we examine the main features of these seven regulatory results. In the next section we will draw some comparisons among these regulatory regimes and discuss the implications.

Under the *LT* mechanism the output levels in table 7.2 correspond to a price (by customer per month) for local exchange service that ranges from \$9.00 (for the most efficient firm) to \$9.61 (for the least efficient firm) while average cost and marginal cost are, respectively, in the range \$4.34–\$7.57 and \$0.90–\$1.52. Under $C+$ and $C + T$ there are greater variations in price, ranging from a low of \$5.62 under $C+$ for the most

Table 7.5
Information rent, $\eta = -0.2$ (10^6 annualized US$)

β	U^{CI}	U^{LT}	U^{BM}	U^{PCT}	U^{PC}	U^{C+}	U^{C+T}
0.50	0.00	10.44	12.52	10.18	12.64	0.00	0.00
0.60	0.00	9.20	11.25	9.15	11.36	0.00	0.00
0.70	0.00	7.99	9.97	8.12	10.07	0.00	0.00
0.80	0.00	6.83	8.71	7.09	8.80	0.00	0.00
0.90	0.00	5.72	7.44	6.07	7.52	0.00	0.00
1.00	0.00	4.66	6.19	5.05	6.25	0.00	0.00
1.10	0.00	3.64	4.94	4.03	4.99	0.00	0.00
1.20	0.00	2.66	3.70	3.02	3.74	0.00	0.00
1.30	0.00	1.73	2.46	2.01	2.49	0.00	0.00
1.40	0.00	0.85	1.23	1.00	1.24	0.00	0.00
1.50	0.00	0.00	0.00	0.00	0.00	0.00	0.00

Table 7.6
Rate of return, $\eta = -0.2$ (%)

β	RoR^{CI}	RoR^{LT}	RoR^{BM}	RoR^{PCT}	RoR^{PC}	RoR^{C+}	RoR^{C+T}
0.50	0.00	40.96	49.09	39.40	49.20	0.00	0.00
0.60	0.00	34.36	42.03	33.77	42.11	0.00	0.00
0.70	0.00	28.49	35.59	28.62	35.66	0.00	0.00
0.80	0.00	23.30	29.73	23.91	29.78	0.00	0.00
0.90	0.00	18.69	24.38	19.61	24.42	0.00	0.00
1.00	0.00	14.60	19.47	15.67	19.50	0.00	0.00
1.10	0.00	10.96	14.96	12.04	14.98	0.00	0.00
1.20	0.00	7.72	10.80	8.68	10.81	0.00	0.00
1.30	0.00	4.84	6.93	5.58	6.94	0.00	0.00
1.40	0.00	2.28	3.35	2.69	3.35	0.00	0.00
1.50	0.00	0.00	0.00	0.00	0.00	0.00	0.00

efficient firm to a high of $8.54 under $C+$ or even to $9.88 under $C+T$ for the least efficient firm. Both types of cost-plus schemes require higher production levels from more efficient firms, namely from lower-β firms (see table 7.2), and we observe that the welfare of consumers is higher for these types of firms (see table 7.4).

The resolution of the pure price-cap regulatory program yields for each customer a cap $\bar{p}$ equal to $7.50 per month,[5] which is binding (i.e., smaller than the monopoly price) for all types of firms, whereas the price-cap with sharing-of-earnings regulatory program leads to a

Table 7.7
Output, $\eta = -0.6$

β	Q^{CI}	Q^{LT}	Q^{BM}	Q^{PCT}	Q^{PC}	Q^{C+}	Q^{C+T}
0.50	5.45	5.45	5.45	3.71	3.71	4.70	5.29
0.60	5.43	5.42	5.42	3.71	3.71	4.58	5.27
0.70	5.41	5.40	5.40	3.71	3.71	4.44	5.25
0.80	5.39	5.38	5.38	3.71	3.71	4.30	5.23
0.90	5.37	5.35	5.35	3.71	3.71	4.15	5.21
1.00	5.35	5.33	5.33	3.71	3.71	3.99	5.19
1.10	5.33	5.31	5.31	3.71	3.71	3.82	5.17
1.20	5.31	5.28	5.28	3.71	3.71	3.64	5.16
1.30	5.30	5.26	5.26	3.71	3.71	3.45	5.14
1.40	5.28	5.24	5.24	3.71	3.71	3.23	5.12
1.50	5.26	5.21	5.22	3.71	3.71	2.97	5.10

Table 7.8
Effort, $\eta = -0.6$

β	e^{CI}	e^{LT}	e^{BM}	e^{PCT}	e^{PC}	e^{C+}	e^{C+T}
0.50	0.69	0.69	0.69	0.63	0.63	0.00	0.00
0.60	0.69	0.67	0.69	0.63	0.63	0.00	0.00
0.70	0.69	0.64	0.69	0.63	0.63	0.00	0.00
0.80	0.69	0.62	0.69	0.63	0.63	0.00	0.00
0.90	0.69	0.60	0.69	0.63	0.63	0.00	0.00
1.00	0.69	0.58	0.69	0.63	0.63	0.00	0.00
1.10	0.69	0.56	0.69	0.63	0.63	0.00	0.00
1.20	0.69	0.54	0.69	0.63	0.63	0.00	0.00
1.30	0.69	0.52	0.69	0.63	0.63	0.00	0.00
1.40	0.69	0.50	0.69	0.63	0.63	0.00	0.00
1.50	0.69	0.48	0.68	0.64	0.64	0.00	0.00

tax rate applied to the firm of 19.44 percent and a cap of $7.70 (with an average cost of about $5.80), which is also binding for all types of firms.

A striking feature of table 7.2 is the high output level induced by the regulatory schemes PC and C+ relative to that induced by all of the other schemes. This may be explained as follows. For the regulatory mechanisms that allow for transfers from consumers to general revenue, namely CI, LT, BM, PCT, and C + T, in low-elasticity markets (elasticity equal to −0.2, which is the value we use for calibration in our base case), society finds it worthwhile to subsidize the general activity through local-exchange revenues.[6] This is achieved by restraining quantity (thus

Table 7.9
Consumers' welfare, $\eta = -0.6$ (10^6 annualized US$)

β	CW^{CI}	CW^{LT}	CW^{BM}	CW^{PCT}	CW^{PC}	CW^{C+}	CW^{C+T}
0.50	78.17	63.37	60.74	56.03	56.03	71.11	71.73
0.60	76.39	63.34	60.74	56.03	56.03	69.18	70.07
0.70	74.61	63.23	60.74	56.03	56.03	67.12	68.35
0.80	72.84	63.06	60.74	56.03	56.03	64.95	66.60
0.90	71.09	62.83	60.74	56.03	56.03	62.67	64.84
1.00	69.34	62.53	60.73	56.03	56.03	60.28	63.08
1.10	67.60	62.17	60.73	56.03	56.03	57.75	61.32
1.20	65.87	61.75	60.73	56.03	56.03	55.04	59.57
1.30	64.15	61.27	60.73	56.03	56.03	52.09	57.82
1.40	62.43	60.73	60.72	56.03	56.03	48.80	56.08
1.50	60.72	60.14	60.72	56.03	56.03	44.91	54.35

Table 7.10
Information rent, $\eta = -0.6$ (10^6 annualized US$)

β	U^{CI}	U^{LT}	U^{BM}	U^{PCT}	U^{PC}	U^{C+}	U^{C+T}
0.50	0.00	11.38	13.41	12.49	12.49	0.00	0.00
0.60	0.00	10.04	12.04	11.22	11.22	0.00	0.00
0.70	0.00	8.73	10.67	9.96	9.96	0.00	0.00
0.80	0.00	7.48	9.31	8.69	8.69	0.00	0.00
0.90	0.00	6.28	7.96	7.43	7.43	0.00	0.00
1.00	0.00	5.12	6.62	6.18	6.18	0.00	0.00
1.10	0.00	4.01	5.28	4.94	4.94	0.00	0.00
1.20	0.00	2.94	3.95	3.69	3.69	0.00	0.00
1.30	0.00	1.92	2.63	2.46	2.46	0.00	0.00
1.40	0.00	0.94	1.31	1.23	1.23	0.00	0.00
1.50	0.00	0.00	0.00	0.00	0.00	0.00	0.00

increasing prices). In our base case we find that local-exchange revenues consistently exceed total costs under these mechanisms. In contrast, in high-elasticity markets (elasticity equal to -0.6), the subsidy goes from the general revenue to the local exchange business. Indeed, we find that in the high-elasticity case, output is lower for the mechanisms PC and $C+$ than for CI, LT, BM, and $C + T$ (see table 7.7), and costs come to exceed revenues under these latter mechanisms.[7]

Under the complete information benchmark (CI) the more efficient firms produce higher output, and hence consumers have higher welfare (see tables 7.2 and 7.4). Effort, which equates marginal disutility and

Table 7.11
Rate of return, $\eta = -0.6$ (%)

β	RoR^{CI}	RoR^{LT}	RoR^{BM}	RoR^{PCT}	RoR^{PC}	RoR^{C+}	RoR^{C+T}
0.50	0.00	41.83	49.27	49.16	49.16	0.00	0.00
0.60	0.00	35.14	42.16	42.08	42.08	0.00	0.00
0.70	0.00	29.20	35.70	35.63	35.63	0.00	0.00
0.80	0.00	23.92	29.82	29.76	29.76	0.00	0.00
0.90	0.00	19.23	24.45	24.40	24.40	0.00	0.00
1.00	0.00	15.05	19.53	19.49	19.49	0.00	0.00
1.10	0.00	11.33	15.01	14.97	14.97	0.00	0.00
1.20	0.00	8.01	10.83	10.80	10.80	0.00	0.00
1.30	0.00	5.03	6.96	6.94	6.94	0.00	0.00
1.40	0.00	2.38	3.36	3.35	3.35	0.00	0.00
1.50	0.00	0.00	0.00	0.00	0.00	0.00	0.00

marginal cost saving, slightly decreases with increasing efficiency for the less efficient group of firms and increases for the more efficient firms (see table 7.3).[8] From tables 7.2 through 7.11 we see that all of the endogenous variables are monotically decreasing in β for the optimal regulatory mechanism with ex post cost observability (*LT*). More efficient firms are induced to produce higher output and exert higher effort, allowing them to trade off higher consumers' welfare for higher information rents. The optimal regulatory mechanism without cost observability (*BM*) also has the more efficient firms produce more. As in the case of complete information, effort is U-shaped (see table 7.3).

There is no distortion in effort (relative to *CI*) for the most efficient firm under either *LT* or *BM* regulation (see table 7.3). Because cost is not observable to the regulator under the *BM* scheme, and is therefore fully borne by the firm, effort is socially optimal for every type of firm, conditional on output in this scheme. Indeed, we note that (except for the most efficient firm) effort is higher under the *BM* mechanism than under *LT*.[9] Correspondingly the information rent to be given up to the firm is higher under *BM* (see table 7.5).[10] A cross-examination of the regulatory schemes shows that higher rents are generally associated with lower consumers' welfare, as can be seen in tables 7.4 and 7.5.[11] We also note that despite the higher effort levels under *BM* (and therefore higher levels of disutility of effort), the higher rents under *BM* lead to higher rate of return than under *LT* (see tables 7.6 and 7.11). We will later see, however (in table 7.12), that the downward distortion in effort under *LT* is more than offset, from a social-welfare point of view, by the higher information rent extracted from the firm. This latter result is not surprising, since the option of ignoring cost observations is available to the regulator under the scheme.

Under *PCT*, part of the financial profits of the firm are returned to society. Consequently the firm exerts lower effort than under pure price cap *PC* (see table 7.3 for the low-elasticity case since for the high-elasticity case *PC* and *PCT* coincide). The sharing mechanism leads to lower rents and rates of return (see tables 7.5 and 7.6), and consumers' welfare is higher (table 7.4).

To conclude this broad presentation of the data produced by the resolution of the various regulatory schemes, we assess the relative importance of transfers from the regulator to the firm under the optimal regulatory mechanism *LT*. Recall that the firm's rent U, given by

$$U = t - \psi(e) \tag{7.3}$$

where t is the net transfer and ψ is the disutility of effort, which can be written in terms of the gross transfer $\hat{t}$ as

$$U = \hat{t} + pq - C - \psi \tag{7.4}$$

If transfers from the regulator were not explicitly allowed, they still could be implemented through menus of two-part tariffs $T = A + pq$.[12] If we restrict ourselves to a single two-part tariff, the fixed part A can be set equal to the gross transfer $\hat{t}$ at the average value of the technological parameter, and by (7.3) we would have

$$A = \hat{t} = t + C - pq \tag{7.5}$$

In the low-elasticity case (-0.2), production is contracted (average of 3.75 *CCS*); correspondingly the marginal price is high (average of $9.28) and is associated with a negative value of A, namely an average subsidy per customer per month of $6.50. In the high-elasticity case (-0.6), production is expanded (5.33 *CCS*); correspondingly the marginal price is low ($3.65) and is associated with a positive value of A, namely an average charge of $10.90.

7.4   Comparisons and Implications

7.4.1   Relative Performance

In this section we seek to compare the various regulatory mechanisms presented in section 7.2 by assessing their relative performance,

Table 7.12
Expected values of social welfare, consumers' welfare, firm's rent (10^6 annualized US$), and rate of return (%)

Regulatory mechanism	$E_\beta W$	$E_\beta CW$	$E_\beta U$	$E_\beta RoR$
CI	187.85	187.85	0.00	0.00
LT	186.19	181.35	4.85	16.53
BM	185.99	179.77	6.21	21.14
PCT	185.90	180.84	5.06	17.00
PC	185.69	179.41	6.28	21.18
C + T	182.47	182.47	0.00	0.00
C+	181.80	181.80	0.00	0.00

measured in terms of expected social welfare ($E_\beta W$). The basic data used for these comparisons and some of our later analysis are presented in table 7.12. Besides expected social welfare this table gives expected consumers' welfare ($E_\beta CW$), expected rent ($E_\beta U$), and expected rate of return ($E_\beta RoR$).

Since the range of parameters used in the simulations limits the *variability* of the results, it is instructive to draw comparisons in relative rather than absolute terms. One possibility is to analyze the performance of the various regulatory mechanisms relative to that of the regulation that would be implemented in a complete-information world (CI). To assess the (social) gain associated with the use of the LT mechanism relative to the C+ mechanism, one might proceed as follows: Let L^{C+} designate the loss in (expected) welfare, with respect to the complete-information social welfare, of cost-plus regulation. From table 7.12, we have

$$L^{C+} = E_\beta W^{CI} - E_\beta W^{C+} = 6.05 \times 10^6 \qquad (7.6)$$

Then, the following simple calculation shows that optimal regulation with ex post cost observability (LT) allows the regulator to recover 72.56 percent of this loss in welfare:

$$\frac{E_\beta W^{LT} - E_\beta W^{C+}}{L^{C+}} \times 100 = \frac{4.39 \times 100}{6.05} = 72.56 \qquad (7.7)$$

We can use the above technique to compare each of the possible forms of incentive regulation with each of the traditional forms of regulation. These results are summarized in table 7.13. We see that in each of the eight possible pairwise comparisons, more than about 55 percent of the welfare loss associated with traditional regulation can be recovered by

Table 7.13
Incentive versus traditional regulation: Percentage welfare losses recovered

Incentive regulation	Traditional regulation	C+	C + T
PC		64.30	53.22
PCT		67.77	56.70
BM		69.26	58.18
LT		72.56	61.49

Table 7.14
Value of transfers: Percentage welfare losses recovered

Regulation with transfers	Regulation without transfers	PC	C+
LT		23.15	—
BM		13.89	—
C + T		—	11.07

switching to incentive regulation. The need to create incentives for cost minimization has been one of the main driving forces behind recent regulatory reforms in developed economies. The results of table 7.13 both explain and justify the popularity of these reforms.

Using the same techniques, we can also measure the gains associated with observability of cost and with the regulator's ability to use transfers. A comparison of the LT and BM mechanisms can be interpreted as an indication of the value of good auditing procedures, assuming that accounting manipulations can be easily detected.[13] Using the figures presented in table 7.12, one can show that the use of ex post accounting data allows the regulator to recover 10.75 percent of the loss associated with the BM regulatory mechanism. A comparison of the PC mechanism with either LT or BM shows the consequences of constraining the regulator from using direct transfers to the firm, a constraint that is often institutionally imposed for political reasons or by fear of capture. A similar comparison can be made between the C+ and C + T mechanisms. These results are summarized in table 7.14. Finally, a comparison of PCT and PC demonstrates that the use of one-way transfers and cost observability simultaneously allows the regulator to recover 9.72 percent of the loss associated with simple price-cap regulation.

Additional instruments of regulation generally enable the regulator to improve social welfare. From this viewpoint, we found that for

$\beta \leq 0.8$ and for the low-elasticity case, a price cap with profit sharing (one-way transfers) dominates the Baron-Myerson regulation with two-way transfers but no cost observability. This is because, in using PCT, we presume an observability of cost, and that with the low elasticity transfers can go in the direction of the general budget, so the one-way transfer in PCT is actually not a restriction. In the high-elasticity case we indeed find that BM dominates PCT for all values of β.

7.4.2   Redistributive Consequences

We now examine the redistributive consequences of the various forms of incentive regulation in more detail. Price-cap regulation was introduced in the early 1980s as an alternative to traditional rate-of-return regulation. The innovative feature was that pricing decisions became completely decentralized. Consequently transfers from the regulator to the firm are no longer being used. The main idea behind establishing price ceilings was to simultaneously restrain monopoly power and to give incentives to the firm for cost minimization. Indeed, because under a price cap the firm becomes the residual claimant of any cost reductions, greater efficiency is achieved with PC since it induces higher effort and quantity levels than under both BM and LT (see tables 7.2 and 7.3). The pitfall associated with PC, however, is that higher rents (see tables 7.5 and 7.12) and rates of return (see tables 7.6 and 7.12) are obtained by the firm, resulting in lower consumer welfare (see tables 7.4 and 7.12) and social welfare (see table 7.12). Thus the efficiency achieved through decentralization comes at a social cost.

Given the high performance of the PC mechanism in terms of incentives for efficiency, profit-sharing rules were introduced to improve its rent extraction. The direct comparison of the PC and PCT mechanisms in table 7.12 and in the preceding discussion nevertheless suggests that the gains associated with the use of transfers to the firm and cost observability (equal to 9.72 percent of the difference between aggregate welfare under CI and PC) are relatively modest. We see this particularly as compared to the substantial gains associated with adopting any form of incentive regulation over traditional regulation. How then are we to explain the use of sharing rules whenever price-cap forms of regulation are adopted? The answer may lie in a deeper analysis of the distributional consequences of imposing incentive regulation.

Figure 7.2 illustrates the trade-off between consumers' welfare and firm's rent under alternative forms of regulation. Although consumers

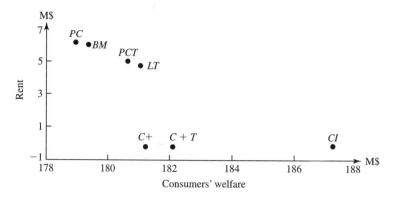

Figure 7.2
Rent–consumers' welfare trade-off

benefit most from cost-plus regulation, expected social welfare is lowest under this traditional form of regulation. In other words, if higher social welfare is the main objective, to achieve this goal through higher production efficiency, society needs to sacrifice consumer welfare in favor of rents. This fundamental trade-off is shown in figure 7.2, which reports the (ex ante) distribution of social welfare between consumers (surplus) and the firm (rent) under each of the regulatory regimes. This figure provides an empirical foundation for the resistance of various interest groups to certain forms of regulation; in particular, it suggests that incentive regulation will be promoted by firms.

We now present a more formal analysis of these issues. Recall that in all of the regulatory mechanisms considered in section 7.2, the objective of the regulator is the maximization of a Benthamite social welfare function, that is, the unweighted sum of consumers' and the firm's welfares. A generalization of this objective, which assigns a weight δ to the firm's utility, has been suggested in the literature:[14]

$$GW = CW + \delta U \qquad (7.8)$$

This generic welfare measure can be used to generate an incomplete information (second-best) Pareto frontier. The regulator's generalized objective function (GW) then takes the form

$$GW = \{V(q) - (1 + \lambda)[C(\beta, e, q) + t]\} + \delta U \qquad (7.9)$$

$$= V(q) - (1 + \lambda)[C(\beta, e, q) + \psi(e)] - (\lambda + 1 - \delta)U \qquad (7.10)$$

and, with cost observability and two-way transfers, its maximization under the incentive compatibility and the (ex post) individual rationality constraints yields the following program:

$$\max_{q(\cdot),e(\cdot)} \int_{\underline{\beta}}^{\overline{\beta}} \left\{ V(q(\beta)) - (1+\lambda)[C(\beta,e(\beta),q(\beta)) + \psi(e(\beta))] \right.$$

$$\left. + (\lambda + 1 - \delta)\frac{F(\beta)}{f(\beta)}\psi'(e(\beta))\frac{C_{\beta}(\beta,e(\beta),q(\beta))}{C_{e}(\beta,e(\beta),q(\beta))} \right\} f(\beta)\,d\beta \quad (7.11)$$

The class of regulatory mechanisms defined by the program (7.8) will be designated $LT(\delta)$. Indeed, an examination of (7.10) and (7.11) reveals that when $\delta = 1$, we achieve the results of the LT mechanism analyzed under the assumption of a Benthamite social welfare function, since (7.11) coincides in that case with equation (6.5) of chapter 6. When $\delta = 1+\lambda$, we also see from (7.10) that the social welfare function has the same functional form as that of the complete information program defined in (7.2), although the information structures of those two problems are different.[15] For values of δ greater than $1 + \lambda$, the regulator's objective function (7.10) is unbounded, and the problem (7.11) is not well defined. The resolution of this program for various values of δ between 0 and $1 + \lambda$ allows us to construct a second-best Pareto frontier representing the trade-off between rent and consumers' welfare under optimal incentive regulation.

This frontier is convex to the origin and is exhibited in figure 7.3. The figure also shows a complete information Pareto frontier, consisting of a line of slope $-1/(1 + \lambda)$ passing through the CI solution.[16] Under

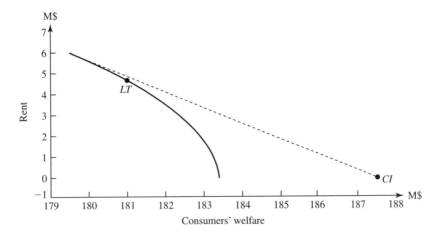

Figure 7.3
Incomplete- and complete-information Pareto frontiers

complete information, every dollar that the regulator wishes to transfer to the firm must be raised at a social cost of $$(1 + \lambda)$. The complete-information frontier is tangent to the second-best frontier at the point corresponding to $\delta = 1 + \lambda$.

Since the mechanisms $BM, PC, PCT, C+$, and $C + T$ impose additional constraints on the regulator, the corresponding consumers' welfare–rent pairs lie inside the second-best frontier. For any of the social welfare allocation points corresponding to one of the regulatory mechanisms defined in section 7.2, there exists a weight δ that leads to a welfare allocation on the second-best frontier that (weakly) Pareto-dominates it. Accordingly, these points may be joined to yield a third-best Pareto frontier, which is depicted in figure 7.4.

We observe, in conclusion, that the price-cap regulatory mechanism with sharing of earnings (PCT) Pareto-dominates a convex combination (labeled LT^{cc} in figure 7.4) of the two extreme points of the second-best frontier $LT(\delta)$.[17] Following Laffont (1996), we can view the allocation LT^{cc} as resulting from a political process, likely one-quarter controlled by a lobby of rent owners who can choose their most favored mechanism in the class $LT(\delta)$, namely the allocation obtained with $\delta = 1 + \lambda$ (1.3), and the remaining three-quarters controlled by a consumers' lobby, which can choose the allocation corresponding to $\delta = 0$. Hence constitutionally imposing PCT leads to an allocation that Pareto-dominates the outcome LT^{cc} of such a political process in an ex ante sense.

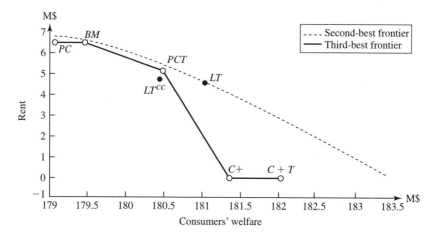

Figure 7.4
Second-best and third-best Pareto frontiers

7.4.3   Effect of the Cost of Public Funds

Because it reflects the social cost associated with transfers from consumers to the firm, the parameter λ, referred to as the shadow cost of public funds, plays a crucial role in the analysis of welfare. While a thorough study of the factors that determine this parameter is beyond the scope of our current analysis, we expect its value to be higher for economies with less efficient taxation systems, such as developing countries. In the next exercise, we seek to investigate empirically how this parameter affects regulatory outcomes for both low-elasticity and high-elasticity markets.

Tables 7.15 and 7.16 summarize the results of the computation of expected social welfare for each of the seven regulatory mechanisms for various values of the cost of public funds, assuming low (-0.2) and high (-0.6) demand elasticities, respectively. For each regulatory mechanism that allows for a transfer from consumers to general revenue, the performance of the mechanism will be sensitive to the cost of public funds. From (7.2) we can see that the derivative of the complete information social welfare function with respect to λ is given by

$$\frac{\partial W}{\partial \lambda} = pq - C - \psi \tag{7.12}$$

For small values of λ this quantity is negative (i.e., revenues are less than total cost), but as λ increases, it becomes increasingly attractive

Table 7.15
Expected social welfare as a function of cost of public funds in low-elasticity markets, $\eta = -0.2$ (10^6 annualized US$)

λ	$E_\beta W^{CI}$	$E_\beta W^{LT}$	$E_\beta W^{BM}$	$E_\beta W^{PCT}$	$E_\beta W^{PC}$	$E_\beta W^{C+}$	$E_\beta W^{C+T}$
0.0	188.91	188.91	188.91	185.69	185.69	181.80	184.31
0.1	187.18	186.57	186.54	185.69	185.69	181.80	182.32
0.2	186.97	185.81	185.71	185.75	185.69	181.80	181.85
0.3	187.85	186.19	185.99	185.90	185.69	181.80	182.47
0.4	189.54	187.42	187.07	186.12	185.69	181.80	183.88
0.5	191.82	189.27	188.78	186.40	185.69	181.80	185.89
0.6	194.58	191.63	190.95	186.73	185.69	181.80	188.37
0.7	197.71	194.38	193.51	187.09	185.69	181.80	191.21
0.8	201.14	197.44	196.36	187.49	185.69	181.80	194.35
0.9	204.81	200.76	199.46	187.91	185.69	181.80	197.74
1.0	208.67	204.29	202.76	188.36	185.69	181.80	201.31

Table 7.16
Expected social welfare as a function of cost of public funds in high-elasticity markets, $\eta = -0.6$ (10^6 annualized US$)

λ	$E_\beta W^{CI}$	$E_\beta W^{LT}$	$E_\beta W^{BM}$	$E_\beta W^{PCT}$	$E_\beta W^{PC}$	$E_\beta W^{C+}$	$E_\beta W^{C+T}$
0.0	74.51	74.51	74.51	62.23	62.23	59.61	69.06
0.1	72.12	71.46	71.43	62.23	62.23	59.61	66.40
0.2	70.48	69.23	69.13	62.23	62.23	59.61	64.48
0.3	69.38	67.58	67.38	62.23	62.23	59.61	63.08
0.4	68.66	66.37	66.03	62.23	62.23	59.61	62.06
0.5	68.25	65.48	64.99	62.23	62.23	59.61	61.34
0.6	68.06	64.85	64.19	62.25	62.23	59.61	60.84
0.7	68.06	64.43	63.58	62.32	62.23	59.61	60.52
0.8	68.20	64.16	63.11	62.44	62.23	59.61	60.34
0.9	68.45	64.03	62.77	62.61	62.23	59.61	60.28
1.0	68.81	64.01	62.53	62.82	62.23	59.61 ،	60.31

to restrict quantities in order to extract revenues from local-exchange telephone customers to subsidize the general budget. Hence the social-welfare function under complete information is U-shaped as a function of λ.[18] In the higher-elasticity example, it is more costly, in terms of forgone surplus, to extract revenues from local-exchange consumers, and social welfare is therefore declining with respect to λ over a larger range of values of λ. Similar observations apply to each of the regulatory mechanisms involving transfers (although for LT and BM the effect shows for values of λ greater than 1).

The value of transfers as a regulatory tool has already been discussed in the previous sections. The remarks above imply that in absolute terms, a comparison of welfare levels under a mechanism using transfers (CI, LT, BM, PCT, or C + T) with a corresponding mechanism without transfers (PC or C+) will show the value of transfers initially declining in λ but eventually increasing in λ, beyond some critical value. Our benchmark value of 0.3, which applies to developed economies, happens to be close to the minimum of expected social welfare as a function of λ for each of our mechanisms in the low-elasticity case. The minimum expected social welfare is reached at a higher value of λ (close to 0.7 for CI and PCT, and close to 1.0 for LT, BM, and C + T) in our high-elasticity case.[19] This suggests that in terms of the value of regulatory transfers in less developed economies, transfers in low-elasticity markets are more desirable in these economies. In high-elasticity markets, on the other hand, the situation is reversed, and transfers are less desirable in the less developed economies.

Tables 7.15 and 7.16 can also be used to illustrate the results of a controlled experiment in which the existence of transfers is given and the incentive power of regulation is the variable. A comparison of incentive regulatory mechanisms (LT, BM) with traditional regulation $(C + T)$ reveals that the gains from incentive effects decline modestly as the cost of public funds increases. In the low-elasticity case, a comparison of PCT and $C + T$ leads to an even stronger conclusion—the relative ranking of the mechanisms depends on λ. For $\lambda \leq 0.5$, PCT gives higher expected welfare, while for $\lambda \geq 0.6$, $C + T$ outperforms PCT.[20] Finally, a comparison of the LT and BM mechanisms reveals that the benefits associated with cost observability are increasing with λ in both low- and high-elasticity markets.[21]

7.5   Conclusion

In this chapter we showed how data generated by engineering process models and calibration techniques can be used to compare different types of regulation. In specifying the ranges of asymmetric information that are reasonable for the cost uncertainty that they imply, we could provide an empirically meaningful evaluation of the social value of the various instruments—cost observability (cost auditing), transfers, and taxes—that the regulator can use. Despite the drawbacks of the analysis (in particular, due to the static character of the model), we illustrated some important results of the economics of regulation and derived some new empirical insights.

We considered the trade-off between rent extraction and the consumer's surplus associated with the various regulatory mechanisms, and we also situated it in a general welfare analysis under incomplete information. The importance of the cost of public funds in regulation and its implications for developing countries was clearly established. The usefulness of this type of normative analysis even for a positive approach to regulation was illustrated.

Empirically, the most striking result is the reasonably good performance of price-cap regulation combined with taxation of profits. This mechanism appears to be the most practical way of implementing a quasi-optimal regulation. Also the empirical analysis has revealed the sensitivity of the results to the elasticity of demand and some implications for the possibility of using the industry as an instrument of taxation.

8   Universal Service

8.1   Introduction

We now turn to some practical aspects of a formidable challenge that faces the telecommunications industry at the turn of the millennium: Can the fundamental historical goal set by countries, to provide a phone to anyone in any particular geographical area who needs it, be fulfilled in the new information age characterized by a general trend toward global deregulation of the industry? To be more specific, local telecommunications service has traditionally been provided by a monopoly under a regulated price structure. In most countries and jurisdictions, an explicit goal of regulation has been the provision of service to customers in high-cost areas at "affordable" prices, and this has been achieved by cross-subsidies within the regulated monopoly. In recent years, however, changing technologies and an increased appreciation of the benefits of competition in traditional natural monopoly industries have generated powerful forces for deregulation of local telecommunications. These forces threaten the viability of this traditional method of universal service funding. In this chapter we evaluate these trade-offs empirically with special attention to parameter values that are relevant for developing economies.

The liberalization of telecommunications is proceeding at a pace faster than in most other network industries. Issues of vertical disintegration, incentive regulation, and access pricing reform have been raised and dealt with in recent years. In telecommunications the compatibility of competition and universal service obligations is the object of intense political and economic debates. Competition destroys to a great extent cross-subsidies so that some areas might be left with very high costs of provision of telecommunications (maybe even the breakdown of provision), resulting in prices that are not considered socially reasonable or affordable.

Various mechanisms have been proposed to fund, with tax money, the provision of telecommunications in those areas in order to ensure universal service. However, in some countries, and this is particularly so in LDCs, the tax system is very inefficient, sometimes even corrupted, to the point where such transfers are socially very costly. This raises the question of what is the best way to introduce competition to limit the deadweight losses due to these transfers. The historical alternative has been to finance the development of telecommunications in high-cost areas from cross-subsidies derived from the low-cost areas with a regulated monopoly. More recently in Argentina, the country has been divided in two regions, each one with an urban area and a rural area. Cross-subsidies are maintained within each region, but some form of yardstick competition exists between regions.[1] Still some alternative competitive solutions might be envisioned and one would like to compare those solutions for the new telecommunications technologies and for various levels of efficiency of the tax systems. That is the issue explored in this chapter.[2]

The rapid evolution of technologies prevents us from using field data and econometric techniques to model all the technological and regulatory choices. Instead, as in previous chapters, we use the engineering simulation model LECOM to evaluate empirically alternative complete and incomplete information regulatory schemes that ensure provision of service in high-cost areas. This methodology allows us to simulate the various asymmetries of information of the adverse selection or moral hazard type that play an important role in the modern regulation literature.

Section 8.2 describes the various theoretical solutions that we wish to compare for a community composed of an urban area and a rural area. Assuming first complete information, we start with the (Hotelling) marginal-cost pricing solution supplemented by costly transfers from the national budget in order to finance the implied deficit of the firms. The implementation of this scheme in a duopoly setting enables us to compare from a purely technological efficiency point of view the solution in which competitive entry takes place only in the (profitable) urban area with the solution in which entry is organized as a yardstick competition between two equal-size regions each of which is composed of an urban area and a rural area.

Next the relative performance of these solutions is reexamined when the regulator requires that the firms balance their budgets. We compare two regulatory scenarios. In the first, entry is allowed in the urban sector and prices are unregulated, while a regulated monopoly provides service in both urban and rural areas. In the second scenario, the community is divided into two equal areas with balanced-budget provision within each region and yardstick competition between regions. This step allows us to appraise the consequences of the destruction of cross-subsidies due to urban competition (in the former solution) and the value of a yardstick competition which maintains cross-subsidies (in the latter solution). We then see how the availability of tax money affects the comparisons. Finally, we explore how asymmetric information alters these comparisons.

Section 8.3 describes the way the cost proxy model LECOM (see chapter 2) is used to implement a simulation-calibration procedure. The empirical results are discussed and summarized in section 8.4, and section 8.5 concludes the chapter. An appendix to the book (appendix A) presents additional data for the scenarios.

8.2   The Theoretical Alternatives

We consider a territory composed of two distinct areas, an urban area (area 1) and a rural area (area 2), with N_1 and N_2 local telephone subscribers. For area $i = 1, 2$, we denote by q_i, $P_i(q_i)$, and $S_i(q_i)$, respectively, output (usage), the inverse demand function, and the associated gross consumer surplus.[3]

Our first objective is to examine the relative technological efficiencies associated with two alternative entry scenarios. The first scenario is an "urban-targeted" entry scenario labeled UT in which entry, targeted toward the urban area only, leads to a split of the urban market in half between the entrant and the incumbent. The latter also serves the rural area. The second scenario is a "territory-constrained" entry scenario labeled TC in which entry takes place in both the urban and rural areas, leading to an equal division of both markets between the two firms. We initially examine these two scenarios by imposing (socially efficient) marginal-cost pricing (mc) and financing with public subsidies (ps) the implied deficit in each case.[4]

The cost function of an integrated monopolistic firm serving the whole territory is

$$C = C(\beta, e, q_1, q_2; N_1, N_2) \tag{8.1}$$

where β is a technological efficiency parameter belonging to an interval $[\underline{\beta}, \bar{\beta}]$ and e represents an endogenous efficiency parameter (the firm's effort) that may take any nonnegative value.[5] The value of β is private information to the firm, but the regulator knows the distribution function $F(\beta)$ and its density $f(\beta)$. An increase in the effort variable, e, decreases observable cost, C, but also imposes a disutility $\psi(e)$ on the firm's manager and workers. The level of effort carried out will depend on the regulatory mechanism implemented.

Under UT duopoly the cost function of the incumbent (firm 1) that serves half of the urban area and the whole rural area is

$$C_1^{UT}(\beta, e_1, q_{11}, q_{21}) \equiv C\left(\beta, e_1, q_{11}, q_{21}; \frac{N_1}{2}, N_2\right) \tag{8.2}$$

where e_1 is the incumbent's effort and q_{11} and q_{21} are the incumbent's output in the urban area and the rural area, respectively. The cost function of the entrant (firm 2) under this scenario is

$$C_2^{UT}(\beta, e_2, q_{12}) \equiv C\left(\beta, e_2, q_{12}, 0; \frac{N_1}{2}, 0\right) \tag{8.3}$$

where e_2 is the entrant's effort and q_{12} is its output.[6]

Under TC duopoly the cost function of both the incumbent and the entrant ($j = 1, 2$) is

$$C_j^{TC}(\beta, e_j, q_{1j}, q_{2j}) \equiv C\left(\beta, e_j, q_{1j}, q_{2j}; \frac{N_1}{2}, \frac{N_2}{2}\right) \tag{8.4}$$

where q_{1j} and q_{2j} represent firm j's output in the urban and rural area respectively. Figure 8.1 illustrates the generic competitive market structures that will be the focus of our analysis.[7]

As a benchmark case, let us first consider the marginal-cost pricing schemes (supplemented by public subsidies) under the two types of equilibrium duopoly markets discussed above. Scenario UT_{mc}^{ps} features (regulated) competition targeted toward the urban sector in which we assume that an entrant captures half of the market and the incumbent matches the entrant's price at marginal cost. Accordingly the incumbent serves the other half as well as the whole rural area. The hypothesis of complete information allows the regulator to impose the optimal effort level on both the incumbent (e_1^*) and the entrant (e_2^*).[8] Those firms solve, respectively, the first-order conditions that require the marginal disutility of effort for each firm to be equal to the marginal benefit for cost-reducing activities and prices to marginal costs. These conditions are represented in equations (8.5) through (8.8) where C_1^{UT} and C_2^{UT}

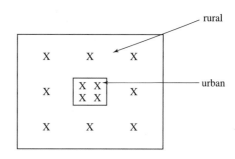

• Monopoly

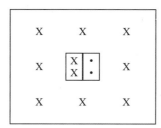

• *UT* entry scenario
(destroys cross-subsidies)

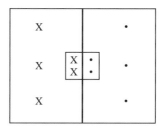

• *TC* entry scenario
(allows some competition while
preserving cross-subsidies)

Figure 8.1
Generic market structures

are the cost functions of the incumbent and the entrant defined in (8.2)
and (8.3), respectively.[9]

$$\psi'(e_1) = -\frac{\partial C_1^{UT}}{\partial e_1}(\beta, e_1, q_{11}, q_{21}) \tag{8.5}$$

$$\psi'(e_2) = -\frac{\partial C_2^{UT}}{\partial e_2}(\beta, e_2, q_{12}) \tag{8.6}$$

$$p_1 = \frac{\partial C_2^{UT}}{\partial q_{12}}(\beta, e_2^*, q_{12}) \tag{8.7}$$

$$p_2 = \frac{\partial C_1^{UT}}{\partial q_2}(\beta, e_1^*, q_{11}, q_{21}) \tag{8.8}$$

By our accounting convention, an aggregate (financial) deficit occurs under marginal-cost pricing and is funded through public funds, expressed by

$$\mathcal{D}^{UT_{mc}^{ps}} = C_1^{UT}(\beta, e_1^*, q_1, q_{21}) + C_2^{UT}(\beta, e_2^*, q_1) - N_1 p_1 q_1 - N_2 p_2 q_2 \qquad (8.9)$$

In (8.9) we make use of the fact that $q_{11} = q_{12} \equiv q_1$, and for simplicity of notation we write q_{21} as q_2. Social welfare to be maximized with respect to q_1 and q_2 is then written as

$$W^{UT_{mc}^{ps}} = N_1 S_1(q_1) + N_2 S_2(q_2) - C_1^{UT}(\beta, e_1^*, q_1, q_2) - C_2^{UT}(\beta, e_2^*, q_1)$$
$$- \psi(e_1^*) - \psi(e_2^*) - \lambda \left[\mathcal{D}^{UT_{mc}^{ps}} + \psi(e_1^*) + \psi(e_2^*) \right] \qquad (8.10)$$

The parameter λ, which represents the social cost of public funds, is generally assumed to range from a value of 0.3 in the most developed countries to 1 and higher in LDCs.

In scenario TC_{mc}^{ps}, entry occurs in both the urban and the rural zones. Again, complete information allows the regulator to impose the (same) optimal level of effort on each firm, e_j^{**}, which solves

$$\psi'(e_j) = -\frac{\partial C_j^{TC}}{\partial e_j}(\beta, e_j, q_{1j}, q_{2j}) \qquad (8.11)$$

where C_j^{TC} is the incumbent's (and the entrant's) cost function defined in (8.4) above. Marginal-cost pricing in both the urban and rural areas amounts to

$$p_1 = \frac{\partial C_j^{TC}}{\partial q_{1j}}(\beta, e_j^{**}, q_{1j}, q_{2j}) \qquad (8.12)$$

$$p_2 = \frac{\partial C_j^{TC}}{\partial q_{2j}}(\beta, e_j^{**}, q_{1j}, q_{2j}) \qquad (8.13)$$

and this leads to an aggregate deficit

$$\mathcal{D}^{TC_{mc}^{ps}} = 2C^{TC}(\beta, e^{**}, q_1, q_2) - N_1 p_1 q_1 - N_2 p_2 q_2 \qquad (8.14)$$

where, because of the symmetry of the problem, we make use of the fact that $e_1^{**} = e_2^{**} \equiv e^{**}$, $q_{11} = q_{12} \equiv q_1$, $q_{21} = q_{22} \equiv q_2$, and $C_1^{TC} = C_2^{TC} \equiv C^{TC}$. Social welfare to be maximized with respect to q_1 and q_2 in this case is then

$$W^{TC_{mc}^{ps}} = N_1 S_1(q_1) + N_2 S_2(q_2) - 2C^{TC}(\beta, e^{**}, q_1, q_2)$$
$$- 2\psi(e^{**}) - \lambda \left[\mathcal{D}^{TC_{mc}^{ps}} + 2\psi(e^{**}) \right] \qquad (8.15)$$

Let us now turn to competitive alternatives. Under competition, the regulator does not attempt to set either prices or effort levels. However, a profit-maximizing firm can be assumed to select a competitive price (we assume Bertrand competition) and for each price an optimal level of effort conditionally on the level of output. The regulator's only role is to enforce a market segmentation according to the UT or TC scenarios. Firms must comply with the universal service obligation, namely the obligation to provide service in (high cost) rural areas at an affordable price, which we take here as meaning the same price as in urban areas.[10] Second, we now impose a budget balance condition on the regulated firm, and take account of the fact that public funds are a scarce resource.[11]

Once again, let us examine the framework in which entry occurs in the urban sector only. Bertrand-like competition in the urban area is assumed to set the price of urban service at the average cost of the entrant who serves one-half of the market. If the incumbent matches this price in the urban area and serves the rural area at average (remaining) cost, then any cross-subsidies going from the urban to the rural sector are eliminated, but the incumbent may not be able to satisfy the universal service obligation.[12] One way to resolve this difficulty is to impose the urban price in the rural area and finance the subsequent incumbent's deficit through public subsidies. This is scenario UT_{ac}^{ps}, which we derive next.[13]

Optimal output of the entrant in the urban sector (which is also that of the incumbent) q_1^* ($\equiv q_{11}^* = q_{12}^*$) maximizes

$$\frac{N_1}{2} S_1(q_1) - C_2^{UT}(\beta, e_2^*, q_1) \tag{8.16}$$

under the constraint

$$\frac{N_1}{2} P_1(q_1) q_1 = C_2^{UT}(\beta, e_2^*, q_1) + \psi(e_2^*) \tag{8.17}$$

where e_2^* is the entrant's optimal effort level that satisfies (8.6). This yields the optimal urban price p_1^* which is matched by the incumbent.[14] The (residual) cost function for the incumbent is

$$C_1^{UT}(\beta, e_1^*, q_1^*, q_2) + \psi(e_1^*) - \frac{N_1}{2} p_1^* q_1^* \tag{8.18}$$

where e_1^* is the incumbent's optimal level of effort that solves (8.5),

$$p_1^* = S_1'(q_1) \tag{8.19}$$

and again for simplicity of notation, we write q_{21} as q_2. If the incumbent applies the same price in the urban and the rural areas and its implied deficit is financed with public subsidies, then social welfare is given in this scenario by

$$W^{UT_{ac}^{ps}} = N_1 S_1(q_1^*) + N_2 S_2(q_2^*) - C_1^{UT}(\beta, e_1^*, q_1^*, q_2^*)$$

$$- \psi(e_1^*) - C_2^{UT}(\beta, e_2^*, q_1^*) - \psi(e_2^*)$$

$$- \lambda \left[C_1^{UT}(\beta, e_1^*, q_1^*, q_2^*) + \psi(e_1^*) - \frac{N_1}{2} p_1^* q_1^* - N_2 p_1^* q_2^* \right] \quad (8.20)$$

where q_2^* is determined by

$$p_1^* = S_2'(q_2^*) \quad (8.21)$$

An alternative view of competitive entry with a balanced budget (as already seen in scenario TC_{mc}^{ps} above) would be to assume that the whole territory is divided in half. In this scenario, labeled TC_{ac}, social welfare is given by

$$W^{TC_{ac}} = \max_{q_1, q_2} \left\{ N_1 S_1(q_1) + N_2 S_2(q_2) - 2[C^{TC}(\beta, e^{**}, q_1, q_2) + \psi(e^{**})] \right\}$$
$$(8.22)$$

s.t. $\quad P_1(q_1)N_1 q_1 + P_2(q_2)N_2 q_2 = 2[C^{TC}(\beta, e^{**}, q_1, q_2) + \psi(e^{**})] \quad (8.23)$

and

$$P_1(q_1) = P_2(q_2) \quad (8.24)$$

where the cost function C^{TC} is the one that is defined in (8.4), $q_1 \equiv q_{11} = q_{12}$, $q_2 \equiv q_{21} = q_{22}$, and e^{**} satisfies equation (8.11).

Both of the preceding (competitive) scenarios satisfy the universal service obligation, which is uniform pricing across the urban and rural areas. However, while TC_{ac} uses urban-to-rural cross-subsidies, UT_{ac}^{ps} relies on public subsidies to finance universal service. Clearly, the relative attractiveness of these scenarios will depend on the cost of public funds λ applicable to UT_{ac}^{ps}, in relation with the distortions created by the cross-subsidies in TC_{ac}. This issue is addressed in our empirical analysis.

Still another alternative way to finance universal service is by using explicit taxes or surcharges.[15] In fact, since it imposes average-cost pricing, TC_{ac} may be interpreted as a scenario that imposes a particular (implicit) tax on the low-cost urban subscribers through price averaging.

Moreover one could rely on explicit taxes applied to the urban sector in a UT-type entry scenario to finance universal service, that is, to cover the incumbent's deficit from using uniform pricing over the whole territory. Let us succinctly describe the main features of such a scenario, which we label UT_{ac}^τ.

Let τ designate the tax rate applied in the urban sector. Note that since the incumbent has to match the entrant's price in the urban area and apply that same price in the rural area, we have $q_{11} = q_{12} \equiv q_1$ and $P_1(q_1) = P_2(q_2)$. Furthermore, assuming that p_1 represents the after-tax price (which is then applied across the whole territory), the firm's per unit revenue in the urban and rural markets is given by $p_1/(1 + \tau)$. This yields the following budget balance constraint for the entrant:

$$\frac{N_1[P_1(q_1)q_1]/2}{1 + \tau} = C_2^{UT}(\beta, e_2^*, q_1) + \psi(e_2^*) \tag{8.25}$$

where e_2^* is the entrant's optimal effort which satisfies (8.6). Now assume that only a fraction δ of the tax revenues collected from the urban subscribers is kept within the system, or that equivalently a fraction $(1 - \delta)$ is driven out of the system for private motives (through corruption or waste). The incumbent's budget balance condition now requires that revenues from the telephone service in one-half of the urban area and the entire rural area augmented by tax revenues collected from the urban population be equal to the incumbent's total cost. This constraint is given by

$$\delta\left(\frac{\tau}{1 + \tau}\right)P_1(q_1)q_1 N_1 + \frac{N_1[P_1(q_1)q_1]/2}{1 + \tau} + \frac{N_2 P_2(q_2)q_2}{1 + \tau}$$

$$= C_1^{UT}(\beta, e_1^*, q_1, q_2) + \psi(e_1^*) \tag{8.26}$$

where e_1^* is the incumbent's optimal effort level which satisfies (8.5) and q_2 is its output in the rural area. Comparing the levels of social welfare achieved under this scenario $SW^{UT_{ac}^\tau}$ with $SW^{TC_{ac}}$ will give us some indication on the relative importance of the distortions associated with implicit (TC_{ac}) and explicit (UT_{ac}^τ) taxation, accounting for the fact that in the latter case tax money is vulnerable to corruption.

The final step of the analysis consists in taking account of the asymmetric information with respect to the firm's technologies. There are various ways to introduce competition in the context of asymmetric information. In order to make the most favorable case for competitive entry into the urban sector only, we assume that the entrant has the most efficient technology, corresponding to $\underline{\beta}$, and that the incumbent is regulated as in scenario UT_{ac}^{ps}, meaning that the regulator still has complete information. This scenario will be designated by $\underline{UT_{ac}^{ps}}$ and the social welfare achieved by $W^{\underline{UT_{ac}^{ps}}}$. We then compare this scenario with the optimal price cap (PC) with asymmetric information obtained when the whole territory is divided in half (scenario $TCPC$ yielding social welfare W^{TCPC}).[16] This allows us again to assess the value of cross-subsidies as a means of financing universal service when asymmetric information is taken into account.

8.3   Empirical Procedure

Having completed our formal analysis in the previous section, we now turn to a detailed specification of the cost function of a representative local exchange telecommunications firm as is required for our empirical analysis. We begin by calibrating the cost function for the local exchange markets, using LECOM. Again, the areas that we seek to model are a densely populated urban area and a sparsely populated rural area. By specifying appropriate input parameters pertaining to the size and population of a central business district, and a mixed and residential district, with LECOM we can devise a stylized local exchange territory (see figure 8.1). The inner rectangle, representing the urban district, has a population of 50,000 subscribers spread uniformly over an area of 24 square miles. The outer rectangle, representing the rural district, has an additional population of 2,000 subscribers spread in an area of approximately 183 square miles. Thus the urban population density is approximately 2,083 subscribers in a square mile, whereas the rural population density is approximately 11 subscribers in a square mile.

Our analysis also requires a method of accounting for the costs of traffic that originates on one network and terminates on a different network, and as in chapter 5, we rely on LECOM to estimate such interconnection costs. The methodology for accounting for interconnection costs described in section 5.3.3 (chapter 5) applied in the present context yields cost-adjustment factors for switching and transport of 1 and 12 percent, respectively, in the case of a TC-type entry scenario and 1 and 13 percent in the case of a UT-type entry scenario.

We use LECOM to simulate the different cost functions implied by our scenarios, and these functions are generically defined in terms of three variables: output, technology, and effort. As in chapters 6 and 7, we use traffic volume expressed in units of hundreds of call seconds, *CCS*. Recall that LECOM allows for the independent specification of demands for access, switched local and toll usage, and local and toll private line services. To keep the analysis and the number of simulations within tractable limits, we hold the number of subscribers fixed and constrain the other outputs to vary proportionally with our measure of traffic volume, which is on a per line basis. As in the previous chapters we use multipliers for the cost of capital and labor *PK* and *PL* as measures of technological uncertainty and effort. Holding all other LECOM inputs fixed, we simulate the cost functions by repeatedly running LECOM for values of the arguments *PK* and *PL* within the range (0.5, 1.5) and for values of output in *CCS* in the range (2, 10).[17] The outcome of a typical simulation exercise (which may involve as many as 1,300 simulation runs) is a detailed map of the cost function.[18]

Recall that entry is envisioned in a variety of duopolistic market structures. We have labeled entry as type *UT* when it is targeted toward only the (profitable) urban zone and as type *TC* when it occurs in both the urban and rural areas. Hypothetical firms operating in such different market structures are likely also to differ in their production cost functions. By appropriately specifying some internal LECOM parameters to reflect a certain market structure, we are able to generate different cost data sets that we use to estimate these various cost functions.[19] More specifically, we can generate data to estimate the following cost functions: a cost function for an incumbent who serves the rural area while facing entry in the urban area, a cost function for an entrant who serves half of the urban area only, and a cost function for an entrant who serves half of both the urban and the rural areas.

In order to evaluate welfare, we must specify both the inverse demand functions and the cost of public funds λ. As in the previous chapters, we take the exponential form, which is widely used in empirical studies of local telecommunications markets, for the demand functions.[20] Calibration of demand is done as in the previous chapters, and the cost of public funds λ will vary within a wide range that includes the standard value of 0.3 for developed countries but also much larger values applicable to less developed ones. Also a quadratic disutility of effort function is calibrated, and when appropriate, we assume that the technological parameter is uniformly distributed in the range (0.5, 1.5).

8.4   Empirical Results

8.4.1   Technological Efficiency

Recall that both the urban-targeted entry scenario UT^{ps}_{mc} and the territory-constrained entry scenario TC^{ps}_{mc} impose marginal-cost pricing in each of the (low-cost) urban and (high-cost) rural areas. Clearly, the universal service obligation to serve both areas at the same price is violated. Yet a comparison of these two alternatives will provide us with useful information on their relative merits on pure technological efficiency grounds.

In entry scenarios UT^{ps}_{mc} and TC^{ps}_{mc} social welfare deteriorates with increasing values of the cost of public funds λ, since both scenarios rely on costly public funds to finance the deficit. Examination of the data shows that these two scenarios are quite close in social welfare, with the urban-targeted scenario UT^{ps}_{ms} slightly dominating the territory-constrained scenario TC^{ps}_{mc}.[21] Figure 8.2 depicts the situation. In the figure the slight improvement of the performance of the urban-targeted scenario relative to the territory-constrained scenario as λ increases may be explained by the relative size of the deficit, which is found to be slightly larger for TC^{ps}_{mc} than for UT^{ps}_{mc}. To summarize, we could say that under complete information, marginal-cost pricing, and access to

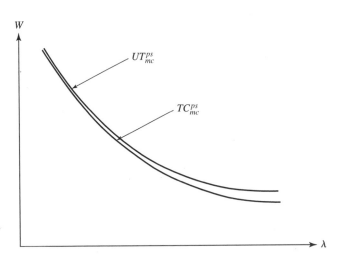

Figure 8.2
UT versus TC under marginal-cost pricing

public subsidies to finance the firms' deficits, the social welfare achieved under the urban-targeted entry scenario UT_{mc}^{ps} is slightly higher than that achieved under the territory-constrained entry scenario TC_{mc}^{ps} with the difference getting larger for greater values of the cost of public funds.

Nevertheless, under marginal-cost pricing both scenarios fail to satisfy either the budget balance constraint or the universal service obligation. In the rest of this chapter we will consider alternative versions of these scenarios that satisfy both constraints.

8.4.2   Universal Service Obligation and Budget Balance

Let us now examine the results for the competitive solutions that satisfy both the universal service obligation and the balanced-budget constraint.[22] Scenario UT_{ac}^{ps} assumes that the entrant captures half of the urban area and that the incumbent serves the other half and the whole rural area. Under this scenario the incumbent has to match the entrant's (average-cost) price in the urban area and apply that same price in the rural area because of the obligation to offer service at affordable prices. This implies a deficit which is financed from external funds provided by public subsidies.[23] In contrast, under scenario TC_{ac}, which assumes that the whole territory is divided in half, the universal service obligation is financed internally through urban-to-rural cross-subsidies imposed by the budget balance in each half of the territory. Consequently, while the performance of TC_{ac} is independent of λ, socially costly public subsidies make social welfare achieved under scenario UT_{ac}^{ps} decrease with increasing values of λ. Figure 8.3 shows the critical value of the cost of public funds λ^* beyond which TC_{ac} outperforms UT_{ac}^{ps}. This parameter is found to satisfy $0.1 < \lambda^* < 0.2$.

We can then state that under complete information and a balanced-budget constraint, for any value of the cost of public funds $\lambda > \lambda^*$, the territory-constrained entry scenario TC_{ac}, that allows for urban-to-rural cross-subsidies, achieves a strictly higher level of social welfare than the urban-targeted entry scenario UT_{ac}^{ps}, in which public subsidies are used to finance the incumbent's deficit due to uniform pricing.

In view of the fact that UT slightly dominates TC, as was found in the previous subsection, the current result has some interesting policy implications. Since our default value of λ for highly developed countries is equal to 0.3, it suggests that the territory-constrained solution can be expected to yield higher expected social welfare in both developed and

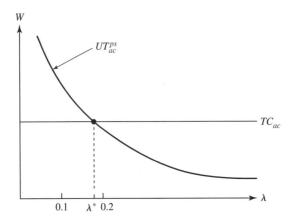

Figure 8.3
UT versus TC under average-cost pricing

developing countries when a uniform price is imposed in both urban and rural regions. Our analysis suggests that even highly efficient public funds transfer systems may impose a social cost that is greater than the deadweight losses associated with uniform pricing regimes, at least for the demand elasticities that we assume.

To conclude this subsection, we note that we have obtained an additional piece of information. Since scenario TC_{ac} relies on transfers internal to the firm whereas UT_{ac}^{ps} uses public funds to finance universal service, the critical value λ^* provides us with an evaluation of the social cost associated with the distortions created by the cross-subsidies in scenario TC_{ac}. We note that the implicit cost of public funds associated with the territory-constrained solution is quite low. This is due to the low price-elasticity of the demand (-0.2) for local telecommunications service, so that, as we have noted throughout the book, this is an attractive sector in which to raise public funds.

8.4.3   Implicit and Explicit Taxation of the Urban Sector

While, in scenario UT_{ac}^{ps} analyzed in the previous subsection, funds are used from the general budget to finance universal service, we might think of a more restricted fiscal basis, such as the urban telecommunications sector, that could generate the needed funds. As we noted in section 8.4.1, in scenario TC_{ac} the government imposes an implicit tax on the urban customers because average-cost pricing within the territory served by the operator forces them to subsidize some of the high cost of serving rural customers. An alternative way to achieve uniform pricing across the urban and rural areas, and within an urban-targeted entry framework, is to impose an explicit tax on the urban sector and to use the tax revenues to cover the incumbent's deficit arising from this universal service obligation. This scheme is labeled UT_{ac}^{τ}.

In the previous subsection we assessed the social cost of the distortions created by the cross-subsidies within the territory-constrained entry framework TC_{ac}. Such a cost was found to be estimated by a shadow price of public funds of the order 0.2. The economic distortion associated with an urban-targeted entry framework using explicit taxation UT_{ac}^{τ} is twofold. First, taxation distorts consumption, and one might assess the extent of this distortion by empirically evaluating the magnitude of the deadweight loss it creates.[24] Second, and the issue is particularly relevant for developing countries, revenues generated by taxes may or may not be fully used in financing universal service. In particular, institutions that leave substantial discretionary decision power to executives may open the door to corruption, and this can easily cause a leakage of a nonnegligible part of the tax revenues from the economy.[25] In our empirical analysis we attempt to take account of this phenomenon by assuming that a fraction δ of the tax revenues, which we let vary from 0.5 to 1 by increments of 0.1, is actually used to finance universal service, and therefore a fraction $1 - \delta$ of these public funds is embezzled by private interests.

We observe that in the no corruption state, namely when all the tax revenues are used to finance universal service ($\delta = 1$), the performance of scenario UT_{ac}^{τ} would be as good as that of scenario TC_{ac} in the absence of a technological advantage to TC. Then both scenarios could be expected to create distortions of the same magnitude, that is, corresponding to a shadow price of public funds λ^* close to 0.2. Yet, as we argued above, the cost of public funds would generally be greater than λ^* in developing countries, so we can expect UT_{ac}^{τ} to be dominated by TC_{ac} in such countries. Clearly, decreasing values of δ would increase the social cost of the distortions associated with explicit taxation and hence would favor the territory-constrained entry scenario TC_{ac}. We have evaluated scenario UT_{ac}^{τ} for each of the six values of δ and derived the corresponding values of the implicit cost of public funds $\hat{\lambda}$. Table 8.1 exhibits the results. As expected, the calculations show that as the portion of tax revenues actually used to finance universal service (δ) increases, the deadweight loss due to taxation decreases, and

Table 8.1
Funding of universal service through explicit taxation: Implicit cost of public funds

Value of δ	$\hat{\lambda}$
0.5	1.35
0.6	0.94
0.7	0.64
0.8	0.43
0.9	0.26
1.0	0.13

this financing tool becomes more and more attractive as reflected in a decreasing implicit cost of public funds.

8.4.4   Impact of Incomplete Information

So far we have conducted the analysis under complete information, even though competition was motivated by informational reasons, and we have presumed that all types of competition eliminate information rents. However, because of the importance of asymmetric information in both developed and developing countries, we need to examine further how it affects our comparisons.[26] We now investigate in more depth the desirability of cross-subsidies as a means of financing universal service when the (social) cost of incomplete information is taken into account. A UT type of entry scenario is considered once more, but the entrant in the urban area is assumed now to have the most efficient technology and, as in scenario UT_{ac}^{ps}, with affordability through complete information regulation. This scenario, labeled $\underline{UT}_{ac}^{ps}$, is compared with a TC-type scenario in which the incumbent and the entrant each serve half of the territory and are regulated under incomplete information with price cap ($TCPC$).[27] Because the performance of $\underline{UT}_{ac}^{ps}$ decreases with λ, we find the critical values of this parameter λ^{**}, which is between 0.4 and 0.5, beyond which the TC-type scenario $TCPC$ dominates it despite the incomplete information (see figure 8.4).[28]

The immediate implication of this result is that if taxation of the urban telecommunications is not feasible and one must only rely on the general budget to fund universal service, as long as the cost of public funds is sufficiently high (which is the case of LDCs), a TC-type solution is to be preferred to a UT-type, even if the informational costs of regulation are accounted for in the TC solution.

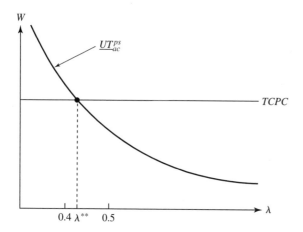

Figure 8.4
UT under average-cost pricing versus TC under price-cap regulation with asymmetric
information

This result also provides us with an evaluation of the social cost imposed by both the distortions tied to cross-subsidies in $TCPC$ and the
rents left to the firms in order to give them incentives for production
efficiency in this asymmetric information context. The corresponding
implicit cost of public funds is seen to be within the range $[0.4, 0.5]$.
Now suppose that taxation is feasible within an urban-targeted entry
framework with no corruption ($\delta = 1$). Recall that the implicit cost of
public funds is found to be equal to 0.134 (see table 8.1). Hence in this
case taxation is more attractive than cross-subsidies. An examination of
table 8.1, however, shows that for some δ around 0.8, that is, for a relatively low level of tax money waste or corruption (around 20 percent),
cross-subsidies become more attractive.

8.5 Conclusion

This chapter has contributed to the debate on the financing of universal
service in the context of the deregulation of telecommunications by ar-
guing that cross-subsidies may still be regarded as a valuable means, in
particular, for developing countries. The analysis presented here suggests that this and other important issues facing the telecommunications
industry today can be dealt with in a framework that combines engineering process models and the tools of modern industrial organization.

As stressed throughout this chapter, the objective of universal service technically amounts to imposing uniform pricing across the urban and rural areas despite the difference in the cost of serving a typical customer in those two areas. This therefore rules out any price discrimination based on cost of service. This uniform pricing constraint creates, one way or another, economic distortions whose extent depends on the unit cost of making the transfers necessary to offset those distortions. Comparing social welfare achieved under the various scenarios allows us to obtain some estimates of the magnitude of these distortions.

An analysis of the performance of the urban-targeted (UT) and territory-constrained (TC) frameworks (see section 8.2) in an economic distortion-free environment (beyond that created by the cost of public funds) provides us with useful information on the relative attractiveness of these two industry configurations on the basis of technological efficiency. This was the purpose of the preliminary exercise in which we compared the marginal-cost pricing scenarios UT_{mc}^{ps} and TC_{mc}^{ps}. From the standpoint of the sole technological efficiency, we found that for all values of the cost of public funds, the urban-targeted configuration is slightly preferred to the territory-constrained one. Then we imposed the USO and budget balance. A comparison of the performance of scenario UT_{ac}^{ps} (funding of USO through the general budget) with scenario TC_{ac} (funding of USO through urban-to-rural cross-subsidies or equivalently through implicit taxation of the urban sector) showed that the distortions associated with the TC solution are rather small, corresponding to a shadow cost of public funds in the range (0.1, 0.2). This implicit cost of public funds provides us with an estimate of the deadweight loss created by explicit taxation of the urban sector in an urban-targeted framework (UT_{ac}^{τ}) that uses (all of) the tax revenues to finance the USO.

A comparison of scenario $\underline{UT}_{ac}^{ps}$ (an improved version of UT_{ac}^{ps} in which the entrant is the most efficient firm in our grid) with scenario $TCPC$ (which allows for cross-subsidies, or implicit taxation of the urban sector, under price cap regulation) yields a shadow cost of the distortions created by the TC solution in the range (0.4, 0.5). What can we then conclude from this comparison? While under complete information the distortions associated with the cross-subsidies in the TC solution turned out to be small, (socially costly) information rents increase them quite a bit (from the 0.1–0.2 range to the 0.4–0.5 range), and hence make this solution noticeably less attractive than explicit taxation of the urban sector. However, we find that when a fraction of the tax revenues close to 20 percent is taken out of the USO financing system, the TC solution becomes desirable again. More specifically, under a regime with this level of tax money waste, despite the complete information on the technology of the incumbent and the entrant who is assumed to be efficient in a UT scenario and the incomplete information on technology in a TC scenario, the latter solution is favored as it creates distortions corresponding to a smaller shadow cost of public funds. Figure 8.5 below summarizes our discussion.[29]

We conclude this section with a few comments on the robustness of the results. Abstracting away from revenue effects, we could think of telecommunications demand in terms of the relative availability of communications means that can be good substitutes to the phone. We consider the case where those substitutes are practically nonexistent (very low elasticity of the demand for telephone usage of -0.1) and the case where there exist good substitutes to the telephone service (very high demand elasticity of -0.6). Tables 8.2 and 8.3 give some estimates obtained through linear interpolation of the critical values of the parameters λ^* and λ^{**} (see figures 8.4 and 8.5) for various combinations of the demand elasticities. An examination of these tables shows that the

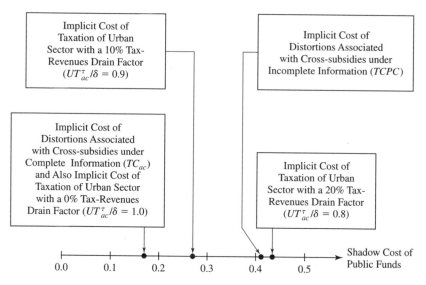

Figure 8.5
Cross-subsidization versus taxation

Chapter 8

Table 8.2
Sensitivity analysis: Elasticity of demand in urban, $\eta_1 = -0.2$

Elasticity in rural (η_2)	λ^*	λ^{**}
-0.1	0.19	0.43
-0.2	0.19	0.43
-0.6	0.20	0.43

Table 8.3
Sensitivity analysis: Elasticity of demand in rural, $\eta_2 = -0.2$

Elasticity in urban (η_1)	λ^*	λ^{**}
-0.1	0.12	0.31
-0.2	0.19	0.43
-0.6	0.43	1.10

estimated values remain generally low for the alternative configurations of demand elasticities.[30] This says that the main policy implication of our empirical findings still holds, namely cross-subsidies are attractive for the financing of universal service in developing countries.[31]

9

Strategic Cross-subsidies and Vertical Integration

9.1 Introduction

When competition is introduced in markets for services using an infrastructure, an important structural decision to be made concerns the vertical disintegration of the incumbent firm that provides both the infrastructure and the services. Preventing the owner of the infrastructure to compete in services, as Judge Greene decided in the AT&T case, may destroy potential economies of scope, create more transaction costs, but eliminate most incentives for favoritism because of the incumbent's internal use of the infrastructure.

In Europe the liberalization reforms have maintained the vertical integration of incumbent operators accompanied with a requirement of accounting separation between services and infrastructure activities. In the United States the FCC has issued a series of rulemakings, known as the Computer Inquiries, that have progressively weakened the separation requirements by moving from a regime of structural safeguards to various forms of accounting safeguards.[1] In this chapter we provide an empirical evaluation of these types of policies as a means of introducing competition in services markets. In particular, we examine the impact on the competitive process in these markets of the cross-subsidies allowed by vertical integration of the incumbent.

We consider a situation where two segments use a common (telecommunications) infrastructure. We envision the introduction of competition in one segment and service by an incumbent regulated firm in the other segment. In section 9.2 we seek to model the manipulation phenomenon, via cross-subsidies, that could result from the accounting procedure of allocating common costs between the two services.

Even with accounting separation, the manipulation of moral hazard variables such as effort levels creates cross-subsidies when the regulated segment is subject to cost-plus regulation while the firm is residual claimant of its costs in the competitive segment. Section 9.3 shows how the size of such cross-subsidies varies with the power of incentives in the regulated sector, while section 9.4 studies how these cross-subsidies may affect entry.

Section 9.5 presents some empirical results based on a LECOM simulation of costs for the case in which potential cross-subsidies may exist between the markets for basic (switched) telephone service and enhanced services supplied to a (unswitched) competitive sector using leased lines. Section 9.6 contains some concluding remarks.

9.2   Size of Cross-subsidies due to Allocation of Common Costs

Consider a service territory composed of two markets. Market 1 is open to competitive entry, and market 2 has the technological characteristics of a natural monopoly. An incumbent firm operates in both markets with a technology described by a cost function C which can be written as

$$C(\beta, e_0, e_1, e_2, q_1, q_2) = C_1(\beta, e_1, q_1, q_2) + C_2(\beta, e_2, q_1, q_2) \\ + C_0(\beta, e_0, q_1, q_2) \tag{9.1}$$

where $C_1(\cdot)$, $C_2(\cdot)$, and $C_0(\cdot)$ are functions that represent, respectively, incremental costs of the activities in markets 1 and 2 and costs that are common to the two activities; β is a technological parameter; e_0, e_1, and e_2 are efforts that reduce the respective components of the total cost; and q_1 and q_2 are output levels in markets 1 and 2.

Equation (9.1) assumes a particular decomposition of the cost function C in which both the effort variables e_0, e_1, and e_2 and the output variables q_1 and q_2 can be assigned to the functions C_0, C_1, and C_2, respectively. An important assumption in this decomposition is that the effort levels e_0, e_1, and e_2 can be individually applied to the component cost functions. This assumption is carried over to the function that gives the aggregate disutility generated by these effort levels for the incumbent. More specifically, we assume that this disutility of effort function is

$$\psi(\beta, e_0, e_1, e_2, q_1, q_2) = \psi_1(\beta, e_1, q_1) + \psi_2(\beta, e_2, q_2) + \psi_0(\beta, e_0) \tag{9.2}$$

This approach is in contrast to an alternative approach in which effort is viewed as a "public" input that is applied equally to all of the firm's activities. As explained in more detail in section 9.5, the latter approach is the one that we adopted in previous chapters, and it is the one that is consistent with our LECOM simulations of the total cost function, where we use the price of labor as a proxy for aggregate effort. In the present chapter, since we primarily deal with incremental cost functions, the interpretation of effort as a "private" input to each activity is more appropriate.[2]

We also assume that the decomposition property holds for the stand-alone cost functions corresponding to the two activities, $SAC_1(\cdot)$ and $SAC_2(\cdot)$:

$$SAC_1(\beta, e_0, e_1, q_1) = C_1(\beta, e_1, q_1, 0) + C_0(\beta, e_0, q_1, 0) \qquad (9.3)$$

$$SAC_2(\beta, e_0, e_2, q_2) = C_2(\beta, e_2, 0, q_2) + C_0(\beta, e_0, 0, q_2) \qquad (9.4)$$

Let us initially focus on cross-subsidies that the firm could achieve through the allocation of the common costs $C_0(\beta, e_0, q_1, q_2)$. Assume that the exogenous technological parameter β is known and that output and effort levels that affect the different cost components are given. Furthermore let $\delta \in [0, 1]$ represent a parameter that specifies the way common costs are allocated between the two activities. Specifically, δ represents the proportion of the common costs that is allocated by the firm to the potentially competitive segment (market 1). Omitting the arguments for simplicity, total cost of the firm can be written as

$$C = C_1 + C_2 + C_0 = [C_1 + \delta C_0] + [C_2 + (1 - \delta)C_0] \qquad (9.5)$$

Equation (9.5) merely shows the decomposition of the total cost C into two parts corresponding to the total costs associated with each of the two activities.

A straightforward way of assessing the potential that the firm has for subsidization of activity 1 by activity 2 via the allocation of common costs is by evaluating the relative importance of these common costs. Clearly segment 1 would benefit from the highest (cross-)subsidies when the common costs are totally allocated to segment 2. More formally, let $s(\delta)$ represent the total cost allocated by the vertically integrated firm to segment 1, namely

$$s(\delta) = C_1 + \delta C_0 \qquad (9.6)$$

This function increases with δ from $s(0) = C_1$ to $s(1) = C_1 + C_0$ (figure 9.1 displays the function s). If the parameter δ is under the

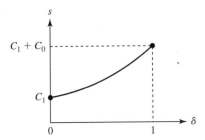

Figure 9.1
Size of cross-subsidies through allocation of common costs

control of the firm, the function s may be used as a basis for constructing some measures of the cost advantage that the vertically integrated firm possesses over its potential competitors in the liberalized sector. This advantage is due to the incumbent firm's ability to subsidize activity 1 from revenues earned in activity 2. This type of cross-subsidy may be particularly attractive to the firm when the market for activity 1 is competitive while activity 2 is regulated by a low-powered cost-based scheme.

9.3   Size of Effort Allocation Cross-subsidies

When strict accounting rules are in place, cross-subsidization may still be possible for an integrated firm through its control of the effort variables e_0, e_1, and e_2. In order to evaluate the size of these strategic cross-subsidies, let us examine more closely how the incumbent firm sets these effort levels. We go back to the total cost function given in equation (9.1) and assume that the scheme under which the incumbent is regulated can be described by a cost-reimbursement rule. More specifically, we assume that the firm bears some given fractions α_1, α_2, and α_0 of the costs of activities 1 and 2, respectively, and of the costs common to these activities.[3]

To determine effort allocation between the two activities and common costs, the firm minimizes

$$\alpha_1 C_1(\beta, e_1, q_1, q_2) + \alpha_2 C_2(\beta, e_2, q_1, q_2)$$
$$+ \alpha_0 C_0(\beta, e_0, q_1, q_2) + \psi(\beta, e_0, e_1, e_2, q_1, q_2) \quad (9.7)$$

where ψ is given in equation (9.2). The first-order conditions of this problem are

$$\frac{\partial \psi_1}{\partial e_1}(\beta, e_1, q_1) \geq -\alpha_1 \frac{\partial C_1}{\partial e_1}(\beta, e_1, q_1, q_2) \tag{9.8}$$

$$\frac{\partial \psi_2}{\partial e_2}(\beta, e_2, q_2) \geq -\alpha_2 \frac{\partial C_2}{\partial e_2}(\beta, e_2, q_1, q_2) \tag{9.9}$$

$$\frac{\partial \psi_0}{\partial e_0}(\beta, e_0) \geq -\alpha_0 \frac{\partial C_0}{\partial e_0}(\beta, e_0, q_1, q_2) \tag{9.10}$$

where (9.8), (9.9), and (9.10) must hold as equalities if, respectively, $e_1 > 0$, $e_2 > 0$, or $e_0 > 0$. These first-order conditions can be solved to yield optimal effort levels $e_1^*(\beta, q_1, q_2, \alpha_1, \alpha_2, \alpha_0)$, $e_2^*(\beta, q_1, q_2, \alpha_1, \alpha_2, \alpha_0)$, and $e_0^*(\beta, q_1, q_2, \alpha_1, \alpha_2, \alpha_0)$. For given β, q_1, and q_2, substitution of the cost-minimizing effort levels into the respective component cost functions yields the "reduced form" cost functions $C_1^* = C_1^*(\alpha_1, \alpha_2, \alpha_0)$, $C_2^* = C_2^*(\alpha_1, \alpha_2, \alpha_0)$, and $C_0^* = C_0^*(\alpha_1, \alpha_2, \alpha_0)$.

By analogy to the function $s(\delta)$ defined in section 9.2, we may define the function $t(\alpha_2, \delta)$ as

$$t(\alpha_2, \delta) = C_1^*(1, \alpha_2, \alpha_2) + \delta C_0^*(1, \alpha_2, \alpha_2) \tag{9.11}$$

This expression assumes that competition in segment 1 makes the incumbent a residual claimant of its costs in that segment while a uniform regulatory regime with power α_2 is applied to the remaining costs of the firm. For a given δ, the function t is expected to decrease from $t(0, \delta) = C_1^*(1, 0, 0) + \delta C_0^*(1, 0, 0)$ to $t(1, \delta) = C_1^*(1, 1, 1) + \delta C_0^*(1, 1, 1)$ (see figure 9.2), and it could be used as a basis for measuring the size of

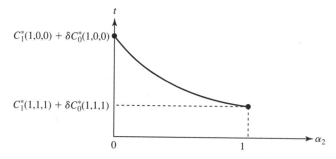

Figure 9.2
Size of cross-subsidies through allocation of efforts

the cross-subsidies that the incumbent can achieve through effort allocation.

9.4 Strategic Cross-subsidies through Effort Allocation under Accounting Separation

Section 9.3 defined the range of potential strategic cross-subsidies in a measure that is roughly comparable to the measure of the potential range for accounting cross-subsidies defined in section 9.2. In this section we explore the possibility that strategic cross-subsidies may be used by an integrated firm to blockade entry when full accounting rules are in place that seek to prevent accounting cross-subsidization. To simplify the empirical analysis that we present in a later section, we seek to identify separately the two channels through which an integrated incumbent may interfere with entry. First we consider a setting where the incumbent does not have any technological cost advantage, and we show how it can still have the ability to manipulate effort in order to undercut the entrant through disutility of effort. Then we consider the case where aggregate disutility of total effort is "neutral" (i.e., held constant) and analyze the conditions under which the allocation of effort of the incumbent gives it a technological cost advantage.

9.4.1 The Cost-of-Effort Channel

Consider the situation where the incumbent (I) faces competition in segment 1 but is a cost-plus regulated monopoly in segment 2. We assume that strict accounting separation holds between its two subsidiaries. We further assume that imputation of common costs is defined on the basis of output so that total allocated costs $\hat{C}_1$ and $\hat{C}_2$ of the two subsidiaries are generically given by

$$\hat{C}_1 = C_1(\beta, e_1, q_1, q_2) + \frac{q_1}{q_1 + q_2} C_0(\beta, e_0, q_1, q_2) \tag{9.12}$$

$$\hat{C}_2 = C_2(\beta, e_2, q_1, q_2) + \frac{q_2}{q_1 + q_2} C_0(\beta, e_0, q_1, q_2) \tag{9.13}$$

Suppose that a firm E considers entry into the liberalized segment market (market 1) by relying on the same technology as the incumbent. Such an entrant, assumed to have "fair" access to the facilities that are common to the two segments, would have a total allocated cost function given by

$$\hat{C}_E = C_E(\beta, e_{E1}, q_{E1}, q_{I2}) + \frac{q_{E1}}{(q_{I1} + q_{E1}) + q_{I2}} C_0(\beta, e_{I0}, (q_{I1} + q_{E1}), q_{I2})$$

(9.14)

where C_E is the incremental cost of the entering firm, e_{E1} and q_{E1} are its effort and output levels, respectively, and e_{I0}, q_{I1}, and q_{I2} are the incumbent's (common) cost-reducing effort and output levels in the competitive and regulated segments, respectively, once entry has occurred. We assume that C_E has the same functional form as C_1, the incumbent's incremental cost function in market 1.[4]

Since the entering firm uses the same technology as the incumbent and competition takes place in segment 1, efforts are conditionally optimal, and one can assume that the incumbent and the entrant share the market at the same level of output ($q_{I1} = q_{E1}$). The pecuniary costs of the incumbent are given by

$$\hat{C}_I = C_1(\beta, e_{I1}, q_{I1}, q_{I2}) + \frac{q_{I1}}{(q_{I1} + q_{E1}) + q_{I2}} C_0(\beta, e_{I0}, (q_{I1} + q_{E1}), q_{I2})$$

(9.15)

where e_{I1} is the incumbent's (incremental) cost-reducing effort in the competitive segment. If the incumbent matches the entrant's price, these costs are the same as the entrant's, and the incumbent must therefore match the entrant's effort level in the competitive segment. Under these conditions $e_{I1}^*(q_{I1}) = e_{E1}^*(q_{E1})$.

Although there are no intrinsic technological cost advantages to the incumbent, the latter might still have the ability to block entry. Indeed, we might well have

$$\psi_E(\beta, e_{E1}^*, q_{E1}) \leq \psi(\beta, e_{I0}^*, e_{I1}^*, e_{I2}^*(q_{I2}), q_{I1}, q_{I2})$$

(9.16)

yet

$$\psi_E(\beta, e_{E1}^*, q_{E1}) > \psi(\beta, e_{I0}^*, e_{I1}^*, e_{I2}^{min}, q_{I1}, q_{I2})$$

(9.17)

where ψ_E is the disutility of effort function of the entrant (in the competitive segment), e_{E1}^* is the entrant's optimizing value of e_1, e_{I0}^* and e_{I2}^* are the incumbent's optimizing values of e_0 and e_2, and e_2^{min} is the minimal effort level that the incumbent can exert in reducing the corresponding cost component.

Inequalities (9.16) and (9.17) suggest that if the incumbent firm has its cost reimbursed at a minimum level of effort in the regulated segment (incremental cost and common costs), then it may have the ability to reduce its total disutility of effort to the point that it is lower than the disutility of effort of the entrant. Hence, despite perfect accounting separation, complemented by a fair access price to the regulated sector, the incumbent can, by strategically manipulating effort levels, undercut an entrant, even if the latter happens to possess a comparable or even somewhat superior technology.

If the entrant uses a significantly better technology ($\beta_E \ll \beta$), than the incumbent, the analysis of strategic manipulation of effort levels would allow us to compute the cost advantage it provides to the incumbent, but nothing general can be said about whether or not entry can be blockaded by the incumbent.

9.4.2 The Cost-of-Production Channel

We have just examined the possible ability that an incumbent would have to blockade entry into a liberalized sector by manipulating effort levels to the point of making its disutility of effort in the regulated sector lower than what first-best efficiency would dictate. A critical (perhaps too critical) role is played in this analysis by the disutility of effort functions of the incumbent and the entrant. From the standpoint of empirical analysis, this reliance on the properties of the disutility of effort functions is problematical because these functions are inherently unobservable, and we obtain them solely through calibration. Therefore in the remainder of this section we consider a similar argument (blockade of entry) that is based only on the cost functions that LECOM allows us to estimate.

We impose, on both the incumbent and the entrant, a fixed level of disutility of effort $\bar{\psi}$.[5] We assume that the entrant and the incumbent have the same disutility of effort functions so that disutility for the entrant can be expressed as

$$\psi_E(\beta, e_{E0}, e_{E1}, q_{E1}) = \psi(\beta, e_{E0}, e_{E1}, 0, q_{E1}, 0) \tag{9.18}$$

Consider an entering firm that uses its own facilities and allocates effort between incremental and common costs. Hence it would determine levels of e_0 and e_1 by minimizing its stand-alone cost SAC_E (see equation 9.3) subject to the constraint

$$\psi(\beta, e_{E0}, e_{E1}, 0, q_{E1}, 0) = \bar{\psi} \tag{9.19}$$

The first-order conditions of this problem, given by (9.19) and

$$\frac{\partial C_0/\partial e_0}{\partial \psi/\partial e_0} = \frac{\partial C_1/\partial e_1}{\partial \psi/\partial e_1} \tag{9.20}$$

can be solved to yield optimal efforts $e_{E0}^*(\beta, q_{E1})$ and $e_{E1}^*(\beta, q_{E1})$ and a stand-alone cost function for the entrant given by

$$C_E(\beta, q_{E1}) \equiv C_1(\beta, e_{E1}^*(\beta, q_{E1}), q_{E1}, 0) + C_0(\beta, e_{E0}^*(\beta, q_{E1}), q_{E1}, 0) \tag{9.21}$$

Substituting back these optimal efforts into the entrant's disutility of effort function yields the reduced form disutility of effort function

$$\psi_E(\beta, q_{E1}) \equiv \psi(\beta, e_{E0}^*(\beta, q_{E1}), e_{E1}^*(\beta, q_{E1}), 0, q_{E1}, 0) \tag{9.22}$$

While the entrant exerts effort to reduce only its incremental and common costs, the incumbent has to allocate its effort among the three components of its cost function. Furthermore the incumbent is subject to regulation, which we assume is represented by a three-part cost-reimbursement scheme with powers α_1, α_2, and α_0 applied to the respective cost components. The incumbent's optimal choices of e_1, e_2, and e_0 are therefore obtained by minimizing total supported cost given by (9.7) subject to the constraint

$$\psi(\beta, e_0, e_1, e_2, q_1, q_2) = \bar{\psi} \tag{9.23}$$

The first-order conditions to the incumbent's effort allocation problem are given by

$$\frac{\alpha_i(\partial C_i/\partial e_i)}{\partial \psi/\partial e_i} = \frac{\alpha_j(\partial C_j/\partial e_j)}{\partial \psi/\partial e_j} \tag{9.24}$$

for $i, j = 0, 1, 2$, $i \neq j$, and equation (9.23). These conditions implicitly define optimal effort functions $e_{I1}^*(\beta, q_{I1}, q_{I2}, \alpha_1, \alpha_2, \alpha_0, \bar{\psi})$, $e_{I2}^*(\beta, q_{I1}, q_{I2}, \alpha_1, \alpha_2, \alpha_0, \bar{\psi})$, and $e_{I0}^*(\beta, q_{I1}, q_{I2}, \alpha_1, \alpha_2, \alpha_0, \bar{\psi})$. Assuming accounting separation and imputation of common costs according to output as in the previous subsection, the cost function of the incumbent in activity 1, $\hat{C}_I(\beta, q_{I1}, q_{I2}, \alpha_1, \alpha_2, \alpha_0, \bar{\psi})$, which is the relevant one to consider as far as comparison with the entrant is concerned, is given by

$$C_1(\beta, e_{I1}^*(\beta, q_{I1}, q_{I2}, \alpha_1, \alpha_2, \alpha_0, \bar{\psi}), q_{I1}, q_{I2})$$

$$+ \frac{q_{I1}}{q_{I1} + q_{I2}} C_0(\beta, e_{I0}^*(\beta, q_{I1}, q_{I2}, \alpha_1, \alpha_2, \alpha_0, \bar{\psi}), q_{I1}, q_{I2}) \tag{9.25}$$

The two functions C_E in equation (9.21) and $\hat{C}_I$ in equation (9.25) can be compared. For given values of the arguments, one can define the cost advantage of the incumbent (or handicap of the entrant) as the difference between these two costs, $\Delta \equiv (C_E - \hat{C}_I)$. Four factors are at work in the determination of Δ: the (dis)economies of scope between the two activities, the power of incentives of regulation, the common costs imputation rule, and the fact that the entrant firm has to allocate effort between only the two components of its stand-alone cost whereas the incumbent has to allocate it among three components.[6] It is worthwhile to note that the cost gap Δ depends on the respective powers of the incentive schemes. In the following section we will empirically analyze this dependence.

9.5 Empirical Results

9.5.1 Simulation of LECOM: Basic versus Enhanced Services

Previously we used LECOM to simulate a telecommunications cost function in which outputs were represented as traffic, measured in CCS per access line (see chapters 6, 7, and 8), and access lines (see chapter 5).[7] Here we again consider cost as a function of the number of access lines, but we separate access lines into two distinct kinds, depending on the type of telecommunications service that they provide. Basic switched services, primarily sold to residential and small business users, are essentially used for voice and low-speed data traffic. High-capacity leased lines (also called private lines) are primarily used by larger business users for high-speed data and other enhanced services.

In both advanced and less developed countries, business and enhanced services have been open to competitive entry for many years, while the markets for residential switched services have retained the characteristics of natural monopoly, even where entry has been allowed or encouraged by the regulator. Thus switched access lines are priced subject to regulatory control in nearly all countries, while enhanced services are generally provided in a highly competitive environment. The issues of cross-subsidization, which this chapter seeks to investigate, are therefore relevant for these markets.

Using LECOM we are able to estimate the cost of providing both switched and unswitched access lines. We assume a city of fixed size consisting of three zones, a central business district, a mixed commercial and residential district, and a residential district. We also assume that customer density progressively increases as we move from the residential to the mixed and to the business districts.[8]

LECOM allows the user to specify the proportion of unswitched access lines in each region of the city. For the simulations, the percentage of private line customers varied from 0 to 100 percent in increments of 20 percent. The total population of the city varied from 6,000 to 100,000 subscribers.[9] Thus, by varying both the population of subscribers and the percentage of unswitched lines, we define a grid of output values that we use to simulate the total cost function of the integrated firm. The grid also includes a range of values for the multipliers of the price of capital and labor PK and PL, which are supposed to represent, respectively, the technology type β and effort e.[10] In order to simulate the stand-alone cost functions for both switched and unswitched access lines, we set the unswitched percentages equal to 0 and 1, respectively, and vary the total number of access lines in a manner consistent with our first grid. This exercise allows us to create the data for estimating the cost functions $C(\beta, e, q_1, q_2)$, $C_1(\beta, e, q_1, q_2)$, and $C_2(\beta, e, q_1, q_2)$ which are described above.[11]

We next explain the techniques that allow us to estimate the stand-alone cost functions defined in (9.1), (9.3), and (9.4) through simulations of LECOM and how we use these functions to derive the incremental and common cost functions. By letting the variables PK (the multiplier for the price of capital, our proxy for the technological parameter β), PL (the multiplier for the price of labor, our proxy for effort e), and q_1 and q_2 (measures of levels of output in markets 1 and 2) vary within a grid, we obtain the cost function $\tilde{C}(\beta, e, q_1, q_2)$.[12] This function represents the stand-alone cost of an integrated firm (the incumbent) serving markets 1 and 2. Using the same grid and restricting the outputs so that only $q_1 > 0$ and $q_2 > 0$, we estimate the cost functions $\widetilde{SAC}_1(\beta, e, q_1)$ and $\widetilde{SAC}_2(\beta, e, q_2)$, which represent the stand-alone costs of a nonintegrated firm serving markets 1 and 2, respectively. We note that these stand-alone cost functions do not correspond exactly to the theoretical stand-alone cost functions $C(\beta, e_0, e_1, e_2, q_1, q_2)$, $SAC_1(\beta, e_0, e_1, q_1)$, and $SAC_2(\beta, e_0, e_2, q_2)$, since they do not allow the firm to assign different effort levels to different activities or markets.

Using these three basic LECOM-generated cost functions $\tilde{C}$, $\widetilde{SAC}_1$, and $\widetilde{SAC}_2$, we define the empirical counterparts of the incremental cost functions C_1 and C_2 and the common cost function C_0 as follows:

$$\tilde{C}_1(\beta, e_1, q_1, q_2) = \tilde{C}(\beta, e_1, q_1, q_2) - \widetilde{SAC}_2(\beta, e_1, q_2) \tag{9.26}$$

$$\tilde{C}_2(\beta, e_2, q_1, q_2) = \tilde{C}(\beta, e_2, q_1, q_2) - \widetilde{SAC}_1(\beta, e_2, q_1) \tag{9.27}$$

$$\tilde{C}_0(\beta, e_0, q_1, q_2) = \widetilde{SAC}_1(\beta, e_0, q_1) + \widetilde{SAC}_2(\beta, e_0, q_2) - \tilde{C}(\beta, e_0, q_1, q_2) \tag{9.28}$$

Substituting from (9.26) and (9.27) yields

$$\tilde{C}_0(\beta, e_0, q_1, q_2) = \tilde{C}(\beta, e_0, q_1, q_2) - \tilde{C}_1(\beta, e_0, q_1, q_2) - \tilde{C}_2(\beta, e_0, q_1, q_2) \tag{9.29}$$

Before discussing results on economies of scope between basic switched service and enhanced high-capacity service, let us say a few more words on the theoretical interpretation of the above simulated-LECOM cost functions.

Our use of the LECOM input PL as a proxy for the firm's effort level implies a constraint on the way effort is allocated among the components of the cost function represented in equation (9.1). For any 4-tuple (PK, PL, q_1, q_2), which is our proxy for (β, e, q_1, q_2), a LECOM run searches for the network configuration and technological characteristics (number of switches, location, types of switches, distribution and transport plant, etc.) that minimize the total cost. For each run a common value of PL, representing a level of effort e, is used in both markets and for the common costs.[13]

Thus the cost function $\tilde{C}(\beta, e, q_1, q_2)$ that LECOM simulates is that for an integrated firm that minimizes the sum of its three components

$$C_1(\beta, e_1, q_1, q_2) + C_2(\beta, e_2, q_1, q_2) + C_0(\beta, e_0, q_1, q_2) \tag{9.30}$$

subject to the constraint $e_0 = e_1 = e_2 \equiv e$. Indeed, the solution to this minimization problem yields a total cost function

$$C_1(\beta, e, q_1, q_2) + C_2(\beta, e, q_1, q_2) + C_0(\beta, e, q_1, q_2) \tag{9.31}$$

that has $\tilde{C}(\beta, e, q_1, q_2)$ as its empirical counterpart as can be verified using (9.26), (9.27), and (9.28).

Note that (9.28) gives a direct indication of whether or not economies of scope between basic switched service and enhanced service exist. If these two services are provided by two separate firms, each firm would have to support the corresponding stand-alone cost and the total multifirm cost would then be equal to $(\widetilde{SAC_1} + \widetilde{SAC_2})$. A single firm offering both services would bear the total cost $\tilde{C}$. The difference between these two costs $[(\widetilde{SAC_1} + \widetilde{SAC_2}] - \tilde{C}]$, which represents the costs that are common to the two services, indicates the presence of economies or diseconomies of scope. For various combinations of outputs q_1 (number of unswitched access lines) and q_2 (number of switched access lines) in the range of output levels for which our LECOM cost functions were defined, and for the average values of the multipliers of price of capital and labor PK and PL (both equal to 1), we found this difference to be consistently positive, indicating the presence of economies of scope.[14]

9.5.2 Accounting and Strategic Cross-subsidies

When strict separation of the accounts of the regulated (switched service) and the unregulated (unswitched service) sectors is not imposed, the integrated firm clearly has an incentive to allocate as much of the common costs as possible to the regulated sector.[15] In the notation of section 9.2, this is achieved when $\delta = 0$, when the totality of the common costs are recorded on the regulated sector accounts. In contrast, when $\delta = 1$, then all of the common costs are born by the unregulated sector. In fact, given the absence of strict accounting safeguards, a natural albeit imperfect measure of the potential for cross-subsidization that the integrated firm has would merely be the magnitude of the common costs relative to total costs. Table 9.1 gives an evaluation of these common costs as a percentage of total cost for various combinations of outputs given in thousands (K) of access lines.[16]

From table 9.1 we see that as q_i increases relative to q_j, $i, j = 1, 2, i \neq j$, the relative importance of common costs diminishes. Note that since the area of the city in our simulations is held constant, an increase in access lines corresponds to an increase in customer density. As any of the two types of markets relative to the other or both markets simultaneously gain in maturity, the two activities can be (technologically) separated leaving less room for cross-subsidization of segment 1 with segment 2 through accounting manipulation of the costs that are common to these segments.

An alternative way to express this ability of the integrated firm to use the allocation of common costs as a means of cross-subsidization is the potential per unit subsidy σ, which we define as $\sigma = \tilde{C}_0/q_1 = [s(1) - s(0)]/q_1$. Table 9.2 gives the value of this measure for different

Table 9.1
Cross-subsidies through allocation of common costs, $[\check{C}_0/\check{C}] \times 100$

	$q_2 = 5K$	10K	15K	20K	25K	30K	35K	40K	45K	50K
$q_1 = 5K$	48.21	39.27	32.98	28.35	24.83	22.08	19.90	18.14	16.71	15.53
10K	32.23	27.23	23.50	20.63	18.37	16.57	15.12	13.94	12.97	12.17
15K	22.51	19.46	17.09	15.23	13.73	12.52	11.54	10.74	10.08	9.54
20K	16.10	14.13	12.57	11.32	10.30	9.48	8.81	8.27	7.83	7.48
25K	11.67	10.34	9.28	8.42	7.73	7.17	6.71	6.35	6.07	5.85
30K	8.49	7.58	6.84	6.25	5.77	5.39	5.10	4.87	4.69	4.57
35K	6.18	5.54	5.02	4.61	4.29	4.04	3.85	3.71	3.63	3.58
40K	4.49	4.03	3.67	3.38	3.17	3.01	2.90	2.84	2.81	2.81
45K	3.25	2.92	2.66	2.47	2.33	2.24	2.19	2.18	2.19	2.24
50K	2.35	2.12	1.94	1.81	1.73	1.69	1.68	1.71	1.75	1.83

Table 9.2
Potential per unit cross-subsidization due to accounting manipulation, $\sigma = \bar{C}_0/q_1$

	$q_2 = 5K$	10K	15K	20K	25K	30K	35K	40K	45K	50K
$q_1 = 5K$	528.18	515.84	505.06	495.84	488.17	482.07	477.53	474.54	473.11	473.25
10K	227.86	222.12	217.16	212.97	209.57	206.94	205.09	204.03	203.74	204.23
15K	129.74	126.20	123.17	120.67	118.68	117.22	116.27	115.84	115.94	116.55
20K	82.17	79.73	77.67	76.00	74.73	73.84	73.34	73.24	73.52	74.19
25K	54.82	53.03	51.56	50.40	49.55	49.01	48.78	48.87	49.26	49.97
30K	37.58	36.23	35.14	34.32	33.75	33.44	33.40	33.61	34.08	34.82
35K	26.11	25.08	24.27	23.68	23.32	23.18	23.26	23.56	24.09	24.84
40K	18.26	17.46	16.86	16.45	16.24	16.22	16.40	16.77	17.34	18.10
45K	12.81	12.20	11.76	11.49	11.40	11.48	11.73	12.15	12.75	13.53
50K	9.05	8.58	8.27	8.11	8.12	8.27	8.59	9.05	9.68	10.46

Note: Units are in annualized dollars per unswitched access line.

combinations of outputs.[17] This table shows that, for any level of q_2, σ decreases with q_1. A slightly different result holds when we fix the level of q_1 and let q_2 vary. In this case σ decreases up to some level of q_2 and then increases beyond that level. As the fixed value of q_1 increases, the minimum value of σ is reached for smaller values of q_2.

The capability of an integrated firm to cross-subsidize through an allocation of common costs can be substantially reduced by strict accounting rules. However, as discussed in section 9.3, besides common costs, the firm could also allocate unobservable effort between its two activities. Such a discretionary action allows the firm to cross-subsidize, and we first seek to quantify this type of cross-subsidization.

Effort allocation depends on the power of the incentive schemes that regulate the two activities of the firm. Equations (9.8), (9.9), and (9.10) define the optimal effort levels e_1^*, e_2^*, and e_0^* that are allocated to the three components of the cost function. We assume that the integrated firm is a residual claimant of any reductions of its costs on the unswitched service market ($\alpha_1 = 1$) and that the incremental costs associated with the switched service market and the common costs are under regulation with the same incentive power ($\alpha_2 = \alpha_0$). From the results on the size of cross-subsidization due to the accounting manipulation discussed above, we let $\delta = 1$ in order to calibrate the level of cross-subsidization due to effort allocation.[18] We then calculate the optimal effort levels for different combinations of outputs q_1 and q_2 and for different values of α_2. These effort levels can be substituted back into the incremental cost function C_1 and the common cost function C_0 to find the value of the total allocated cost function t defined in (9.11).[19] It is worthwhile to note that in contrast with the function s previously analyzed, the value taken by this allocated cost function t depends on the power of the incentive scheme (α_2) that regulates the switched service sector.

In the same vein as σ, we can compute a per unit subsidy τ on the basis of the function t as $\tau = [t(0, 1) - t(1, 1)]/q_1$. Table 9.3 gives the value of τ for different combinations of outputs. Note that besides nearly following the same pattern as the potential per unit subsidy due to the accounting manipulation of common costs σ (see table 9.2), this potential subsidy due to effort allocation represents less than 1 percent of the former for high values of outputs but can get as large as 40 percent for low values of outputs.[20] We should also note that this subsidy potential decreases with jointly increasing outputs. This is because

Table 9.3
Potential per unit cross-subsidization due to effort allocation, $\tau = [t(0, 1) - t(1, 1)]/q_1$

	$q_2 = $ 5K	10K	15K	20K	25K	30K	35K	40K	45K	50K
$q_1 = $ 5K	224.00	220.84	217.71	214.60	211.51	208.44	205.39	202.37	199.37	196.39
10K	91.19	89.76	88.35	86.95	85.56	84.18	82.81	81.45	80.11	78.78
15K	48.34	47.50	46.66	45.83	45.00	44.18	43.38	42.58	41.78	41.00
20K	27.99	27.43	26.88	26.33	25.79	25.26	24.73	24.21	23.69	23.18
25K	16.63	16.25	15.87	15.49	15.12	14.76	14.40	14.04	13.69	13.34
30K	9.77	9.50	9.24	8.98	8.72	8.47	8.22	7.97	7.73	7.49
35K	5.48	5.30	5.11	4.94	4.76	4.59	4.42	4.25	4.09	3.93
40K	2.80	2.68	2.56	2.44	2.32	2.21	2.10	1.99	1.89	1.79
45K	1.19	1.11	1.04	0.97	0.90	0.84	0.77	0.71	0.65	0.60
50K	0.33	0.29	0.26	0.22	0.19	0.16	0.14	0.11	0.09	0.07

Note: Units are in annualized dollars per unswitched access line.

as the two activities become more important, they independently require higher effort, so effort allocation cross-subsidization is less of a problem.

So far our main objective was to get a sense of how much an integrated firm can use its regulated activity to cross-subsidize its competitive one. We chose exercises that provide useful information on the ranges of cost variations associated with the allocation of both common costs and effort. We now seek to explore further the conditions under which the allocation of effort, which remains a cross-subsidization instrument at the firm's disposal even under strict accounting safeguards, can affect entry. While assuming that the integrated incumbent firm has to comply with a strict rule of allocation of common costs, we will identify conditions under which the mechanism of effort allocation among its cost components enables the firm to undercut potential entrants into the competitive unswitched service segment.

Our empirical exercise follows the analysis presented in section 9.4.2. Recall that we imposed a fixed level of disutility of effort $\bar{\psi}$ on both the incumbent and the entrant and that, as was mentioned, this level of disutility corresponds to an implicit level of effort that can be used as an indicator of the aggregate level of effort in the industry. We therefore organize the empirical results according to low, medium, and high level of effort, or equivalently, low, medium, and high level of disutility of effort.

Given accounting separation and the rule of allocating common costs imposed on the incumbent firm, one way to "neutralize" strategic cross-subsidization is by implementing a high-powered incentive scheme. To show how this works, we first assume that the incumbent firm is subject to regulation described by the triplet of incentive power values $(\alpha_1, \alpha_2, \alpha_0) = (1, 1, 1)$.[21] Given these fixed values of the power of incentives and that a common costs imputation rule is imposed, two effects can still be identified from this exercise: that of the (dis)economies of scope and that of the number of activities among which effort should be allocated (see section 9.4.2). Table 9.4 gives the value of the incumbent's cost advantage (per unswitched access line) over a potential entrant due to effort allocation for this reference case of "perfect" regulation, under a medium level of industry effort that corresponds to a value of PL that is in the midrange of our data points.[22] Tables with the results for high and low levels of effort are given in appendix A.

Table 9.4
Incumbent per unit cost advantage under high-powered regulation and medium effort, $\Delta/q_1 = (C_E - \hat{C}_1)/q_1$

	$q_2 = 5K$	10K	15K	20K	25K	30K	35K	40K	45K	50K
$q_1 = 5K$	224.01	292.18	320.70	334.35	341.39	345.33	347.95	350.21	352.69	355.78
10K	53.43	81.01	95.21	103.20	108.01	111.15	113.47	115.45	117.40	119.55
15K	15.19	28.35	35.71	40.08	42.81	44.66	46.06	47.30	48.55	49.95
20K	1.16	8.13	12.05	14.36	15.78	16.72	17.44	18.11	18.84	19.70
25K	−5.42	−1.44	0.65	1.78	2.39	2.75	3.01	3.29	3.65	4.14
30K	−9.06	−6.58	−5.50	−5.06	−4.94	−4.96	−5.00	−4.99	−4.88	−4.64
35K	−11.31	−9.61	−9.08	−9.04	−9.22	−9.47	−9.71	−9.88	−9.94	−9.87
40K	−12.84	−11.50	−11.28	−11.47	−11.82	−12.21	−12.57	−12.85	−13.03	−13.08
45K	−13.96	−12.76	−12.69	−12.99	−13.43	−13.90	−14.33	−14.68	−14.93	−15.06
50K	−14.83	−13.63	−13.61	−13.96	−14.44	−14.95	−15.41	−15.80	−16.10	−16.28

Note: Units are in annualized dollars per unswitched access line.

These various tables show that for each level of (fixed) aggregate disutility of effort in the industry, the entrant firm has a cost advantage (since $\Delta < 0$) provided that q_1 is large relative to q_2. As the competitive market becomes increasingly important relative to the regulated market, the integrated firm has less leverage in terms of subsidizing the former by the latter. A cross-examination of these three tables also shows that entry becomes viable for smaller outputs of q_1 as the aggregate level of disutility of effort imposed on the firms is larger. Indeed, as effort increases, costs decrease and the strategic allocation of costs is less of a problem.

The next step is to examine the sensitivity of the difference between the incumbent's cost and the entrant's cost to the "quality" of regulation in market 2 as measured by the power of the incentive scheme that regulates the market. As expected, less than perfect regulation of activity 2 opens the door for more cross-subsidization, and a comparison of table 9.4 with tables 9.5 and 9.6 illustrates the point for the medium level of effort. Tables 9.5 and 9.6 show the values of Δ/q_1 under incentive schemes whose power values are 0.5 and 0.2, respectively. In the three effort levels, we find that for some representative combinations of output, the incumbent's cost advantage Δ changes sign from negative to positive when α_2 decreases. This says that for some given market size, as the quality of regulation deteriorates in terms of the incentives that regulation gives the firm for cost minimization, entry can be blockaded more easily by the incumbent.

As an illustration, consider the output combination $(q_1, q_2) = (30,000, 35,000)$. Under high-powered regulation $(\alpha_2 = 1)$, Δ/q_1 is negative, suggesting that entry is viable. However, for this same output combination and under medium-powered regulation $(\alpha_2 = 0.5)$, the incumbent firm acquires a cost advantage, as shown by the positive value of Δ/q_1, by which the incumbent can implement a pricing strategy for blockading entry. The same effect can be seen in proceeding from medium-powered to low-powered regulation $(\alpha_2 = 0.2)$ for the combination of outputs $(q_1, q_2) = (45,000, 50,000)$. The implication is that if an incumbent firm's noncompetitive segments are not properly regulated, through effort allocation the firm can succeed in protecting its competitive segments by cross-subsidizing them with its regulated segments, and thus affect the market's structure. Thus regulation can be circumvented by an incumbent firm to blockade entry into liberalized markets.

Table 9.5
Incumbent per unit cost advantage under medium-powered regulation and medium effort, $\Delta/q_1 = (C_E - \hat{C}_1)/q_1$

	$q_2 = 5K$	10K	15K	20K	25K	30K	35K	40K	45K	50K
$q_1 = 5K$	237.41	312.99	345.03	360.69	368.99	373.80	377.04	379.78	382.64	386.03
10K	61.52	94.73	112.30	122.50	128.87	133.16	136.34	138.99	141.48	144.06
15K	22.45	39.66	49.78	56.16	60.43	63.47	65.83	67.85	69.74	71.66
20K	8.66	18.50	24.62	28.65	31.46	33.54	35.20	36.67	38.07	39.51
25K	2.58	8.61	12.42	14.99	16.82	18.21	19.36	20.41	21.44	22.52
30K	-0.51	3.39	5.81	7.45	8.63	9.54	10.32	11.05	11.80	12.62
35K	-2.26	0.39	1.96	2.99	3.73	4.31	4.82	5.32	5.87	6.50
40K	-3.35	-1.44	-0.42	0.22	0.66	1.01	1.33	1.67	2.07	2.55
45K	-4.11	-2.63	-1.95	-1.57	-1.32	-1.13	-0.94	-0.72	-0.43	-0.06
50K	-4.68	-3.45	-2.98	-2.76	-2.64	-2.56	-2.46	-2.32	-2.11	-1.82

Note: Units are in annualized dollars per unswitched access line.

Table 9.6
Incumbent per unit cost advantage under low-powered regulation and medium effort, $\Delta/q_1 = (C_E - \hat{C}_1)/q_1$

	$q_2 = 5K$	10K	15K	20K	25K	30K	35K	40K	45K	50K
$q_1 = 5K$	234.03	321.94	360.79	380.96	392.59	400.01	405.40	409.95	414.40	419.20
10K	57.84	97.17	118.83	132.06	140.81	147.06	151.91	156.01	159.78	163.50
15K	20.94	41.52	54.23	62.69	68.69	73.22	76.88	80.06	83.00	85.88
20K	8.96	20.76	28.57	34.07	38.16	41.38	44.07	46.48	48.74	50.99
25K	4.22	11.38	16.34	19.97	22.77	25.05	27.03	28.84	30.58	32.34
30K	2.10	6.63	9.84	12.26	14.18	15.80	17.25	18.61	19.97	21.36
35K	1.07	4.00	6.10	7.73	9.05	10.20	11.26	12.30	13.35	14.47
40K	0.49	2.43	3.82	4.90	5.81	6.63	7.41	8.21	9.05	9.95
45K	0.10	1.42	2.34	3.06	3.69	4.27	4.85	5.47	6.14	6.89
50K	−0.21	0.71	1.32	1.80	2.23	2.65	3.09	3.58	4.13	4.76

Note: Units are in annualized dollars per unswitched access line.

9.6   Conclusion

In this chapter we introduced a methodology that combines theoretical ideas from regulation and an empirical analysis in order to explore the impact of cross-subsidies allowed by vertical integration on entry into liberalized segments of the telecommunications industry. Our first task was to quantify the phenomenon of cross-subsidies in the case of an incumbent regulated in a market for switched access lines, and facing competition in a market for unswitched access lines. From the properties of some basic cost functions estimated using LECOM, we produced measures of two types of cross-subsidies that an incumbent firm might enjoy against a potential entrant. The first of these involved evaluating a range of straightforward cross-subsidies favoring the incumbent's competitive segment to which a small fraction of the common costs are allocated by an accounting manipulation. The second exercise concerned cross-subsidies stemming from the allocation of effort by the incumbent between its competitive and regulated segments. These two types of cross-subsidies were expressed in terms of the potential cost advantage that the incumbent would have over a potential entrant for each unswitched access line. From this measure we obtained an idea of the extent to which an incumbent can (unfairly) undercut its competitors.

While the adverse effect on entry of the first type of cross-subsidy can largely be alleviated by imposing strong accounting safeguards, since effort is inherently unobservable, the second type of cross-subsidy is considerably more difficult for the regulator to monitor. Much of this chapter was devoted to the impact of cross-subsidies on the process of entry into liberalized segments. Using LECOM, we were able to proxy the incumbent's effort and thus to closely examine the mechanism by which the incumbent can allocate effort among its (regulated) switched service segment and its (competitive) unswitched segments. In analyzing this mechanism of effort allocation, we emphasized the role of the power of an incentive regulatory scheme in affecting costs and, we identified situations where the incumbent achieved lower costs than a potential competitor. Our analysis illustrated that regulation, which is designed to foster competition, may actually hinder competition if it does not give the incumbent firm appropriate incentives to efficiently allocate managerial effort among the divisions of the firm.

10   Conclusion

We initiated our line of empirical research on regulatory mechanisms in the fall of 1994. At that time the theory of incentive regulation was already well developed, but it was becoming increasingly apparent that the prospects for empirical tests of the theory were limited. One source of difficulty, at least for empirical tests of the theory of regulation in the telecommunications industry, is the relatively poor quality of data for firms in that industry.[1] Historical data are recorded at most on a quarterly basis, and for a limited number of firms, since the industry has been characterized by regulated or public monopoly for most of its history. Thus the opportunity to construct meaningful time series or panel sets of data for firms facing different regulatory constraints has been limited. Furthermore the available data are generally presented in highly aggregate form, and in categories based on accounting purposes that are not necessarily appropriate for an analysis of incentive effects.[2]

A greater barrier to empirical analysis, however, is the nature of the testable implications that the theory suggests. As our survey in chapter 4 illustrates, it is possible to characterize fully the social welfare consequences of various forms of regulation, and in other chapters we pursue a similar approach to a wide variety of policy issues in the industry. Our common theme in these chapters is that the testable implications of the theory, in large part, depend on very detailed properties of the cost function of a representative firm in the industry. For example, in the characterization of optimal regulation of a natural monopoly supplier, the optimal mechanism is shown to depend on the detailed relationship of the derivatives of the cost function with respect to the technology and effort variables. From historical data we would be unable to adequately characterize these relationships.

Very early in this project we therefore began to consider an alternative approach to cost estimation using engineering process, or cost proxy, models. We were aware of a long tradition of economic analysis using engineering models, but the real impetus to our research program was the discovery of a recently developed public domain proxy model of local exchange telephony.[3] Armed with a proxy model as a tool, we could clarify our research objectives, but we still did not have a well-conceived plan for achieving those objectives. Our endeavor was very much an exercise in learning by doing. To some extent, as we proceeded by trial and error in using the model to generate data for our empirical analysis, our research objectives were correspondingly modified. In this chapter we describe briefly the most important results of our research program to date, the methodological lessons that we have learned, and some directions for future research.

10.1   What Have We Learned?

10.1.1   Implications for Incentive Regulation and Telecommunications Policy

Our primary objective was to fully characterize the cost function of a representative local exchange telecommunications firm, and to apply this representation to a variety of economic models representing current issues in telecommunications policy. The major innovation in the cost analysis was to allow for incomplete information of the regulator, a cornerstone of the new economics of regulation. In this we believe that our efforts were successful, although our representation of the technology was admittedly crude and capable of substantial refinement. We will consider in later sections of this chapter some of the promising areas for refinement of our analysis, but in this section we briefly summarize the main conclusions of our efforts to date.

We began in chapter 5 with a reexamination of the proper characterization of natural monopoly in a traditionally regulated industry such as local telecommunications. Conceptually our analysis led us to suggest that a proper definition of natural monopoly should take account not only of the traditional technological characteristics of the industry, meaning the properties of the cost function alone, but in addition a variety of social welfare measures.

We considered two entry scenarios. Under targeted entry, an entrant succeeds in ultimately attracting all of the customers in a portion of the incumbent's service territory. Under uniform entry, both the incumbent and entrant share the entire market territory, and customer densities for each firm depend on their respective market shares. We also made various strong assumptions on the basis of a few simple economic models of the regulatory regime and firm behavior under both monopoly and free-entry duopoly. In our "access as usage" model, we found that the performance of a deregulated market clearly depends on the assumptions made about the way in which firms compete. Under either regulated (i.e., yardstick) competition or highly competitive unregulated competition, we found that duopoly outperforms traditional cost-plus regulated monopoly under both uniform and targeted entry scenarios. Under the more favorable targeted entry scenario, yardstick competition outperforms simple price-cap regulation, while competitive unregulated duopoly achieves slightly lower aggregate social welfare than incentive regulation.

In chapter 6 we took a close look at the properties of optimal incentive regulation. As noted above, this task required a detailed examination of the firm's cost function in terms of the firm's technology and managerial effort input variables. This representative cost function, and some additional assumptions about consumer demand, the nature of the firm's disutility of effort function, and the regulator's beliefs allowed us to work out precisely an optimal regulatory contract. This contract specifies the level of output for the firm and the transfer that the regulator will make to the firm at each level of output. We were also able to determine the optimal regulation as would be approximately set by prices according to the Ramsey rule plus a monetary transfer to the firm.[4] In addition we showed that the optimal transfer could be implemented by a menu of linear contracts presented to the regulated firm.

In chapter 7 we extended our analysis of the regulated monopoly by introducing a variety of regulatory mechanisms that differ in the quality of information available to the regulator and in the feasibility of making transfers to the regulated firm. Full information (a benchmark but not a realistic prospect for any regulator) requires the observability of both cost and effort. Cost observability (ex post) requires minimal accounting procedures, while other mechanisms such as price caps do not rely on any observation of current cost. Transfers can be bi-directional, in which case they can be used to induce the firm to choose an efficient (at the margin) level of effort given the transfer. Alternatively, a uni-directional transfer from the firm to the regulator (and consumers) can be used to improve the distributional consequences of the regulatory mechanism. Our analysis confirms the widely held belief that incentive regulation generally, including the widely observed use of simple price caps, can significantly increase aggregate social welfare relative to traditional cost-plus regulation. However, pure price-cap regulation and pure cost-plus regulation have vastly different distributional consequences, with price caps favoring the profits of the regulated firm and cost plus favoring the welfare of consumers. Optimal incentive regulation, in our simulations, offers consumers a welfare level close to that achieved under cost plus, while allowing the firm to achieve rents that are also close to the rents they achieve under price caps. Somewhat surprisingly, a price-cap mechanism with profit sharing achieves a very similar result.

In chapter 8 we again considered the role of competition policy and deregulation in the context of a public mandate to finance a universal service subsidy to telecommunications customers in high-cost areas. We modeled the cost structure of a service territory consisting of a low-cost urban area and a higher-cost rural area. We assumed in an "urban-targeted" scenario that if entry is unconstrained, a rational entrant would choose to serve only the lower-cost urban customers. In this case we postulated a Bertrand-like price competition to determine the price in the urban market and a regulated incumbent faced with a universal service obligation to serve rural customers at the same price. The implied budget deficit for the incumbent was to be financed through a public subsidy. As an alternative, in a "territory-constrained" scenario, the regulator could impose a universal service obligation on both the entrant and the incumbent firm. In this case the universal service objective could be achieved under competition without the use of a public subsidy, but the price to urban (and rural) customers turned out to be higher than that under the urban-targeted scenario.

Our analysis revealed that because of the presence of cross-subsidies, the territory-constrained scenario appears to be an efficient method of financing the universal service objective when the cost of public funds (given by λ) is sufficiently high. Under complete information, the territory-constrained scenario even dominates the urban-targeted scenario for virtually all reasonable values of λ. A similar result held under price-cap regulation (for the territory-constrained scenario), though for higher critical values of λ.

Finally, in chapter 9, we considered an issue of some importance in newly deregulated telecommunications markets. Participation in unregulated markets raises the issue of cross-subsidization between regulated and unregulated activities of the incumbent. We considered the case in which some markets where the incumbent was active are fully open (and attractive) to competitive entrants, while other markets are served exclusively by the incumbent monopolist. Using LECOM we simulated the cost structure of a firm that serves markets for both switched access lines, which we assumed to be fully regulated, and unswitched access lines, which we assumed to be competitive. We then decomposed the resulting cost function into a common cost term and incremental costs associated with the regulated and unregulated activities, and based on this decomposition derived a cost function for firms serving only the unregulated market.

We were able to characterize both the magnitude of cross-subsidies due to accounting manipulation and cross-subsidies due to the allocation of effort by the incumbent firm between regulated and unregulated activities. We found that strategic cross-subsidies (from effort allocation) are always lower in magnitude than accounting cross-subsidies, but for lower values of output reflecting small-scale entry, they are nevertheless significant. Accounting cross-subsidies can, in principle, be easily observed and controlled by accounting safeguards. However, effort misallocation is difficult or impossible to observe, and therefore this empirical finding is policy relevant. We further examined the potential role of strategic cross-subsidies by asking whether, under strict accounting safeguards, a regulated incumbent can use its ability to allocate effort strategically to blockade the entry of an otherwise efficient entrant. This analysis revealed that the possibility of entry deterrence depends critically on the power of the regulatory incentive scheme.

10.1.2   Lessons for the Use of Proxy Models in Empirical Research

In addition to the policy implications of our telecommunications cost function, there were some useful lessons learned on the use of proxy models in an empirical research program. These can be grouped broadly into data issues, including the choice of proxies for technology and managerial effort, computational issues, and the extension of the proxy model approach to new markets and new technologies.

One of the first issues to be decided was the definition of an appropriate set of inputs and outputs for our cost function. From our theoretical presentation, recall that we have consistently assumed that a cost function for local telecommunications could be represented in a form $C(\beta, e, q)$ where β represents a technology parameter (known to the firm but not the regulator), e represents cost reducing effort by the firm that is not observable by the regulator, and q represents output. Tables A.14 and A.15 in the appendix illustrate representative LECOM input and output files from which prospective inputs and outputs could be chosen. As indicated, the output file represents the total annual cost of a serving area, which is broken down into the cost of distribution plant, feeder plant, switching plant, interoffice plant, and the cost of the main distribution frame. As potential quantity variables, LECOM specifies the number of switched access lines and the number of private lines (both distributed among business, mixed, and residential lines), traffic volume per line measured in CCS (also distributed among business, mixed, and residential lines), and the ratio of local to toll usage. We have used one or more of these variables to represent the cost function for a local exchange company.

A somewhat more difficult task was the choice of a pair of input parameters to represent β and e. Initially we considered using a specific technological input variable, such as "plcost" (the cost markup for private access lines due to additional line conditioning and higher reliability standards traditionally required by business customers) or the utilization rate (giving spare capacity when loop and switching plant is deployed). Experiments with these input variables did not prove successful, however, largely because the range of cost variation for plausible ranges of input variation was not significant when all other inputs were held constant. As a proxy for managerial effort, e, we briefly considered the theoretically attractive possibility of using the LECOM optimization parameters "ftol" and "itmax" (which essentially instructed the computer algorithm how hard to search for an optimal solution). However, these experiments also produced only minor cost variation, and had the added drawback of introducing a significant noise factor for low levels of computer "effort." We therefore settled on the convenient, but perhaps unintuitive, choice of the variables PK and PL to represent technology and effort. Those variables, PK and PL, act as multipliers for a large number of other LECOM input parameters, and they have an impact on the capital and labor inputs to production, respectively. We thus chose to view technology as something embodied in the capital stock of a representative firm and effort as a function of the labor input, which we interpret as the efficiency price of labor.

Given the full set of quantity and price input variables, we next created a grid of values and proceeded to generate a set of "pseudodata" through a large number of simulations. Since the number of potential data points was limited only by the speed and number of computers used for these simulations, our first intention was to create a very large data set in order to conduct an analytical analysis based on the resulting discrete data.[5] We found, however, that the interpretation of the discrete data was difficult for several reasons. For example, the characterization of optimal incentive regulation depends on a solution of first-order conditions involving the ratio of partial derivatives of the cost function with respect to β and e. Since LECOM generates only an estimate of minimum cost for any given set of inputs, we found that in some cases the realized values of the cost function were not monotonic functions of these input parameters. Even when the cost difference at adjacent data points had the expected sign, the process of computing two sets of first differences and taking their ratio proved to introduce a noise factor that made it difficult to accurately characterize a unique solution.

Rather than simply discarding data points representing nonmonotonic cost values or working with a smoothed set of discrete data, we decided to take the simpler approach of using the entire data set to estimate a smooth functional form cost function. Following a long tradition of empirical analysis, we used a translog functional form and were able to successfully generate a smooth numerical valued cost function. We did not impose any of the standard restrictions on the functional form of the cost function, such as input price homogeneity. It is worth noting, however, that in our case the data-generating process relies on an explicit cost minimization algorithm, which by construction satisfies the required homogeneity conditions. Any violation of standard constraints on the cost function parameters could only be an indication of a computational error in the network optimization or the imprecision of the translog approximation to the true underlying cost function. We did not find evidence of either effect.

The use of a translog involved certain compromises in subsequent analysis. For example, a translog function is not well defined for values of inputs or outputs near the origin. We defined the effort variable by $PL_0 - PL$ for values of $PL < PL_0$, where PL_0 represents the efficiency price of labor associated with minimal effort. Therefore our empirical cost function was not well defined for small effort levels, and it was necessary to take this into account where theory suggests that solutions at minimal effort are possible. Similarly, in our analysis of cross-subsidy in chapter 9, it was necessary to obtain a cost function representation of the fixed and variable costs so that outputs at zero were necessarily involved. In the latter case we gave up using the translog form and substituted a simple quadratic functional form instead.

Computational tractability was also an issue with the translog representation of cost. Closed form analytical solutions were not possible for this form, and so numerical solution techniques had to be used. These generally worked well, though they were cumbersome and depended on initial value specification. Generally, the analysis was much easier to conduct using functional forms that permit closed form solutions despite their weaker fit to the underlying data.

Once the basic methodology was in place and the first simulations had been completed (leading to the data used in chapters 6 and 7), we began to recognize the flexibility that the proxy model tool offered for generating new data sets. Our initial simulations took usage as the output, but later in chapters 5, 9, and to some extent in chapter 8, we focused on access lines instead. Chapters 5 and 8 also presented two different approaches to modeling cost as a function of consumer density. We also developed a (crude) way to estimate the costs of interconnection, an important cost in comparing competitive to monopoly networks. Our measure of interconnection costs included both the cost of interconnecting (linking) separate networks and the cost penalty due to the suboptimal location of switches when two networks optimize in isolation.

10.2 Directions for Improvements in Our Approach

In this section we suggest areas where we believe that future work could significantly improve our analysis. These suggestions will include both improvements in the proxy model itself and in the economic analysis.

Our empirical analysis has relied on the LECOM cost model to generate data for each of the empirical chapters. While LECOM was the only computer-based optimization model of local telecommunications in the public domain at the time we started our research, there are now several additional models available for this purpose, and LECOM itself has undergone significant revisions. In many respects the newer models are capable of much more accurate representation due to a number of factors. Significant work has recently been done in developing better data sources for use in telecommunications cost models. In particular, highly accurate geocoded customer location data are now available that specify the location of customers and therefore the density of customer serving areas—a significant driver of cost. In addition detailed terrain data are now commonly used in proxy models to accurately represent the cost of deploying outside plant in different geographical areas.

The version of LECOM that we used was created in 1991, and we did not attempt to update the input values to reflect more recent conditions. Since local telecommunications technologies and input prices were continually changing during this period, we cannot claim that at any point in our study the cost estimates that we achieved represented the most accurate estimate of the absolute cost of providing service. We do not regard this as a serious drawback of the analysis, however, since we were concerned only with the structure of cost rather than the magnitude of total cost.

Newer proxy models also incorporate improvements in the optimization methodology, which is crucial in estimating the forward-looking cost function of an efficient firm in the industry.[6] An accurate portrayal of the substitution possibilities between capital and labor inputs is clearly critical to our framework given our choice of proxies for representing technology and hidden effort. For example, current proxy models account for the substitution possibilities between copper and fiber transmission plant, which allows for a firm to evaluate a trade-off between the higher maintenance cost of copper plant and the potentially higher initial capital cost of fiber.[7]

The modeling of interconnection cost is another area in which significant improvements in technique could perhaps be achieved. When LECOM was created, the natural monopoly status of local exchange was not seriously questioned. The only interconnection arrangements observable at the time consisted of interconnection between carriers serving customers in separate jurisdictions, and there were no serious attempts to model the costs of interconnecting such carriers. In theory, we believe that our approach to interconnection is sound, since it computes the difference between the costs of two carriers optimizing in isolation and the cost of a single firm serving the entire market. However, in practice, it is relatively cumbersome to follow this approach, and as a result we used it to compute only a single interconnection multiplier for equal sized competitors, which we then applied to all outputs of the interconnecting carriers. This approach is likely to overstate the cost of interconnection when the two carriers differ greatly in size. In addition interconnection costs depend in large part on the cost structure of switching machines, and it is not clear that LECOM or any of the more recent proxy models are able to accurately represent this cost.

Perhaps the largest single area for improvement in our analysis is the development of better proxies for technology and hidden effort. While we are generally comfortable with the choice of PK as a proxy for technology, it would be desirable to have available an alternative more direct measure of technology. The use of PL as a proxy for effort is even more troublesome. It is possible that some of the newer proxy models, such as the HCPM model described in appendix B, could be used to provide a better proxy for the labor input, if not for the hidden effort variable itself. For example, a finer disaggregation of output reports is possible in the more recent models, based on expenses associated with specific categories of investment. We note, however, that all proxy models, including the most recent vintages, have difficulty in modeling labor input effectively. For some of the same reasons that the effort variable is unobservable by the regulator, it is difficult for computer-based models to accurately model the efficient use of labor resources. While accounting data on labor and other expense items exists (and are used in cost proxy models), there can be no guarantee that the data represent firms following the most efficient practices. In addition certain activities of the firm, such as research and development and long-run strategic planning, are inherently difficult to model on a forward-looking basis, though they clearly have a potentially significant impact on cost.

Finally, we note that throughout our analysis where we have modeled the costs of an entrant facing an existing incumbent, we have in almost every case assumed that the cost functions of the two firms are identical.[8] It would be a straightforward extension of our methodology to allow for competition between firms of different technology type. In many of the situations where differing technologies are important, it is likely that completely different technologies (e.g., wireless as opposed to wireline local access) should also be considered. In addition many of the interesting questions that could be asked involving competition between firms using different vintages of capital are inherently dynamic in nature, and our cost modeling approach largely ignores the dynamic aspect. Thus a full treatment of these issues goes substantially beyond the scope of our present analysis.

10.3   Some Issues Not Addressed in Our Analysis and Suggestions for Further Research

Besides the various improvements in practice that future empirical work using cost proxy models might incorporate, there are a number of new areas that we believe could be productively examined using the engineering process approach. Some of these have already been hinted at in the preceding discussion, and we devote this section to some further thoughts on these possibilities.

As already noted, we do not claim that the LECOM cost function provides the most accurate possible representation of the current forward-looking cost of the local exchange network. In particular, it does not include recent input prices, detailed customer data, geographic data, or the most recent engineering assumptions. For our analysis of the properties of incentive regulation, we believe that these deficiencies are of relatively minor importance, though it would clearly be a useful exercise to replicate many of our results using an alternative proxy cost simulation. There are many other valid empirical questions, however, where an accurate representation of the level of total cost as well as the structure of cost would be important. An example would be an investigation of the issue of "stranded costs."

As the telecommunications industry has evolved in recent years, both underlying technologies and regulatory constraints have changed dramatically. Generally speaking, technological advances have reduced the costs for potential entrants, but substantial entry barriers remain. Regulatory constraints on pricing behavior of incumbent firms have been substantially relaxed as a result of reforms in incentive regulation, and new potentially profitable markets have been opened to incumbent firms. At the same time, however, regulatory barriers to entry have been eliminated in many jurisdictions, and in many cases, new regulations have been adopted that require incumbent firms to make portions of their network available to competitors at wholesale prices. This complicated mix of events has led to allegations by some incumbent carriers that the new regulations deny them the opportunity to recover fully the costs that were incurred in good faith under a prior regulatory regime. This is the issue of stranded cost.

It is possible that proxy model analysis could be used to shed light on the magnitude of these stranded costs. For example, it would be possible to model the technologies, input prices, and even the incentive structure faced by incumbent firms in a prior regulatory regime when the costs were originally incurred. A test of the stranded cost issue could be accomplished by quantifying these costs and then investigating the pricing constraints faced by these same firms under the new regime where entering firms would be using the most recent technologies.

A related question for potentially useful future research concerns the impact of emerging technologies, such as wireless local access, conversion of broadband cable access facilities to allow switched interactive service, and the provision of voice over IP service on the Internet. All these services are, of course, highly substitutable in demand. Thus the evolution of these markets will likely be driven by the costs of the underlying technologies, whether provided separately or in combinations.

Since regulatory or deregulatory policies can significantly affect the evolution of these markets, we believe that proxy models could provide useful guidance to future regulatory decisions. One such useful research effort could extend our analysis of the universal service provision to take account of possible wireless local access as a substitute for wireline access in high-cost areas.

To this point, we have focused exclusively on the ways in which cost proxy models can be utilized in an empirical economic research program. Another area for future research concerns the ways in which traditional economic analysis can be used to improve the accuracy of proxy cost models. There are three areas in which existing proxy models might be improved. First, as previously noted, existing proxy models are generally weak in their ability to accurately model labor inputs and generally in quantifying the operating expenses of firms. Traditional regulation relies on detailed accounting data to record expenses as well as capital investments. Increasingly, proxy models are being considered, for example, in setting cost-based prices at which an incumbent regulated firm might be required to make an essential facility available to competitors. Hence improvements in the treatment of operating expenses could be of substantial value in pursuing these policies by way of proxy models.

A second area of potential refinement is the capability of proxy models to accurately model the costs of firms operating in a competitive environment. Proxy models were originally designed as models of monopoly service providers. Costs were computed under the assumption that a single firm provides service to all of the customers in a given service area. While it is a simple matter to adjust customer density to reflect expected market shares under competition, there are other cost differences between competitive and monopoly firms. For example, the risk-adjusted cost of capital is presumably higher for a competitive firm, and empirical evidence on the magnitude of this effect would be useful in calibrating a model for a competitive firm.

Finally, the dynamic nature of costs should be continually evaluated and refined in the context of proxy model estimates. While existing proxy models are structured as static optimization models, and are likely to remain so for some time, current proxy models attempt to approximate the intertemporal aspect of investment decision making through appropriate choices of certain model inputs. In some cases it may be possible to simulate a dynamic investment program more directly, and to incorporate this program into the modeling process.

Appendix A

A.1 The Natural Monopoly Test (Chapter 5)

In this section we present the translog estimation of the various cost functions used in chapter 5. The values of the estimated parameters are rounded to the second decimal.[1]

A.1.1 Usage as Output (Section 5.4.1)

$\log C(PK, PL, Q)$
$$= 16.96 + 0.44 \log PK + 0.44 \log PL + 0.15 \log Q + 0.11(\log PK)^2$$
$$+ 0.12(\log PL)^2 + 0.02(\log Q)^2 - 0.18 \log PK \log PL$$
$$- 0.01 \log PK \log Q + 0.01 \log Q \log PL \tag{A.1}$$

A.1.2 Access as Output[2]

- Monopoly

$\log C^M(PK, PL, N)$
$$= 18.64 + 0.52 \log PK + 0.31 \log PL - 1.20 \log N + 0.12(\log PK)^2$$
$$+ 0.12(\log PL)^2 + 0.09(\log N)^2 - 0.18 \log PK \log PL$$
$$- 0.01 \log PK \log N + 0.01 \log N \log PL \tag{A.2}$$

- Duopoly

  Uniform entry without accounting for interconnection costs:

$\log C_U^D(PK, PL, N_i)$
$$= 18.64 + 0.52 \log PK + 0.31 \log PL - 1.20 \log N_i + 0.12(\log PK)^2$$
$$+ 0.12(\log PL)^2 + 0.09(\log N_i)^2 - 0.18 \log PK \log PL$$
$$- 0.01 \log PK \log N_i + 0.01 \log N_i \log PL \tag{A.3}$$

Uniform entry with interconnection costs accounted for:

$$\log C_U^D(PK, PL, N_i)$$
$$= 18.64 + 0.52 \log PK + 0.31 \log PL - 1.20 \log N_i + 0.12(\log PK)^2$$
$$+ 0.12(\log PL)^2 + 0.09(\log N_i)^2 - 0.18 \log PK \log PL$$
$$- 0.01 \log PK \log N_i + 0.01 \log N_i \log PL \qquad (A.4)$$

Targeted entry without accounting for interconnection cost:

$$\log C_T^D(PK, L, N_i, A_i)$$
$$= 14.24 + 0.49 \log PK + 0.35 \log PL - 0.78 \log N_i + 0.73 \log A_i$$
$$+ 0.12(\log PK)^2 + 0.12(\log PL)^2 + 0.09(\log N_i)^2 + 0.09(\log A_i)^2$$
$$- 0.18 \log PK \log PL - 0.01 \log PK \log N_i$$
$$+ 0.01 \log PK \log A_i + 0.01 \log N_i \log PL$$
$$- 0.01 \log A_i \log PL - 0.10 \log N_i \log A_i \qquad (A.5)$$

where $A_i \equiv 57.39 \times N_i/(N_i + N_j)$, $\quad i, j = 1, 2$, $\quad i \neq j$.

Targeted entry with interconnection costs accounted for:

$$\log C_T^D(PK, PL, N_i, A_i)$$
$$= 14.24 + 0.49 \log PK + 0.35 \log PL - 0.78 \log N_i + 0.73 \log A_i$$
$$+ 0.12(\log PK)^2 + 0.12(\log PL)^2 + 0.09(\log N_i)^2 + 0.09(\log A_i)^2$$
$$- 0.18 \log PK \log PL - 0.01 \log PK \log N_i + 0.01 \log PK \log A_i$$
$$+ 0.01 \log N_i \log PL - 0.01 \log A_i \log PL - 0.10 \log N_i \log A_i$$
$$\qquad (A.6)$$

where A_i is as defined above.

A.2 Optimal Regulation of a Natural Monopoly (Chapter 6)

Recall from the text that we assumed that the technological efficiency parameter β had a uniform distribution with support (0.5, 1.5). Asymmetric information allows the firm to enjoy some rent, and we have explored empirically the effect of improving the regulator's information by tightening the support of the uniform distribution and also by using the normal distribution instead of the uniform. Table A.1 presents the level of rent for each β and expected social welfare achieved in those experiments. In this table the index 1 refers to our base case, that is, the calculations that make use of the uniform distribution with support (0.5, 1.5). The index 2 refers to a case where the uniform distribution is

Table A.1
Firm's information rent and expected social welfare (10^6 annualized US\$)

β	U_1	U_2	U_3
0.50	10.44	—	10.06
0.60	9.20	—	8.81
0.70	7.99	7.07	7.59
0.80	6.83	5.81	6.39
0.90	5.72	4.59	5.22
1.00	4.66	3.40	4.09
1.10	3.64	2.23	3.01
1.20	2.66	1.10	2.00
1.30	1.73	0.00	1.09
1.40	0.85	—	0.37
1.50	0.00	—	0.00
$E_\beta W_1 = 186.19$			
$E_\beta W_2 = 186.77$			
$E_\beta W_3 = 186.27$			

still used but its support tightened to $(0.7, 1.3)$, and the index 3 corresponds to a case where the normal distribution with support $(0.5, 1.5)$ is used.

A.3   Universal Service (Chapter 8)

In this section we give the levels of social welfare corresponding to the competitive scenarios in our base case of chapter 8 and the translog estimation of the cost functions used.[3] To help the reader in the examination of these figures, we provide in table A.2 the shorthand designation and a brief description of each scenario considered in the chapter.

Cost function of an incumbent serving the rural area while facing entry in the urban area:

$$\log C_1^{UT} (PK, PL, Q_{11}, Q_{21})$$

$$= 16.35 + 0.47 \log PK + 0.42 \log PL - 0.01 \log Q_{11} + 0.01 \log Q_{21}$$
$$+ 0.12(\log PK)^2 + 0.12(\log PL)^2 + 0.01(\log Q_{11})^2 + 0.02(\log Q_{21})^2$$
$$- 0.018 \log PK \log PL - 0.002 \log PK \log Q_{11}$$
$$- 0.001 \log PK \log Q_{21} + 0.001 \log Q_{11} \log PL$$
$$+ 0.002 \log Q_{21} \log PL - 0.002 \log Q_{11} \log Q_{21}$$

Table A.2
Competitive scenarios considered

Scenario	Description
UT_{mc}^{ps}	Urban-targeted entry, MC pricing, deficit financed with PS
UT_{ac}^{ps}	Urban-targeted entry, AC pricing, USO, deficit financed with PS
UT_{ac}^{τ}	Urban-targeted entry, taxation of urban to finance USO
$\underline{UT}_{ac}^{ps}$	Scenario UT_{ac}^{ps} but with most efficient technology entrant
TC_{mc}^{ps}	Territory-constrained entry, MC pricing, deficit financed with PS
TC_{ac}	Territory-constrained entry, AC pricing
$TCPC$	Territory-constrained entry, (incomplete information) price-cap regulation

Note: PS = public subsidies; USO = universal service obligation.

Table A.3
Competitive solutions relying on public subsidies: Expected social welfare in US$100 M

Value of λ	$W^{UT_{mc}^{ps}}$	$W^{TC_{mc}^{ps}}$	$W^{UT_{ac}^{ps}}$	$W^{\underline{UT}_{ac}^{ps}}$
0.0	1.40	1.40	1.40	1.41
0.1	1.39	1.38	1.39	1.41
0.2	1.37	1.36	1.38	1.40
0.3	1.35	1.34	1.38	1.39
0.4	1.33	1.32	1.37	1.38
0.5	1.31	1.31	1.36	1.37
0.6	1.29	1.29	1.36	1.36
0.7	1.27	1.27	1.35	1.36
0.8	1.25	1.25	1.34	1.35
0.9	1.24	1.23	1.34	1.34
1.0	1.22	1.21	1.33	1.33
1.1	1.20	1.19	1.32	1.32
1.2	1.18	1.17	1.31	1.31
1.3	1.16	1.15	1.31	1.30
1.4	1.14	1.13	1.30	1.30
1.5	1.12	1.11	1.29	1.29
1.6	1.10	1.09	1.29	1.28
1.7	1.09	1.07	1.28	1.27
1.8	1.07	1.05	1.27	1.26
1.9	1.05	1.04	1.26	1.25
2.0	1.03	1.02	1.26	1.24

Table A.4
Competitive solutions relying on cross-subsidies: Expected social welfare in US$100 M

$W^{TC_{ac}}$	W^{TCPC}
1.39	1.38

Table A.5
Competitive solution relying on taxation: Expected social welfare in US$100 M

Value of δ	$W^{UT^\tau_{ac}}$
0.5	1.37
0.6	1.38
0.7	1.38
0.8	1.39
0.9	1.39
1.0	1.39

Cost function of an entrant serving half of the urban area only:

$$\log C_2^{UT}(PK, PL, Q_{12})$$
$$= 15.50 + 0.45 \log PK + 0.43 \log PL + 0.05 \log Q_{12} + 0.12(\log PK)^2$$
$$+ 0.12(\log PL)^2 + 0.03(\log Q_{12})^2 - 0.18 \log PK \log PL$$
$$- 0.01 \log PK \log Q_{12} + 0.004 \log Q_{12} \log PL$$

Cost function of an entrant ($j = 2$) and an incumbent ($j = 1$) serving half of both the urban and the rural areas:

$$\log C_j^{TC}(PK, PL, Q_{1j}, Q_{2j})$$
$$= 16.03 + 0.46 \log PK + 0.42 \log PL - 0.02 \log Q_{1j} + 0.02 \log Q_{2j}$$
$$+ 0.12(\log PK)^2 + 0.12(\log PL)^2 + 0.01(\log Q_{1j})^2 + 0.02(\log Q_{2j})^2$$
$$- 0.18 \log PK \log PL + 0.01 \log PK \log Q_{1j}$$
$$- 0.01 \log PK \log Q_{2j} - 0.003 \log Q_{1j} \log PL$$
$$+ 0.01 \log Q_{2j} \log PL + 0.001 \log Q_{1j} \log Q_{2j}$$

A.4 Strategic Cross-subsidies and Vertical Integration (Chapter 9)

In this section we present in tables A.6 through A.12 empirical results that complement the discussion in chapter 9, and the quadratic estimations of the cost functions used in that chapter.

Table A.6
Incumbent per unit cost advantage under high-powered regulation and low effort, $\Delta/q_1 = (C_E - \hat{C}_I)/q_1$

	$q_2 = 5K$	10K	15K	20K	25K	30K	35K	40K	45K	50K
$q_1 = 5K$	286.05	373.97	412.48	432.20	443.30	450.17	454.97	458.91	462.73	466.87
10K	78.46	116.62	137.36	149.84	157.97	163.67	168.02	171.66	175.00	178.31
15K	30.70	50.23	62.02	69.70	75.04	79.00	82.15	84.87	87.39	89.88
20K	13.07	24.12	31.15	35.95	39.42	42.09	44.29	46.24	48.10	49.96
25K	4.93	11.62	15.95	18.97	21.22	22.99	24.50	25.89	27.24	28.64
30K	0.62	4.89	7.61	9.52	10.96	12.12	13.14	14.11	15.10	16.14
35K	-1.88	0.99	2.72	3.92	4.81	5.55	6.23	6.90	7.61	8.40
40K	-3.43	-1.40	-0.28	0.45	0.99	1.44	1.87	2.33	2.85	3.45
45K	-4.45	-2.91	-2.18	-1.75	-1.45	1.19	-0.93	-0.62	-0.24	0.22
50K	-5.14	-3.89	-3.40	-3.16	-3.01	-2.88	-2.73	-2.53	-2.53	-1.89

Note: Units are in annualized dollars per unswitched access line.

Table A.7
Incumbent per unit cost advantage under high-powered regulation and high effort, $\Delta/q_1 = (C_E - \hat{C}_I)/q_1$

	$q_2 = 5K$	10K	15K	20K	25K	30K	35K	40K	45K	50K
$q_1 = 5K$	168.31	216.78	235.10	242.44	245.16	245.98	246.22	246.63	247.63	249.52
10K	32.22	48.96	56.46	59.80	61.15	61.61	61.78	61.99	62.46	63.35
15K	2.81	9.08	11.78	12.67	12.68	12.32	11.88	11.56	11.47	11.69
20K	-7.88	-5.73	-5.20	-5.45	-6.30	-7.18	-8.02	-8.71	-9.17	-9.36
25K	-13.02	-12.61	-13.09	-14.04	-15.19	-16.35	-17.42	-18.32	-19.02	-19.47
30K	-16.00	-16.32	-17.24	-18.48	-19.80	-21.10	-22.28	-23.30	-24.13	-24.74
35K	-18.00	-18.55	-19.63	-20.96	-22.35	-23.69	-24.92	-26.00	-26.89	-27.59
40K	-19.50	-20.01	-21.10	-22.43	-23.81	-25.15	-26.37	-27.46	-28.39	-29.14
45K	-20.71	-21.05	-22.06	-23.33	-24.66	-25.96	-27.16	-28.23	-29.16	-29.93
50K	-21.74	-21.83	-22.71	-23.89	-25.15	-26.39	-27.55	-28.59	-29.51	-30.28

Note: Units are in annualized dollars per unswitched access line.

Table A.8
Incumbent per unit cost advantage under medium-powered regulation and high effort, $\Delta/q_1 = (C_E - \hat{C}_I)/q_1$

	$q_2 = 5K$	10K	15K	20K	25K	30K	35K	40K	45K	50K
$q_1 = 5K$	191.82	254.5	279.65	290.89	296.07	298.53	299.94	301.21	302.89	305.30
10K	44.68	71.73	85.37	92.78	97.00	99.57	101.34	102.79	104.26	105.94
15K	13.35	27.17	34.90	39.44	42.21	44.01	45.30	46.38	47.45	48.64
20K	2.73	10.54	15.12	17.89	19.64	20.79	21.64	22.38	23.12	23.96
25K	-1.79	2.95	5.73	7.42	8.47	9.16	9.69	10.15	10.65	11.24
30K	-4.05	-0.98	0.73	1.73	2.33	2.70	2.98	3.25	3.56	3.97
35K	-5.35	-3.23	-2.16	-1.60	-1.31	-1.16	-1.05	-0.92	-0.74	-0.46
40K	-6.21	-4.64	-3.96	-3.68	-3.59	-3.58	-3.59	-3.56	-3.47	-3.29
45K	-6.87	-5.59	-5.16	-5.05	-5.08	-5.17	-5.26	-5.30	-5.28	-5.16
50K	-7.44	-6.30	-6.00	-5.99	-6.10	-6.25	-6.39	-6.48	-6.50	-6.43

Note: Units are in annualized dollars per unswitched access line.

Table A.9
Incumbent per unit cost advantage under low-powered regulation and high effort, $\Delta/q_1 = (C_E - \hat{C}_1)/q_1$

	$q_2 = 5K$	10K	15K	20K	25K	30K	35K	40K	45K	50K
$q_1 = 5K$	186.13	316.39	305.85	324.88	335.89	343.00	348.29	352.87	357.44	362.44
10K	38.43	75.55	95.94	108.37	116.59	122.47	127.07	131.01	134.67	138.33
15K	10.52	30.03	42.04	50.02	55.67	59.95	63.43	66.47	69.31	72.12
20K	2.75	14.01	21.44	26.65	30.53	33.59	36.16	38.47	40.66	42.85
25K	0.34	7.24	11.99	15.46	18.13	20.32	22.21	23.96	25.66	27.39
30K	-0.38	4.03	7.14	9.47	11.33	12.89	14.29	15.62	16.95	18.33
35K	-0.56	2.35	4.42	6.00	7.29	8.41	9.46	10.48	11.52	12.63
40K	-0.61	1.37	2.76	3.84	4.74	5.55	6.33	7.12	7.95	8.86
45K	-0.69	0.71	1.65	2.39	3.02	3.61	4.19	4.81	5.49	6.25
50K	-0.84	0.18	0.83	1.34	1.78	2.21	2.66	3.16	3.72	4.36

Note: Units are in annualized dollars per unswitched access line.

Table A.10
Incumbent per unit cost advantage under medium-powered regulation and low effort, $\Delta/q_1 = (C_E - \hat{C}_1)/q_1$

	$q_2 = 5K$	10K	15K	20K	25K	30K	35K	40K	45K	50K
$q_1 = 5K$	290.23	380.24	419.77	440.07	451.55	458.68	463.67	467.76	471.70	475.95
10K	81.37	121.17	142.92	156.08	164.68	170.72	175.34	179.18	182.68	186.13
15K	33.47	54.13	66.75	75.05	80.86	85.18	88.63	91.59	94.31	96.96
20K	16.00	27.78	34.45	40.77	44.67	47.69	50.18	52.38	54.45	56.49
25K	8.08	15.20	20.02	23.48	26.09	28.19	29.97	31.60	33.16	34.74
30K	4.00	8.48	11.56	13.82	15.57	17.02	18.29	19.49	20.67	21.90
35K	1.69	4.61	6.59	8.07	9.24	10.23	11.13	12.01	12.92	13.88
40K	0.30	2.25	3.54	4.50	5.26	5.94	6.58	7.23	7.92	8.69
45K	-0.58	0.77	1.60	2.21	2.71	3.16	3.62	4.10	4.64	5.26
50K	-1.17	-0.19	0.35	0.73	1.05	1.35	1.67	2.04	2.47	2.98

Note: Units are in annualized dollars per unswitched access line.

Table A.11
Incumbent per unit cost advantage under low-powered regulation and low effort, $\Delta/q_1 = (C_E - \hat{C}_I)/q_1$

	$q_2 = 5K$	10K	15K	20K	25K	30K	35K	40K	45K	50K
$q_1 = 5K$	289.15	383.20	424.93	446.65	459.18	467.11	472.75	477.40	481.81	486.50
10K	80.19	122.03	145.15	159.32	168.70	175.39	180.55	184.86	188.78	192.59
15K	33.05	54.80	68.29	77.28	83.67	88.47	92.36	95.70	98.77	101.74
20K	16.22	28.59	36.83	42.64	46.96	50.36	53.19	55.70	58.05	60.36
25K	8.78	16.20	21.39	25.19	28.13	30.52	32.58	34.45	36.25	38.06
30K	5.03	9.65	12.97	15.48	17.48	19.15	20.65	22.05	23.44	24.86
35K	2.98	5.90	8.04	9.70	11.06	12.24	13.32	14.38	15.45	16.58
40K	1.77	3.64	5.02	6.11	7.03	7.86	8.65	9.45	10.29	11.20
45K	1.02	2.22	3.10	3.81	4.43	5.01	5.59	6.20	6.87	7.62
50K	0.52	1.29	1.85	2.30	2.72	3.13	3.56	4.04	4.59	5.21

Note: Units are in annualized dollars per unswitched access line.

Table A.12
Average cost

	$q_2 = 5K$	10K	15K	20K	25K	30K	35K	40K	45K	50K
$q_1 = 5K$	547.78	437.9	382.87	349.79	327.68	311.84	299.91	290.60	283.12	276.97
10K	471.34	407.82	369.65	344.14	325.87	312.13	301.40	292.79	285.71	279.78
15K	432.29	389.12	360.28	339.63	324.11	311.99	302.27	294.28	287.59	281.91
20K	408.2	376.10	353.12	335.84	322.36	311.55	302.67	295.25	288.94	283.50
25K	391.59	366.32	347.33	332.52	320.64	310.89	302.73	295.81	289.85	284.66
30K	379.25	358.58	342.46	329.54	318.93	310.06	302.53	296.06	290.42	285.47
35K	369.59	352.19	338.24	326.79	317.23	309.11	302.12	296.05	290.71	285.98
40K	361.70	346.75	334.48	324.23	315.53	308.05	301.55	295.84	290.78	286.26
45K	355.06	342.00	331.08	321.81	313.85	306.92	300.84	295.46	290.65	286.33
50K	349.33	337.76	327.94	319.50	312.16	305.72	300.02	294.93	290.36	286.23

Note: Units are in annualized dollars per unswitched access line.

Total cost of a firm providing basic switched service (Q_2) and enhanced service (Q_1):

$\tilde{C}(PK, PL, Q_1, Q_2)$

$= 171091.81 + 1454911.26(PK) + 1104000.39(PL) + 67750298.35(Q_1)$
$+ 31289871.04(Q_2) - 2505.49(PK)^2 + 72057.43(PL)^2 - 0.0003(Q_1)^2$
$- 0.00003(Q_2)^2 - 27128.04(PK)(PL) + 132.28(PK)(Q_1) + 92.70(PK)(Q_2)$
$+ 124.23(PL)(Q_1) + 95.50(PL)(Q_2) - 0.0002(Q_1)(Q_2)$

Stand-alone cost function of enhanced service:

$\widetilde{SAC}_1(PK, PL, Q_1)$

$= 381439.96 + 1522860.60(PK) + 1250412.60(PL) + 26.21(Q_1)$
$- 27484.81(PK)^2 - 22795.98(PL)^2 + 0.0003(Q_1)^2$
$+ 32344.01(PK)(PL) + 113.62(PK)(Q_1) + 102.19(PL)(Q_1)$

Stand-alone cost of basic switched service:

$\widetilde{SAC}_2(PK, PL, Q_2)$

$= 654277.80 + 386698.07(PK) + 1360048.55(PL) + 18.22(Q_2)$
$+ 650541.14(PK)^2 + 137066.82(PL)^2 + 0.0001(Q_2)^2$
$- 446276.91(PK)(PL) + 91.84(PK)(Q_2) + 93.91(PL)(Q_2)$

A.5   Preparation of LECOM Cost Data

In this section we describe how to use LECOM to obtain the cost data of the simulations appearing in the text. The relevant LECOM computer files, data files, and utility programs are supplied on the CD provided with this book under the LECOM directory. It is assumed at this point that the reader has some familiarity with the structure of LECOM after reading chapter 2. While this section of the appendix is intended to provide a self-contained user guide on the operation of LECOM, the reader should, if possible, consult the more extensive documentation available in Gabel and Kennet (1991).

All of the LECOM cost computations reported in this text make use of the freely available DOS version of LECOM, which can be run in any DOS or Windows environment. All of the LECOM programs and support files are contained in the program directory. The user editable input files and certain utility programs are contained in the data directory. It is recommended that the user create a working directory on the user's

Table A.13
A sample populatn.dat file

600			
40	40		
16	16	24	24
8	8	32	32
18,000	54,000	36,000	

hard drive, which we assume for illustrative purposes has been named "C:\Lecom." All of the files from the program and data directories on the CD should be copied into this working directory.

LECOM requires three input files. The file "gaugedst.dat" specifies certain technical information relating copper gauge and loop distance, and we will ignore it for the remainder of this discussion. The file "populatn.dat" contains the dimensions of the representative city. A sample population file is illustrated in table A.13.

The first row specifies the number of target access lines to be placed in each serving area. The next row gives the coordinates of the northeast corner of the region under study, measured in thousands of feet from the southwest corner, which is assumed to be at the origin. The next two rows give the southwest and northeast coordinates of the central business district and the mixed commercial and residential district, respectively. The last row gives the line counts to be placed in the central, mixed, and residential districts, respectively.

The file "dvariabl.dat" specifies the remaining user inputs, which for our purposes contain the input data for usage demands per access line in each city district and input values for the price of capital and price of labor. Various other input prices and algorithm control parameters are also specified in this file. A representative dvariabl.dat file is illustrated in table A.14.

LECOM consists of three executable programs. The first program "Cityinit.exe" is used to create a set of serving areas based on the data in the populatn.dat file. This program needs to be executed only once unless the underlying populatn.dat file is modified. As an output, cityinit writes a file called "rectangl.dat" that defines the upper-right and lower-left boundaries of each serving area. If desired, this file can be created independently of the cityinit program and used in subsequent calculations, as long as the data are consistent with the populatn.dat file.

Table A.14
A sample dvariabl.dat file

0.31300000000	* ac211 = carrying charge for land
0.32690000000	* ac212 = carrying charge for buildings
0.30140000000	* ac22157 = carrying charge for circuit
0.37530000000	* access = carrying charge for analog switches
0.28080000000	* ac244 = carrying charge for conduit
0.28120000000	* ac2422 = carrying charge for underground cable
0.31660000000	* ac2423 = carrying charge for buried cable
0.31660000000	* ac815 = carrying charge for underground fiber
0.34310000000	* ac845 = carrying charge for buried fiber
0.5000	* ccs_per_res_line = ccs per residential customer
0.5000	* ccs_per_med_line = ccs per medium density customer
0.5000	* ccs_per_bus_line = ccs per business customer
0.90000000000	* perund_bus = fraction of cable underground, business
0.50000000000	* perund_med = fraction of cable underground, mixed
0.35000000000	* perund_res = fraction of cable underground, residential
0.068	* perpl[1] = fraction private lines for residential
0.075	* perpl[2] = fraction private lines for mixed customers
0.11	* perpl[3] = fraction private lines for business
0.45000000000	* plcost = cost markup fraction for private lines
0.94	* tollper = percentage toll traffic
0.4	* pltollper = private line percentage toll traffic
1.68244500000	* f1526 = fixed investment per foot for UG 26 gauge cable
1.91939600000	* f1524 = fixed investment per foot for UG 24 gauge cable
1.74269200000	* f1522 = fixed investment per foot for UG 22 gauge cable
2.57593700000	* f1519 = fixed investment per foot for UG 19 gauge cable
2.17225000000	* f4526 = fixed investment per foot for buried 26 gauge cable
2.41109800000	* f4524 = fixed investment per foot for buried 24 gauge cable
2.23356200000	* f4522 = fixed investment per foot for buried 24 gauge cable
3.06785100000	* f4519 = fixed investment per foot for buried 19 gauge cable
0.00752700000	* m1526 = marginal cost per foot for UG 26 gauge cable
0.00966400000	* m1524 = marginal cost per foot for UG 24 gauge cable
0.01343800000	* m1522 = marginal cost per foot for UG 22 gauge cable
0.01305500000	* m1519 = marginal cost per foot for UG 19 gauge cable
0.00990300000	* m4526 = marginal cost per foot for buried 26 gauge cable
0.01204000000	* m4524 = marginal cost per foot for buried 24 gauge cable
0.01581200000	* m4522 = marginal cost per foot for buried 22 gauge cable
0.01543500000	* m4519 = marginal cost per foot for buried 19 gauge cable
1.00000000000	* misc15 = miscellaneous investment for UG copper
1.00000000000	* misc45 = miscellaneous investment for buried copper
300000.000000	* dms100cap = calling capacity of a DMS100 digital switch

(continued)

Table A.14
(*Continued*)

38000.0000000	* dms10cap = calling capacity of a DMS10 digital switch
0.90000000000	* switchutil = utilization of switch capacity
1.00000000000	* looputil = utilization of loop line capacity
0.60000000000	* blockwidth = width of a city block in kilofeet
0.07000000000	* build22157 = loading factor for building, applied to circuit
0.07000000000	* build22177 = loading factor for building, applied to switch
0.00500000000	* land22157 = loading factor for land, applied to circuit
0.00500000000	* land22177 = loading factor for land, applied to switch
53.0000000000	* mdfcost = main distribution frame cost per customer
1.60000000000	* intraht = holding time for intraoffice call
1.60000000000	* interexcht = holding time for interoffice call
1.80000000000	* tollht = holding time for toll call
0.001000000	* ftol = function tolerance for downhill simplex routine
500	* ITMAX = maximum number of AMOEBA iterations
1	* number_of_restarts for AMOEBA when minimum is found
1.03592000000	* droptpi = drop wire tpi 1985 to 1990
1.04484300000	* tpiund80 = tpi underground cable 1990/1985
1.03592000000	* tpibur80 = tpi buried cable 1990/1985
1.11913400000	* tpicond80 = tpi conduit cable 1990/1985
0.00572000000	* condpf = 1985 conduit cost per pair foot of copper cable
0.70645160000	* dig100tp = tpi DMS100 1990/1985
0.57783640000	* dig10tp = tpi DMS10 cable 1990/1985
21.3700000000	* tandem = 1990 tandem investment per ccs
1.07960700000	* tpiosp80 = tpi outside plant 1990/1982
1.18198000000	* tpi5780 = tpi circuit plant 1990/1982
4.60000000000	* loadc = 1990 load coil investment
1.50000000000	* fppercust = feeder pairs per customer
1.05000000000	* fpslcpercust = feeder pairs per SLC customer
2.00000000000	* dppercust = distribution pairs per customer
1.57546000000	* ufibfix = fixed cost of underground fiber
0.18781060000	* ufibmc = per foot cost of underground fiber
2.77804500000	* bfibfix = fixed cost of buried fiber
0.19762650000	* bfibmc = per foot cot of buried fiber
30.0000000000	* fcond = cost per foot of conduit (total investment)
5	* max_remotes attachable to DMS100
14260.0000000	* remotecap = ccs capacity of remote switches
1.00000000000	* remotetpi = 1990/1990 price index for remote switches
1.00000000000	* TPIOSP90 = price index for 1990/1990 outside plant
2	* slc_mode: 1 = unconcentrated, 2 = concentrated
1.00000000000	* tpi5790 = price index for circuit 1990/1990
0.500000	* price of labor

Table A.14
(*Continued*)

0.500000	* price of capital
1.000000	* price of central office material
1.000000	* price of outside plant
1.00000000000	* tpiundf90 = 1990/1990 tpi for underground fiber
1.00000000000	* tpiburf90 = 1990/1990 tpi for buried fiber
1.00000000000	* tpicond90 = 1990/1990 tpi for conduit
0.79166666667	* tutil = t-carrier utilization factor
1.10000000000	* cbd_factor = multiplier for land in CBD
1.00000000000	* meddens_factor = multiplier for land in mixed district
0.90000000000	* lowdens_factor = multiplier for land in residential district
0	* min_DMS10
2	* max_DMS10

After the file rectangl.dat file has been created, the file "dxinit.exe" is run in order to compute copper to fiber crossover values. Finally, the main LECOM program, called "Digital.exe" is run to compute loop investments while optimizing over the number and location of switching machines as described in Chapter 2. The program Digital.exe should always be run with command line options by calling "Digital -f -5." These options tell the program to write its outputs to a file called "digital.oda" that contains all of the necessary outputs for subsequent data analysis. A representative output file is illustrated in table A.15.

In order to automate the process of running large numbers of LECOM simulations in order to generate data for the estimation of cost functions, several utility programs have been provided. The programs "Setpop.exe" and "Setinput.exe" allow the user to set the parameters in the populatn.dat file and the output and price variables in the dvariabl.dat file, respectively. The syntax of each program can be determined by typing the name of the program without arguments as in the following example:

```
C:\Lecom\setinput

Error in command line parameters: 1

Correct syntax is

SETINPUT [ccs res] [ccs med] [ccs bus] [PK] [PL] [P COmat]
[P OSmat]
```

Table A.15
A sample digital.oda file

9066863.79	total annual cost
5	total number of switches
0	number of dms10 switches
4	number of remote switches
2705435.20	annual cost of distribution plant
2644365.83	annual cost of feeder plant
2460468.72	annual cost of switching plant
378012.14	annual cost of interoffice plant
878581.9012	annual cost of main distribution frame
186	number of serving areas
600	target lines per serving area
581	actual lines per serving area
18000	number of business lines
54016	number of mixed density lines
35968	number of residential lines
8477	number of private lines
0.4500	private line cost markup
0.400000	private line toll percentage
0.110000	business private line percentage
0.075000	mixed density private line percentage
0.068000	residential private line percentage
29715.6407	intraoffice message volume
4800.8416	exchange interoffice message volume
10779.9224	toll message volume
95090.0501	intraoffice ccs
15362.6933	exchange interoffice ccs
38807.7206	toll ccs
0.260000	toll percentage
1.500000	business ccs per line
1.500000	mixed density ccs per line
1.500000	residential ccs per line
2455.8235	average loop length
184.8236	length of slc-96
1.0000	price of labor
0.5000	price of capital
1.0000	price of central office materials
1.0000	price of outside plant materials
24.0000 24.0000 16.0000 16.0000	business district coordinates
32.0000 32.0000 8.0000 8.0000	mixed density district coordinates
40.0000 40.0000	city upper right coordinates
22.0745 20.0628 33.3916 26.7297 13.6222 37.9972	switch locations
38.6403 3.7448 29.4541 37.5476	switch locations

Batch files have also been written to set appropriate inputs and run the relevant LECOM programs in order to generate the data sets used in each chapter's analysis. For example, in order to duplicate the data used in chapters 6 and 7, the user should proceed as follows: First make sure that the files pop_Ch6.dat and dvar_Ch6.dat are located in the data directory. Then copy the batch program "run_Ch6.bat" into the working directory, C:\Lecom, and run it by typing the DOS command "C:\Lecom\run_ch6.bat" or by using the Windows "Run" command to execute this file. After the program has completed operation, a set of output files will be located in the directory "C:\Lecom\output." In order to conveniently transfer these files into an Excel spreadsheet for further analysis, the Excel Macro GetLecomData, which is contained in the workbook "data.xls," may be used.

Once the data have been converted to a spreadsheet format, they can be further processed in a variety of ways and used in any standard econometrics package. Since the computations that underlie chapters 5 through 9 were done using the program Mathematica, we have chosen to read the data directly into a Mathematica notebook and use the built-in regression routine to fit a translog cost function. The data and cost functions computed for chapters 5 through 9 are contained in the notebook titled "LECOM_data.nb."

A.6 A Guide to the Mathematica Analysis

A separate Mathematica notebook for each chapter is included in the CD provided with the book to document the analysis used in chapters 5 through 9. These notebooks, however, make no attempt to explain the commands contained in them. Moreover, since the authors are not expert Mathematica programmers, the programming logic contained in these notebooks represents by no means the most efficient method of obtaining our desired results. Mathematica version 3.0 or higher is required in order to make use of the notebooks.

Each notebook has been designed to run on a stand-alone basis in order to perform the necessary analytical computations and derive the results used in the empirical sections of the chapters. For each chapter the interested reader should first evaluate the group of cells labeled "Initialization" which defines all of the relevant functions and constants used in the "Results" sections. It is recommended that only one chapter at a time be evaluated in each Mathematica session, since the definitions and names of functions may differ slightly from one chapter to another. Since the Mathematica kernel "remembers" all definitions until they are explicitly cleared, unintended conflicts may arise if two or more chapters are evaluated in a single session.[4] Each initialization section contains the definitions of all of the functions used in our analysis: the cost function, demand functions, disutility of effort function, and the regulator's probability density function over the type of firm. Based on these functions, all of the analytical results described in chapter 4 and in the theoretical sections of chapters 5 through 9 can be given an explicit representation, and in most cases solved. For the purpose of illustration we consider here the case of optimal (LT) regulation.

Recall from section 6.2 the statement of the regulator's problem, given in equations (6.2) through (6.4). Solving (6.3) and (6.4) for the firm's rent, and substituting into equation (6.2), yields the reduced form regulatory problem given in equation (6.5) and repeated as

$$\max_{q(\cdot),e(\cdot)} \int_{\underline{\beta}}^{\bar{\beta}} \left\{ V(q(\beta)) - (1+\lambda)\left[C(\beta,e(\beta),q(\beta)) + \psi(e(\beta))\right] \right.$$
$$\left. + \lambda \frac{F(\beta)}{f(\beta)} \psi'(e(\beta)) \frac{\partial C(\beta,e(\beta),q(\beta))/\partial\beta}{\partial C(\beta,e(\beta),q(\beta))/\partial e} \right\} f(\beta)\, d\beta. \quad \text{(A.7)}$$

In Mathematica notation the integrand to equation (A.7) is given as

LTIntegrand [q_,e_,b_] := (V[q]−(1+lambda)*(Cost[q,e,b]+psi[e])+
  lambda*(F[b]/f[b])*psi'[e]*dcb[q,e,b]/dce[q,e,b]);

In the expression above, the functions dcb and dce represent the derivatives of cost with respect to β and e, respectively, and the other terms are exactly as defined in chapter 6. The functions q(.) and e(.) that solve the regulator's problem (A.7) are therefore given by the Mathematica functions LTQ[b_] and LTE[b_] which are solved for using the code

LT[b_] := LT[b] = FindRoot[Evaluate[{D[LTIntegrand [q,e,b1],q]==0,
  D[LTIntegrand [q,e,b1],e]==0}/.b1 → b],
  {q,highq},{e,lowe}];

LTQ[b_] := q /.LT[b];
LTE[b_] := e /.LT[b];

The expression above directly solves the first-order conditions found by differentiating social welfare with respect to q and e, respectively, for each value of b. The firm's rent is then determined by integrating equation (6.4) using the optimal values of q and e for each value of b:

LTR[b_] := LTR[b] = NIntegrate[−psi'[LTE[b1]]*
   dcb[LTQ[b1],LTE[b1],b1]/dce[LTQ[b1],LTE[b1],b1],
   {b1,b,highb},PrecisionGoal → 3];

Consumers' welfare is solved using equation (6.1) and the fact that it is equal to social welfare minus the firm's rent, which gives the following Mathematica expressions:

CW[q_,e_,b_,U_] := V[q] − (1+lambda)*(U+psi[e]+Cost[q,e,b])

LTCW[b_] := CW[LTQ[b],LTE[b],b,LTR[b]];

LTSW[b_] := LTCW[b] + LTR[b]

A.7 Contents of the CDRom

Included with this volume is a CD containing programs and data that will allow the reader to verify virtually all of the reported results. The reader is encouraged to experiment with these files by choosing alternative input assumptions. The files on the CD are organized in four directories as follows:

LECOM
   Data
   Programs
   Results
Mathematica
   Chapter 5
   Chapter 6
   Chapter 7
   Chapter 8
   Chapter 9
   LECOM_data

Install HCPM: A program to install the most recent available version of HCPM along with source code and documentation.

Install Mathreader: A free program from Wolfram Research Inc. that allows one to read the Mathematica notebook.

Appendix B

In this appendix we present some recent work on alternative proxy models.

B.1 The Hybrid Cost Proxy Model (HCPM)

In this book we have demonstrated that a particular cost proxy model, LECOM, can be used as an empirical tool in the investigation of telecommunications policy. LECOM became our tool of choice also because it does not rely on proprietary company data for its operation and because it has the novel feature of a fully forward-looking cost function that optimizes the location of switching centers in the local exchange network. Following the divestiture of the local operating companies from AT&T in 1984, a number of other engineering process models of telecommunications were developed by both industry sources and by regulatory bodies. These models have become increasingly sophisticated in their modeling techniques, and in many respects the current generation of cost models are capable of providing a significantly more detailed and accurate representation of cost than LECOM. In this section we briefly review the development of cost proxy models other than LECOM, and we describe in some detail the hybrid cost proxy model (HCPM), which was selected by the FCC in 1998 for use in computing universal service support in high-cost areas served by non-rural companies in the United States.[1] In section B.2 we describe the application of the HCPM outside of the United States.

The proxy models such as the HCPM were developed for explicit regulatory policy objectives, primarily as tools for estimating the costs of universal service support to high-cost areas, setting interconnection prices and purchasing unbundled network elements, and providing regulators with an independent estimate of the forward-looking cost of local telecommunications services, among other things. The analysis of certain issues in incentive regulation in earlier chapters provides an interesting counterpoint to these intended applications, for as this analysis has stressed the regulator's knowledge of the cost function is never perfect. We have formalized the imperfect information of the regulator by separating two crucial input parameters that are outside of the regulator's control. In our standard representation of cost as a function $C(q, \beta, e)$, the variable β represents the technology type of the firm, about which the regulator knows only the probability distribution function. The variable e represents the level of effort of the firm to engage in cost minimization, which is chosen by the firm in response to the form of incentive contract offered by the regulator.

While the availability of cost proxy models offers an important new tool to regulators in the design of pricing and entry rules, the theory of incentive regulation, which our earlier chapters seek to empirically test, suggests that there are limitations in the power of this tool. A proper application of cost proxy models by regulators should be made with full knowledge of these limitations. At the same time, however, the ever-increasing accuracy of proxy models can, and we believe should, be used to obtain new theoretical insights of interest to telecommunications policy makers. It is our hope that the analysis of this book can serve as a contribution to both the theory of regulation and the application of regulatory theory to the actual market.

The HCPM consists of several independent modules—computer programs that read relevant input data, perform the calculations relevant to a portion of the local network, and print output reports for use in succeeding modules. The version of HCPM adopted by the FCC in its universal service proceeding consists of three such modules: a clustering algorithm that groups customer locations into neighborhood serving areas, a cluster interface module that computes the area and line density of each cluster and assigns individual locations to cells in a grid structure, and a loop design module that uses network design algorithms to connect the grid cells in each serving area to a central serving area interface and subsequently connect each serving area interface to the central office switch. The HCPM also includes a module that can be used to compute the cost of switching and interoffice transport. The loop design and interoffice modules report as outputs both total investment in network facilities and an estimate of annual expenses associated with those facilities.

Since the primary intended use of forward-looking cost proxy models in the United States has been to estimate the cost of providing universal service support, most of the development effort for such models in that country has been in the design of distribution and feeder portions of the local exchange network. In this section we review several modeling approaches to this portion of the local network in some detail in addition to describing the HCPM approach. In many countries other than the United States, cost proxy models have been developed with the intention of providing estimates of the cost of interconnection among networks. Accordingly the switching and interoffice portions of the network have received more attention in these models, notably in the German intercity cost model prepared for the German Regulatory Authority for Telecommunications and Posts.[2] The Japanese Ministry of Posts and Telecommunications (MPT) has also sponsored a Long-Run Incremental Cost model of the local and intercity telecommunications networks in Japan.[3]

One of the first engineering process models was developed by Mitchell (1990) for the Rand Corporation under contract with GTE of California and Pacific Bell Telephone Company. This model was a significant departure from a series of earlier econometric studies that sought to estimate the degree of scale economies in the local telephone industry following the divestiture of AT&T. The Rand model developed simple representations of the major components of the local network—loop, switching, and interoffice links—and attempted to calibrate these functions using data supplied by the client companies. The next significant advance in proxy cost modeling was the development of LECOM. LECOM differed significantly from the Rand model by including specific computer algorithms and network optimization routines in the design of the network. Nevertheless, by current standards, both the Rand model and LECOM are relatively crude in certain aspects of their modeling methods.

Recall from chapter 2 the approach that LECOM takes to defining local serving areas.[4] A LECOM city consists of three regions of varying population density: a central business district, a mixed commercial and residential district, and a residential or rural district. Serving areas in LECOM always have a uniform population distribution within them, and they are always rectangular in shape. Moreover, while the size of the serving area, measured as the number of access lines, is specified as a user input, the shape of the area is by default determined by an algorithm that seeks to subdivide each of the city areas into an appropriate number of neighborhoods.

Other cost proxy models have adopted a similar approach to defining distribution areas. For example, the benchmark cost model (BCM), sponsored by an industry consortium consisting of US West, Sprint, NYNEX, and MCI used Census block groups (CBGs) as distribution serving areas, with the justification that CBGs on average have a household count that is reasonably comparable to local serving area line counts and, more important, that CBGs represent a uniform nationwide statistical representation of population by a disinterested government body. Since the original purpose of the BCM was to estimate the relative costs of serving different regions of the country for purposes of providing universal service support for high-cost areas, this latter advantage was justifiably seen as an important modeling principle. A competing industry sponsored model known as the Hatfield model (HM) used the same modeling approach as the BCM, although it differed significantly in its choice of recommended input assumptions.[5]

Later versions of the BCM adopted a somewhat different modeling principle of a rival industry-sponsored model—the cost proxy model sponsored by Pacific Bell and developed by an independent consulting firm. The resulting benchmark cost proxy model (BCPM) followed a grid-based approach that measured population in areas defined by one degree of longitude and one degree of latitude.[6] Serving areas were constructed in the BCPM either by forming collections of grid cells until an appropriate line count was reached or in heavily populated regions by subdividing grid cells. In rural regions, CBGs typically include a large land mass in order to maintain a roughly constant population count throughout the country. Since the BCM and HM assumed that population was uniformly distributed throughout the entire CBG, the grid-based approach offered significant modeling advantages in highly rural areas. Ultimately, however, a uniform distribution within the serving area was assumed for computational tractability.

In response to the grid-based approach of the BCPM, the HM sponsors introduced a clustering algorithm in a later version of that model, which was renamed the HAI model. A clustering approach uses individual customer locations rather than grid cells as primary data points. A statistical algorithm is then used to identify natural groupings of customers that can be served by a common interface point. The HAI clustering approach and the significant customer location data preparation that was required to implement it were ultimately chosen as the most accurate of the modeling approaches by the FCC in its universal service proceeding. The particular clustering method used by the HAI model, and more important, the loop design algorithms, that remained largely intact from earlier versions of BCM and HM was not, however, used in the FCC approach. Instead, the approach of the HCPM in both of these areas was adopted based on evidence indicating that it gave the most accurate modeling results for both urban and rural areas.[7]

HCPM includes a module that performs a type of cluster analysis on the customer location input data. The data consist of the latitude and longitude of each residential and business location and the number of access lines demanded at that location. If location data at this level of detail are not available, the model can also process data at a more geographically aggregated level (e.g., a Census block) where the user provides the location of an interior point of the geographic region, its area, and an estimate of the number of residential and business lines demanded by users within the region. In the latter case the model processes the block-level data by creating a set of surrogate point locations randomly distributed in a square area the size of the original region.

An advantage of the clustering approach over earlier approaches is the ability of the model to explicitly maintain a maximum copper distance constraint. Satisfactory quality for both voice grade and digital services requires that the copper loop plant be restricted to a maximum distance, where the distance depends on the quality of service offered.[8] In LECOM the distribution loop length is allowed to vary according to the endogenously determined size of serving areas, but appropriate adjustments are made in the thickness (gauge) of the copper cables being used. In the clustering approach, distances are controlled, and the model is able to use higher gauge (and therefore less expensive) cable.

Once the clustering process is complete, the customer locations are assigned to a set of grid cells that overlay each cluster. The grid cells resemble those used by BCPM except that the cells are an order of magnitude smaller in size—360 feet on a side instead of approximately 3,000 feet—and the population of each cell is determined endogenously by the model from the more detailed customer location data. A loop design module is then called upon to build both distribution and feeder plant to each grid cell. The smaller size of grid cells allows both distribution and feeder plant to be built to essentially the exact customer locations in the case of distribution plant, and to the exact locations of serving area interface (SAI) points in the case of feeder plant.

Both distribution and feeder portions of the local network are designed based on minimum cost spanning tree algorithms, which seek to determine the minimum cost configuration of network links that connect customers to the SAI and SAIs to the central office switch, respectively. Earlier cost proxy model, including LECOM, BCPM, and HAI, used different variations of a "pine tree" routing algorithm in which locations were connected to a central point (SAI or switch) by a predetermined set of routes along vertical and horizontal axes. No attempt was made to minimize either the distance or the cost of the resulting network.[9]

While the loop design portions of the HCPM represent a significant advance over earlier modeling approaches, the HCPM and proxy models generally have been criticized for failing to take account of geographical barriers, such as bodies of water or extremely mountainous terrain—which real operating telephone companies are forced to recognize when they build loop plants.[10] It is likely that future modeling efforts will seek to incorporate local cost conditions in a more sophisticated manner.

In terms of modeling switching and interoffice investments, there have been relatively minor advances in the current generation of cost proxy models over the approach taken by Mitchell. Most of the approaches define a simple switching cost function of the form

$$C = C_0 + a_1 AL + a_2 T + a_3 CA + a_4 MN$$

where C_0 is getting started cost, AL is the number of access lines, T is the number of trunks, CA is the number of call attempts, MN is the number of minutes, and $a_1, a_2, a_3,$ and a_4 are constants. The difficulty in obtaining an accurate forward-looking representation of this cost has traditionally been in obtaining appropriate data to calibrate it. Neither switch vendors nor switch buyers have been willing to publicly reveal the details of actual contracts, since the market for switching capacity is thin, and both sides have incentives to withhold the relevant information from competitors. LECOM's formulation of switching cost improves somewhat on this situation by designing a stylized Northern Telecom DMS-100 type host-remote switch system from the bottom up, wherein the model sizes switch components according to the demand variables above using actual engineering tables, enabling the reduction of the problem to one of determining component costs rather than cost coefficients, but the information problems persist.

Interoffice investments have been modeled with increasing accuracy, much like investments in the loop plant. As described in chapter 2, LECOM designs a full mesh network for interoffice communications, where the amount of traffic carried between individual switches is assumed to be inversely proportional to the distance between them. While early versions of the BCM did not attempt to model interoffice costs in any manner, choosing instead to represent interoffice investment as a fixed percentage of loop plus switching investment, more recent versions of the BCPM and HAI models have incorporated algorithms that compute the SONET ring technologies now increasingly being used to link both host remote configurations and host to tandem configurations. An international version of the HCPM also computes the cost of SONET rings. The WIK model, which is intended to apply to the entire German intercity network, consists of a hybrid of full mesh and SONET ring connections based on a detailed traffic demand model for projected traffic flows between switches.

B.2 International Applications of HCPM

At this writing, three countries outside the United States are in varying stages of adopting some form of HCPM for use as a regulatory tool, with a likelihood of more adoptions as the need for such a tool grows. In this section we briefly describe the implementation process in two of these countries, Argentina and Portugal. The third country, Peru, is still in the very early stages of HCPM implementation and is not yet in a position suitable for written description.

Argentina and Portugal have approached the model selection process quite differently. In Argentina a research team under the Universidad Argentina de la Empresa (UADE) began the initial work of developing data sources and proposing changes to model logic suitable for the Argentinian situation. This group was able to develop a funding resource in collaboration with the World Bank by working with local telephone operators.[11]

The Portuguese modeling team, by contrast, has always been fully contained within the independent quasi-governmental authority Instituto das Comunicações de Portugal (ICP). The Portuguese team used ICP resources to purchase and develop independent data sources and modify the program for use in Portugal.[12]

Below we describe highlights of both nations' experiences in the use of the model.

B.2.1 Argentina

The UADE team began its process of adapting the model to the Argentinian reality by first approaching local telephone operators to seek their support for developing the tool, with an eye toward eventually turning it over to the Comisión Nacional de Comunicaciones (CNC) for use in arbitrating interconnection disputes and for calculating universal service subsidies.

UADE devoted the first portion of its effort to identifying two representative areas for analysis. In the Argentinian model of liberalization, the country was divided into two "LATA-like" regions in order to create two distinct franchises (which are ultimately intended to be open to completely free entry). These franchises were sold at auction to Telefónica de Argentina, a subsidiary of Telefónica de España, and to Telecom Argentina, a subsidiary of France Telecom. A city from each franchise area was chosen for the initial study. In the case of Telefónica the city chosen was Córdoba; Mendoza was the city from Telecom's area.

The UADE team gathered data from Argentina's Instituto Nacional de Estadistica y Censos (INDEC) at the *manzana*, or city block, level for Córdoba. The INDEC data include information on the number of residences, number of business locations, and number of employees at those locations (business data are only available at the radio level, which is analogous to a Census block group in the United States, and these are distributed uniformly across *manzanas*).[13]

Manzanas are assigned to wire centers according to their proximity to each central office. At the time of the writing of this book, precise data on wire-center boundaries are not available in Argentina. Residential line counts are assumed to equal either the number of residences or the number of residences "adjusted" by weighting according to the total residential line count for each wire center. Business line counts are assigned by dividing total business line count for the wire center evenly over all business locations within the calculated wire center. Letting $RLCM_i$ and RM_i be, respectively, the residential line count assigned to *manzana i* and the number of residences in that *manzana*, and $RLCWC_j$ be the residential line count for the wire center j, we have

$$RLCM_i = \frac{RM_i}{\sum_j RM_j} RLCWC_j$$

Similarly, for business line counts in each *manzana*, we have

$$BLCM_i = \frac{BM_i}{\sum_j BM_j} BLCWC_j$$

where $RLCM_i$ and $BLCM_i$ represent, respectively, residential locations and business line count in *manzana i*, and $BLCWC_j$ represents business line count for the wire center j.

HCPM has also been designed to accept detailed geological and topographical data, such as maximum and minimum grade of elevation, soil type, depth to bedrock, and water table. Unfortunately, such data do not exist in Argentina as yet, so "average" values were used.

One purpose of the UADE exercise was to determine the effect of less-than-optimal customer location data on cost estimates. To that end, Benitez et al. (2000) essentially performed an experiment in which results from *manzana*-based data were compared with data based on geocoded customer locations derived from an address database maintained by Telefónica. A dataset with even less precision than the *manzana* data was also created by aggregating *manzana* data. The study found that cost differentials between the most and least aggregated cases were only 3 to 5 percent for an urban area (Córdoba) presumed to be typical of Argentina. This result is important for developing countries in view of the high cost of collecting data in those countries.

Another objective of UADE research is to estimate the cost of incumbents' universal service obligation. At this writing, the research team is gathering data for other locations in Argentina in order to develop such estimates, but preliminary results have been presented in several academic conferences. Using the Córdoba dataset, Benitez et al. (1999) first calculated cost estimates for serving these urban wire centers at the existing level of penetration. Other exercises included testing the sensitivity of the latter result to changes in the cost of copper cable and the cost of capital. Finally, these authors calculated the incremental cost associated with moving from current penetration levels to 100 percent service penetration.

At this writing, Argentina's Secretaría de Defensa de la Competencia y del Consumidor (Secretariat for the Protection of Competition and Consumers, the Argentinian Federal Trade Commission) of the Economics Ministry, has announced that it plans to use the HCPM for official universal service cost estimates and for refereeing interconnection disputes. A committee consisting of representatives of industry operators, the government, academics, and international experts will be convened to supervise data collection and mandate changes to the structure of the model.

B.2.2 Portugal

The ICP (Instituto das Comunicações de Portugal) has decided to follow a somewhat independent course within the European Union in its approach to handling universal service and interconnection issues. The ICP is in full agreement with EU policy, which mandates that long-run incremental cost be used as the basis for decisions on these issues and that interconnection rates be set at the local, single tandem and double tandem level. While the EU has employed consultants to develop its own forward-looking costing methodology, ICP has been concerned that the modeling approach used may not be sufficiently rich or detailed enough to accurately reflect the reality of Portuguese topography and geography. There are also concerns that the EU's consultants, Europe Economics, following the example set by Oftel in the United Kingdom, is developing a model that merely reflects a stylization of the existing network and does not incorporate the economic notion of long-run cost (e.g., which would include optimization of at least some network components based on prices and usage profiles).

The ICP modeling team has, at this writing, been successful in developing a customer location database in an innovative way. No database exists for Portugal that includes georeferenced customer locations with an indication of demand at each point, and population data collected by the Instituto Nacional de Estatísticas reports only at the level of the *freguesia*, an administrative unit roughly equivalent to a US township. The Portuguese Instituto Geográfico do Exército, or Army Geographic Institute (IGE), has developed digitized maps showing the location and shape of every building, road, and geographical feature in the country. These data are manipulated to work with HCPM as follows.

Each shape record is assigned to a *freguesia* based on the coordinates of its centroid using MapInfo® software. Once all shapes within a *freguesia* are "identified," the number of business and residential lines in that *freguesia* are assigned to each location proportionally to the area of the shape at that location. Residential line counts from the *freguesia* are derived in one of two ways, either by using INE data on number of residences within the *freguesia* or by allocating total wire-center line counts to the *freguesia* based on an allocation rule. When the computer program developed at ICP has assigned a line count to each shape, it then assigns each shape to a wire center either by using a minimum distance criterion (the shape is attached to the nearest wire center) or by accepting information provided by the user on wire-center boundaries. Finally, at the option of the user, total lines within each wire center can be "trued-up" to reflect line counts for the wire center.

Partial data on soil type, depth to bedrock, and water table are available for portions of Portugal, and these data have also been applied to the model. The ICP team has further collected altimetry data to use in calculation of "slope," or grade angle. The altimetry data exist at a resolution of approximately 100 meters latticed throughout the country. A computer program developed at ICP calculates the slope at each point by measuring the change in altitude between the point and each of its neighbors, recording the maximum value. Each value is converted into a grade angle using the appropriate trigonometric identity. A database is thus created for the entire country. MapInfo® assigns each slope value to a *freguesia*, and maximum and minimum values for that *freguesia* are calculated.

At this writing, ICP is engaged in calculating interconnection costs using the HCPM interoffice module as well as calculating universal service costs using another innovative methodology. In the United States universal service cost estimates are obtained by estimating company statewide average costs using HCPM. If the overall company statewide average cost exceeds a benchmark, the difference between the statewide average cost and the benchmark is equal to the amount of subsidy for that company in that state. ICP proposes to calculate universal service costs in a manner more consistent with the understanding of economists. Let B be a benchmark cost calculation. Let $R_i(x)$ be a geographic radius about wire center i such that the average cost of providing service to all customers within $R_i(x)$ is less than x. Let $C(R)$ be the average cost of providing network service to all customers within radius R of the wire center, and $C'(R)$ be the average incremental cost of providing service to customers located outside of R.

Note that $C(R)$ is a "metafunction," or composite, of the HCPM cluster, cluster interface, and feeder/distribution algorithms. That is, as R changes, the number of customer locations to be included in the wire-center "map" varies, and clustering must be redone to establish the locations of serving area interfaces. The universal service subsidy USS for wire center i is defined as

$$USS_i = \max\{C'(R_i(B)) - B, 0\}$$

The value is calculated using the classical bisection technique. The approach permits universal service subsidy calculations to be made for each individual wire center and reflects the incremental cost of only those lines requiring subsidy.

Notes

Chapter 1

1. See, for example, Sharkey (1982).

2. Armstrong (1998) and Laffont et al. (1998a,b) stressed the potential use of interconnection agreements for collusion on final prices and for blockading entry. New Zealand, which eliminated regulation in the telecommunications industry, is returning to it because of the excessive delays created by the settling of interconnection disputes by competition policy.

3. In circuit-switched networks the relative prices charged for interconnection at a tandem switch versus interconnection at an end office will dictate the form of interconnection that competing firms choose. If these prices are set by a regulator, there can be no guarantee that the cost-minimizing form of interconnection will be chosen. Even in the unregulated setting of the Internet, voluntary interconnection agreements among backbone networks can in many cases lead to suboptimal routing decisions by competing networks.

4. *United States of America* v. *AT&T Co.*, Defendants' Third Statement of Contentions and Proof, Civil Action No. 74-1698, March 10, 1980, p. 137.

5. See Brock (1981) for additional discussion of the competitive era in telecommunications.

6. See, for example, Kahn (1970), vol. 1, pp. 20–60, for a more detailed discussion of the operation of cost-based rate of return regulation.

7. See Averch and Johnson (1962).

8. A framework for the analysis of incentives in regulation will be presented in chapter 4.

9. In the United States, price caps were used on an experimental basis for the regulation of Michigan Bell from 1980 to 1983. However, it should be noted that simple forms of price-cap regulation were used in Europe as far back as in the nineteenth century for the regulation of electricity prices at a time when accounting data were not available.

10. See, for example, Baron and Myerson (1982) and Laffont and Tirole (1986) and the synthetic work of Laffont and Tirole (1993, 2000).

11. In an appendix we also provide a description of an alternative cost proxy model (HCPM) that was created at the FCC after the present research project was underway.

12. See Laffont (1994) for a survey.

13. See Green and Laffont (1979) for a survey.

14. This expression was coined later in Myerson (1981).

15. For instance, while the Cobb-Douglas and the CES specifications imply, respectively, a unitary and a constant (not necessarily equal to one) elasticity of substitution between factors, the translog specification does not impose any specific value for this elasticity.

16. Financial statements are generally filed quarterly for publicly traded firms.

17. We should note that econometric methods for the analysis of heterogeneous data sets have been developed and used with some success (see Greene 2000).

18. For example, a universal service fund based on industry average cost parameters may lead to an inadequate transfer from urban to rural subscribers, at least in the short run.

19. LECOM stands for local exchange cost optimization model. This is the engineering cost model that we will use throughout the book (chapter 2 describes this model in great detail).

Chapter 2

1. This model was developed as part of a research grant from the National Regulatory Research Institute (see Gabel and Kennet 1991). A reader not familiar with the technology of voice telecommunications at the local exchange level may wish to consult some outside sources in order to have a better understanding of the LECOM cost model. See, for example, Sharkey (2001).

2. Digital technology is now the dominant technology in telecommunications for both switching and transmission functions. When a subscriber is served by a digital switch, voice signals must be converted from an analog to a digital format, and this can be done either at the central office or at the serving area interface level. If this conversion is done in the field, concentrating the resulting digital signals on a reduced number of pairs of copper or fiber-optic cables leads to some cost savings. This concentration technology is referred to as subscriber-line carrier.

3. While copper cables are available in the model in four different sizes (gauges), 26-, 24-, 22-, and 19-gauge wire, fiber-optic cable comes only in one size (see section 3.1 for the more precise meaning of these gauges). The installed size of copper wire critically depends on the distance to be covered and the desired level of quality of communications. The shorter the distance, the smaller is the diameter of the copper cable that can be used, and hence the lower is the cost. The drawback, however, is that smaller-size cables have more electric resistance than larger ones, which could impede communications. The gauge bears no direct relation with the amount of traffic that a line can handle.

4. LECOM assumes that distribution cables are always copper, the technology of choice for voice-grade only networks. In other words, the model at this time does not handle "fiber to the curb," which is possibly the next generation of distribution technology.

5. Typically a serving area contains 350 to 600 subscribers.

6. See note 2 above for the factors that determine the choice of gauge in the distribution plant. Those same considerations are taken into account when determining the proper gauge of cable in the feeder plant (see section 2.3.2; see also section 2.4).

7. These standards have been established by AT&T in order to allow users to possess a second line and provide spare capacity in the distribution and feeder plants in anticipation of a high level of usage (see Stiles 1978).

8. Note, however, that cable is available only in discrete sizes. Thus suppose that the total pairs required by customers at point A (which is more distant from the switch) are 5, and customers at point B have additional demand for 5 pairs. The smallest cable size used is 6 pairs, and the next larger size is 12 pairs. Thus, from point A to point B, a cable with a capacity of 6 pairs is used, and from point B toward the SAI the cable size must be increased to the next size 12 pairs. This is an example of "telescoping."

9. Recall from section 2.2 that the feeder network connects every area to a central office and that the distribution plant provides a link for every customer in a given serving area to a serving area interface (SAI).

10. T1 is a US standard in which 24 digital channels are carried over 2 copper pairs. The European standard, E1, carries 30 digital channels over 2 pairs. In either case the deployment decision hinges on the relative cost of the copper (a function of the distance the signal must travel), expected traffic (a "concentrated" digital channel shares the capacity of the copper line with other channels, while an analog line is dedicated), and the cost of the electronics required to convert the digital signal to analog so that the customer is able to use it.

11. Long analog copper runs may impede the ability of the network to support high-speed services.

12. SLC-96 (subscriber-line carrier) is the subscriber-line concentrator that has typically been used by the Bell Operating Companies (see note 2 above for a discussion of the role of the subscriber-line-carrier technology).

13. Recently a minimum cost spanning tree type algorithm, which is more general than the pine tree method, was used to model feeder routing (see Bush et al. 1999). For computational efficiency reasons, however, the pine tree algorithm might still be desirable as it requires no iterative procedures, searching, or sorting.

14. Switching capacity can be changed by the LECOM user, although it is usually set once and for all.

15. This parameter may be increased up to 9 by the LECOM user.

16. In general, the greater the peak usage, the larger is the ratio of interoffice trunk lines to single-channel local loops (see, e.g., *Engineering and Operations in the Bell System*, 1983).

17. Note that this interoffice trunk model builds interoffice trunks between every pair of switches. Alternatively, SONET technology only requires that a switch belong to one or more rings of interconnected switches and hence would most likely lead to less interoffice plant overall.

18. LECOM is less successful in explicitly modeling substitution between capital and labor, although implicitly this too is possible. This is accomplished through the model's

use of annual charge factors, which include a labor loading on each piece of capital equipment used in the optimization. Thus the cost of labor is taken into account when the optimization is performed, and trade-offs can be explored by varying the capital and labor cost indexes that are input parameters in LECOM.

19. To alleviate the problem of local optimum, LECOM restarts the optimization a certain number of times specified by the user, by randomly adjusting the initial values.

20. Recall that as distance traversed by copper wire increases, thicker wire is required in order to compensate for electrical energy losses.

21. For the purpose of the example, we simplify the exposition by merging distribution and feeder plants into the loop plant.

22. Note that even though feeder and distribution costs are not directly functions of the number of switches, they are functions of the locations of those switches.

23. The solution to the first-order condition may result in a non-integer-valued number of switches. In this case the exact solution may be the integer on either side of the fractional part, depending on which one gives the lower cost.

24. Recall that in performing the requisite optimizations, LECOM is more flexible than the preceding discussion might indicate. Indeed, LECOM simultaneously optimizes over the number of switches, the technology of the switches, as well as their location within the city served.

25. A multiplex loop is a multichannel connection within a switch. The number of channels depends on usage, since heavy peak usage will occupy more of any given connection, thereby reducing its availability to carry other channels. A line group controller electronically manages a group of line cards; the number of line cards it can handle depends on their peak usage, with heavier usage reducing the effective capacity of the controller.

26. See the discussion following equation (2.4) for a description of these control variables.

27. The complete set of LECOM inputs is shown in tables A.13 and A.14 of appendix A.

28. This is the so-called Shephard's lemma.

29. More specifically, the standard disturbance term reflects the goodness of the approximation of the functional form used.

Chapter 3

1. This chapter is based on Gabel and Kennet (1994). We thank David Gabel for his permission to use the material.

2. See section 3.4.1 for a definition.

3. Leggette (1985) has also used the translog cost function and data from the Statistics of Common Communication Carriers to estimate a multiproduct cost function. Leggette concluded that there were no economies of scope between the two outputs he considered in his study, private branch exchange and main station telephones.

4. When Christensen, Cummings, and Schoech (1981) built the data set that has been used by prior econometricians, they used different price indexes for each of the primary types of facilities.

5. For example, between 1976 and 1980, the price of outside plant increased by 33 percent, while inside plant increased by 12 percent (Bell System Telephone Plant Indexes).

6. See Rey (1983, p. 125). In standard traffic engineering terminology, this level of peak usage corresponds to 0.125 Erlang or 3 CCS. In this example we treat usage as the sum of exchange and toll usage. This simplification does not affect our analysis.

7. See "Usage Forecasting by Class of Service," *American Telephone and Telegraph System Letter*, 83-05-128.

8. *Response of New York Telephone to User Request #147*, Case 28978, New York Public Service Commission.

9. The data set used by Christensen, Cummings, and Schoech (1983), Evans and Heckman (1983), and Charnes et al. (1988) suffers from the same problem.

10. To be more specific, administrative costs are a linear function of the level of investment. Therefore the administrative costs will exhibit the same economies or diseconomies that are present in the use of physical facilities. Evans and Heckman (1983, p. 141) raise the issue of whether managerial diseconomies can exceed engineering economies. Because of this concern, they argue that "Although engineering studies may be useful to businessmen choosing between alternative technologies, they are of little use for determining whether an industry is a natural monopoly." Evans and Heckman express their preference for "hard data" rather than engineering constructs. Unfortunately, the "hard data" approach provides little or no indication on the industry's current or future cost trends. In order to identify prospective costs, in a dynamic, capital-intensive industry, we believe that data generated through an optimization model provides more insights than "hard" but historical data.

11. Sufficient conditions for a multiproduct natural monopoly are economies of scope and declining average incremental costs (see Evans and Heckman 1984, pp. 615–16). Other sufficient conditions for a natural monopoly are discussed in Sharkey (1982, pp. 67–73).

12. Whenever toll or exchange switched service is provided, the customer is connected to the switch via an access line. While this cost is included in the tables below, here we do not list it as a product by itself.

13. See chapter 2 for the shape of the generic city assumed in LECOM.

14. The diseconomies of scope occur between switched services on one hand and private line networks on the other. Since both networks build a trunk to an interoffice POP (see section 2.3.4 of chapter 2), interconnection is already included in the cost, and the diseconomies arise purely because of the fact that the model "forces" the firm in providing the private line network to use the same infrastructure used for the switched plant. In practice, these diseconomies might disappear because a single firm can mimic the two-firm solution modeled by LECOM.

15. No switching costs are incurred with an all private line system.

16. We have not tested for the sufficient conditions of a natural monopoly (see note 11).

17. New York Telephone response to information request CPBCS 199, in Docket 28978, New York Public Service Commission.

18. Within the industry, the cost attributes commonly allocated to the local loop are non-traffic sensitive. The nomenclature reflects a situation with no congestion in the local loop.

19. Memorandum from T. Sheridan to J. Hudson (November 20, 1895), box 1275, American Telephone and Telegraph Corporate Archive.

Chapter 4

1. See Laffont (1994) for a survey of this literature and Laffont and Tirole (2000) for a nontechnical exposition. For a more technical presentation of the basic concepts and yet at a relatively elementary level, the reader might find it useful to go through chapter 1 of Laffont and Tirole (1993), in particular, section 1.3 of that chapter.

2. The gross transfer $\hat{t}$ would be such that $t = \hat{t} + R(q) - C$.

3. To avoid bunching in the regulatory solutions, we make the monotone hazard rate assumption

$$\frac{d}{d\beta}\left(\frac{F(\beta)}{f(\beta)}\right) > 0 \quad \text{for all } \beta$$

Without fear of confusion, we denote by C both the cost function $C(\beta, e, q)$ and the argument $C(\tilde{\beta})$ of the revelation mechanism defined below.

4. Without loss of generality, because of the revelation principle (Gibbard 1973; Green and Laffont 1977; Myerson 1979), any regulation mechanism is equivalent to a truthful revelation mechanism.

5. From now on, we make the arguments of functions explicit only when they are needed for clarity. Derivatives with respect to β of functions, which are only functions of β, are denoted with dots, $\dot{t}(\beta)$, $\dot{q}(\beta)$, $\dot{C}(\beta)$, $\dot{U}(\beta)$. From (4.14) we see that a necessary condition for truthful behavior (i.e., for $\tilde{\beta} = \beta$ to be an optimal announcement or $\hat{U}(\beta, \tilde{\beta})$ to be maximized with respect to $\tilde{\beta}$) is the first-order condition of the maximization of $\hat{U}(\beta, \tilde{\beta})$ with respect to $\tilde{\beta}$.

6. From (4.16), $\hat{U}_{\tilde{\beta}}(\beta, \tilde{\beta})|_{\tilde{\beta}=\beta} = 0$ for any β, $\tilde{\beta}$ or $\hat{U}_{\beta}(\beta, \beta) = 0$ for any β. Since $U(\beta) = \hat{U}(\beta, \beta)$, $\dot{U}(\beta) = \hat{U}_{\tilde{\beta}}(\beta, \beta) + \hat{U}_{\beta}(\beta, \beta) = \hat{U}_{\beta}(\beta, \beta) = -\psi'(e)E_{\beta}$.

7. In this book we do not discuss the second-order conditions. See Laffont and Tirole (1993).

8. They are obtained by the Pontryagin principle or by integrating (4.17) using $U(\tilde{\beta}) = 0$, since the most inefficient type receives no rent, and then substituting the result into (4.18) and integrating by parts.

9. This is the key implication of asymmetric information. It is due to the fact that a β-firm can mimic a less efficient firm with less effort.

10. See Laffont and Tirole (1993). Note that $E_{\beta} = de/d\beta = -C_{\beta}/C_e$. So (4.29) means that the marginal rate of substitution between e and β in the cost function is independent of q.

11. Note again, however, that Ramsey pricing is defined relative to marginal cost, which is affected by the effort level and therefore by the incentives provided by the cost-reimbursement rule.

12. As in the Baron-Myerson regulation the firm is residual claimant for its cost saving.

13. Note that β^* is defined by $p^M(\beta^*) = \bar{p}$.

14. If $C_{qq} > 0$, it is conceivable that (4.42) is not binding. However, we will concentrate on the case where it is binding.

15. The regulatory reforms by the FCC in the 1980s incorporate such sharing rules.

16. Since the regulator cannot observe effort levels, financial rather than actual profits are used as the basis of profit sharing.

17. A less efficient use of these resources would be to reimburse consumers; this is what is often done in practice.

Chapter 5

1. This is particularly true of labor costs which can have a large variance across regions.

2. In this chapter, although we consider the possibility of interfirm rivalry in markets that might be characterized as natural monopolies, we focus on the final outcome of such a process, namely on the equilibrium state.

3. More recently Maher (1999) has estimated a translog cost function in order to measure access costs at the local level. The data set used by Maher consists of observations on the central offices of two companies during the year of 1985. The main findings of the study is that there are differences in access costs across geographical locations but that because of significant economies of scale, "cost-based rates at the local level wouldn't be prohibitively high and would not threaten universal service objective."

4. That is to say, in a forward-looking framework, the relationship between the cost and market structures needs to be taken into account.

5. Using a standard oligopoly modeling framework, von Weizsäcker (1980) shows the importance of accounting for welfare effects when drawing policy conclusions concerning barriers to entry. For example, the author shows that for a given configuration of demand and cost parameters, social welfare is higher under restricted entry than under free-entry Cournot equilibrium. In our analysis we examine Cournot as well as other Bertrand-type duopoly equilibria and contrast those with some regulated monopoly outcomes. Our approach incorporates the impact on welfare of both economies of scale and information rents in the comparisons of monopoly and duopoly.

6. See section 4.3 for a more technical discussion of this trade-off.

7. It is assumed that a higher β corresponds to a less efficient technology and that effort reduces cost at a decreasing rate.

8. Under standard assumptions on demand, the social surplus function V is increasing and concave in output.

9. See chapter 4.

10. This optimal level of effort, which is indicated by an asterisk, solves the equation $C_e = -\psi'(e)$, which equates marginal cost-saving and marginal disutility. Hence this optimal effort is expressed as $e^*(\beta, q)$.

11. The main idea behind yardstick competition is that asymmetric information problems can be alleviated if the principal uses some measure of the relative performance of the economic agents. Shleifer (1985) discusses this concept in the context of regulation.

12. Note that strictly speaking, in the *MC* model one should account for any welfare losses associated with the disconnection of some low-income customers unable to pay for the fixed fee.

13. In this approach we also assume that interconnection costs are negligible and that total subscribership is independent of market structure and prices for usage.

14. A one-dimensional adverse selection parameter makes both the theoretical and empirical analysis considerably more tractable.

15. Note that in our interpretation, *PL* refers to a parameter (effort) that is endogenous to the decision-making within the firm, whereas *PK* refers to an exogenous parameter that describes the technology type of the firm. Both interpretations are permissible since LECOM is not intended to be an explicit behavioral model of economic equilibrium. The function of LECOM is to describe (approximately) the set of cost-minimizing facilities that an efficient firm would choose to deploy given a set of assumed input values. Whenever a LECOM input value such as *PL* is a decision variable for the firm, it is necessary to determine this value as part of the profit maximization problem for the firm, subject to the competitive and regulatory constraints in which it operates. This is the approach we have taken in our empirical work. An alternative interpretation of *PL* is that it represents the unit price of labor input where the latter is measured in efficiency units. Then, if the nominal (exogenous) price of labor is held constant, changes in *PL* are perfectly (inversely) correlated with changes in underlying effort.

16. This corresponds to an area of approximately 150 square kilometers with a density close to 720 subscribers per square kilometer.

17. This range of values corresponds to total cost differences (which can be interpreted as uncertainty on costs) due to adverse selection (modeled through *PK*) and moral hazard (modeled through *PL*) that could be as large as 23 and 30 percent, respectively.

18. This empirical cost function is presented in the section of appendix A corresponding to this chapter. Again, we note that interconnection costs are here neglected.

19. Assuming that the number of lines per subscriber remains constant, our cost function in this approach is equivalently a function of the number of subscribers.

20. In chapter 8 we study the case where an entrant specifically targets the lower-cost business district. This form of targeted entry, however, is not considered in the present analysis.

21. LECOM also reports the disaggregated costs of the feeder and distribution networks. Theory predicts, and our empirical analysis verifies, that the corresponding multipliers for distribution should be equal to one, and for the feeder network, close to one.

22. Total cost increased by about 6 percent.

23. The appendix at the end of the book gives the specific form of the various cost functions.

24. A mean-value estimate of 0.3 for the shadow cost of public funds λ is considered reasonable for a developed country such as the United States (see Ballard et al. 1985; Hausman and Poterba 1987).

25. See Taylor (1994) for an extensive survey of the empirical literature on telecommunications demand.

26. For the purpose of the calibration exercise, both of these assumptions seem plausible for the case of the US local telecommunications. Initially we also used an elasticity of −0.2 for access, and the qualitative results of the monopoly versus duopoly exercise were the same (see Gasmi et al. 1999c). Under both of these assumptions we used $PK = 1$ and $PL = 1.5$; when output is usage, we used $q = 4$ CCS, and when output is access, we used $q = 60,000$ lines.

27. In chapter 6 we give a more detailed description of these two assumptions that we use to calibrate the disutility of effort functions.

28. The issue of the value of information to the regulator certainly deserves a more careful investigation.

29. Expected social welfare, expected consumer surplus, and the firm's rent (see below) are given in hundred million dollars (100 M).

30. The substantial increase in social welfare at higher values of λ is due to the extremely low elasticity of demand for access to the network (equal to −0.05) that has been assumed for this simulation. From (5.1) it follows that social welfare can be expressed as $W = S(q) - [C(\beta, e, q) + \psi(e)] + \lambda[P(q)q - C(\beta, e, q) - t]$. For low-demand elasticities the second term in brackets is positive. Hence under optimal regulation telephone subscribers may contribute to general governmental revenues. At higher elasticities these results would no longer hold. We explore these issues in more detail in chapters 6 and 7 in cases where higher elasticities are more plausible.

31. Note, however, that for less-developed countries (LDCs) one should include the effect of possible corruption of the tax system in the comparisons (in chapter 8 we explore this issue in the context of the financing of universal service).

32. Note that these tables provide only the relevant information. In particular, two pieces of information are implicit in the results and are therefore not presented in these tables. First, for all of the scenarios that do not allow for transfers (PC, $C+$, UM, CD, AC, and MC), the results are independent of the cost of public funds λ. Second, the whole social welfare goes to consumers in the scenarios that do not leave any rent to the firm ($C+$, AC, MC, and YS).

33. For $\lambda = 0.3$, see tables 5.5, 5.8, and 5.9. For $\lambda = 1.0$ and $\lambda = 2.0$, see tables 5.7, 5.8, and 5.9. Note that under YS the firm's rent is nil.

34. Note from tables 5.5 and 5.9 that Bertrand competition (AC) dominates PC from the point of view of consumers.

35. In the next chapter we further compare the results of this study with ours.

36. These average cost functions are calculated at the average values of the adverse selection and moral hazard parameters for both monopoly and duopoly.

Chapter 6

1. At the risk of repeating ourselves, because this chapter focuses on the optimal regulatory mechanism, it is worthwhile recalling from chapter 4 its main theoretical ingredients.

2. See chapter 4 for more details.

3. Appropriate assumptions could be made to ensure that $\partial E/\partial\beta > 0$ so that $U(\beta)$ is decreasing in β. The participation constraint reduces to $U(\bar{\beta}) \geq 0$, and from the objective function it is clear that at the optimum this constraint is binding.

4. A LECOM run takes roughly a minute for a medium-sized city of the type we consider here. A typical simulation with about 600 runs would then approximately take 10 hours on a machine ranging from 200 to 500 MHz.

5. Note that the translog function is viewed as a second-order Taylor expansion (in natural logarithms) that approximates the true underlying cost function. Since we generate our data through a process that may be considered deterministic (LECOM), the disturbance term in the regression might be regarded as merely reflecting the imprecision of this quadratic approximation fit and not as some unobservable random effect.

6. An important point is worth mentioning here, however. While the only requirements for running the standard OLS method on these cost data are the usual Gauss-Markov assumptions, the use of the t-statistic to test the significance of the coefficients necessitates, in small samples, the normality of the disturbance term. On the one hand, because of the large size of our data sample, we benefit from the asymptotic normality of the t-statistic. On the other, because of the deterministic nature of our data-generating process (LECOM), the numbers presented in the third columns of tables 6.1, 6.7, and 6.8 give merely an indication of the goodness of the nul hypotheses. For this reason they will be referred to as t-measures.

7. Also Shin and Ying report an (uncorrected) R-squared of 0.9977 for their cost equation.

8. In contrast, Shin and Ying estimate a cost function using data on firms that serve areas of different sizes and with different population densities, and they compute an overall scale elasticity by summing up their three output (access, local calls, and toll calls) cost elasticities.

9. In our context, these elasticities are given by

$$\sigma_{PK,PL}(PK, PL, Q) = \sigma_{PL,PK}(PK, PL, Q)$$
$$= \frac{\tilde{C}(PK, PL, Q) \cdot \tilde{C}_{PK\,PL}}{\tilde{C}_{PK} \cdot \tilde{C}_{PL}}$$
$$\epsilon_{PK,PL}(PK, PL, Q) = \tilde{C}_{PK} \cdot \left(\frac{PL}{\tilde{C}(PK, PL, Q)}\right)$$
$$\epsilon_{PL,PK}(PK, PL, Q) = \tilde{C}_{PL} \cdot \left(\frac{PK}{\tilde{C}(PK, PL, Q)}\right)$$

10. Taylor (1994) reports a demand elasticity in the range $(-0.38, -0.17)$. In our base case the value of -0.2 is used at an output $q = 4\ CCS$.

11. See section 5.3.4 for some more quantitative details on this demand calibration exercise. Two comments are worth making. First, while LECOM can handle disaggregated output in business, residential, private line, and so on, taking a multidimensional output approach would make both the theoretical exposition and the computational burden much heavier. We circumvent these issues by assuming the existence of a representative customer. Second, we assume that the cost of local exchange services must be fully recovered from local revenues. While telephone rate structures have

traditionally embodied a subsidy from toll to local usage, we believe that given changing technologies and liberalized regulatory regimes, this assumption is appropriate
for future regulation of local exchange companies.

12. As informal evidence in support of this assumption, see the *Wall Street Journal*, October 2, 1995, p. A6, where the following statement appears: "BT [British Telecom] ...
like many phone companies around the world, has been forced to gird for the new
competition by slashing costs. Since 1984, when the former state phone monopoly
was privatized, BT has shed nearly 102,000 jobs, or 43% of its work force."

13. Note that if there is monitoring of effort, then under cost-plus regulation the marginal
disutility of effort is positive but there is a positive cost of monitoring.

14. We evaluate the derivative of C with respect to e at average output $(3\,CCS)$ and at
average value (1) of the technological parameter β.

15. These calculations were carried out using the mathematical software Mathematica.
Strictly speaking, our cost function C defined in equation (6.6) is valid only for positive
values of ϵ. We report in table 6.2 the limiting values for e as $\epsilon \to 0$. We have also directly
estimated a translog cost function $C(PK, PL_0 + \epsilon - PL, Q)$ for positive values of ϵ and
for $\epsilon = 0$ (by eliminating data points where necessary). In all cases the regression
results were qualitatively the same as those that we report.

16. Recall from chapter 4 that the net consumer surplus $CS(q)$ is defined as the gross
consumer surplus $S(q) = \int_0^q P(s)\,ds$ minus the total consumer expense (the firm's
revenue) $R(q) = P(q)q$.

17. Note that the nonmonotonicity of $\hat{T}$ does not prevent W from behaving as its two
other components CS and U, namely monotonically increasing in efficiency.

18. Note that CS is rescaled by dividing by 10.

19. See appendix A.2. We also present in this appendix data showing that using the normal
instead of the uniform distribution decreases rents and increases social welfare. Note,
however, that in this model of optimal regulation under asymmetric information,
an improvement of the information structure even in the strong sense of Blackwell
(1951) is not necessarily beneficial to the principal (the regulator) because it also affects
directly the information rents.

20. The complete information regulatory scheme is found by solving

$$\max_{q,e} V(q) - (1 + \lambda)[C(\beta, e, q) + \psi(e)]$$

21. Note from (6.17) that the incentive correction term is nil for the most efficient firm.

22. When the incentive-pricing dichotomy holds, the first-order condition of the regulator's program (6.5) yields the Ramsey formula

$$\frac{p - C_q}{p} = \frac{\lambda}{1 + \lambda} \cdot \frac{1}{\eta}$$

where η is the demand elasticity (see chapter 4).

23. See Laffont and Tirole (1993, p. 179).

24. Note from table 6.1 that the cross-terms that have been removed are relatively small
in magnitude and have the smallest values of the indicative t-measures.

25. This sufficient condition for linear implementation is given in Laffont and Tirole (1993, p. 171).

26. We also have fitted a specification similar to (6.21), which contains the cross-term $\log(PK + PL) \times \log(Q)$ and found that the coefficient corresponding to this term had a very low t-measure.

27. This measure might be thought of as a generalized average cost.

28. Proposition 3 in Wilson (1989) shows that priority service, which is a form of optimal nonlinear pricing with n priority classes, incurs an efficiency loss which no more than $1/n^2$.

29. Ideally one could optimize over this choice of pairs.

30. To be more explicit, $G(x) = \tilde{G}(0, x) = \tilde{G}(x, 0)$, where $\tilde{G}$ is given in (6.23).

31. See equation (6.4). Note that given the form of our cost function, $E_\beta = 1$.

32. On the basis of a grid of demand and cost parameters defined by Schmalensee (1989), Gasmi et al. (1994) find values that show a much higher welfare loss of linear regulation relative to optimal regulation of about 0.5 percent. Although in using a higher demand elasticity, they found that welfare loss increased by a factor of 4, the comparison of these results should only be done at a methodological level for at least two reasons. First, while the exercise of these authors is based on a grid of parameters built mainly for illustration purposes, ours uses cost data based on real local exchange technology as described by LECOM. Second, our results still depend on our calibration of the unobservable disutility of effort function, and how sensitive the results are to the precise form of this function is still under investigation.

Chapter 7

1. This normative approach should be viewed as a necessary first step. A more complete approach should explicitly take into account political constraints. In section 7.4 we refer to a reduced-form model based on this later type of approach.

2. Note again that the expression of the social welfare function (7.1) shows that the regulator dislikes leaving rent to the firm. This will turn out to be an important determinant of optimal regulatory policies.

3. The compact form of the optimal regulatory mechanism with transfers and cost observability (LT) is given in the previous chapter. When costs are not observable, the regulatory program (BM) can compactly be written as

$$\max_{q(\cdot)} \int_{\underline{\beta}}^{\bar{\beta}} \left\{ V(q(\beta)) - (1+\lambda)[C(\beta, e^*(\beta, q(\beta)), q(\beta)) + \psi(e^*(\beta, q(\beta)))] - \lambda \frac{F(\beta)}{f(\beta)} C_\beta(\beta, e^*(\beta, q(\beta)), q(\beta)) \right\} f(\beta) \, d\beta$$

where e^* refers to optimal effort and $F(f)$ is a cumulative distribution (density) that describes the beliefs of the regulator concerning the technological parameter β.

4. It is useful to recall here (see also chapter 4) that $CW = V(q) - (1+\lambda)(t + C(\beta, e, q))$, where $V(q) = S(q) + \lambda P(q)q$ and $S(\cdot)$ and $P(\cdot)$ are, respectively, the gross consumer

surplus, and the inverse demand function, $U = t - \psi(e)$, where t is the net monetary transfer (if allowed) from the regulator to the firm. We also define RoR as $RoR = 100 \cdot U/(C + \psi)$.

5. With an average cost of about $5.50.

6. The social value of transfers will be further discussed later in this chapter.

7. For CI, LT, and BM, costs exceed revenues except for the most efficient firms in this high-elasticity case. Also in this case PC and PCT coincide.

8. Note that because the first-order condition defines effort in CI, BM, PC, and PCT ($\psi' = C_e$), there is no compelling reason to expect, for general cost functions, monotonicity of effort even if $C_{\beta e} > 0$ (which is the case for our estimated translog cost function, as can be seen from the sign of the coefficient of the cross-product term involving PK and PL in equation (6.7) of chapter 6). This is due to the influence of the production level on cost. In the case of LT, however, the first-order condition in effort has an additional term that leads to a distortion of effort. Monotonicity of effort arises then as a consequence of the optimal trade-off between rent extraction and efficient effort.

9. The fact that in tables 7.2 and 7.7 output levels are practically identical for BM and LT is a result of rounding. Output levels are lower under BM, but the effect is small for these particular simulations.

10. Note that no rent is left for the least efficient firm under these mechanisms.

11. Note, however, that for the highest-cost firms, rents are equal to zero under each form of regulation and that consumer welfare is higher under BM and PC regulation than under LT and PCT regulation. The fundamental trade-offs involved in implementing incentive regulation will be discussed further below.

12. Note, however, that this would require a different interpretation of the deadweight loss associated with transfers, which here would have to allow for the possibility of disconnection of low-income consumers.

13. If the project is small relative to the size of the firm, this assumption may fail to hold, and cost observation may prove less useful than our computations suggest.

14. See Baron (1989) for a good discussion of the rationale behind this specification.

15. Under complete information, maximization is done with respect to q and e in which effort $e(\beta)$ is assumed to be observable for any value of β. In contrast, under incomplete information (i.e., on the second-best frontier), maximization is done with respect to the functions $q(\cdot)$ and $e(\cdot)$ as in equation (6.5) of the previous chapter.

16. Our quasi-linear specification of utility functions leads to a linear Pareto frontier under complete information. Furthermore it limits the meaningfulness of δ to the highest value of $1 + \lambda$. For higher values the regulator would want to transfer unlimited amounts to the firm. Asymmetric information typically convexifies the Pareto frontier, as transfers are costly because of incentive constraints.

17. The point LT^{cc} is obtained by giving weights 0.25 and 0.75 to the allocations on the second-best frontier $LT(\delta)$ corresponding to $\delta = 1.3$ and $\delta = 0$, respectively.

18. The reader may be surprised by the fact that social welfare increases with high values of λ. This is because the telecommunications sector can be used for raising funds which are socially increasingly valuable. Note, however, that our social welfare function is

only a partial one, so it does not take into account the decrease of welfare elsewhere in the economy due to higher inefficiencies in the tax system.

19. For LT and BM the minimum is reached at a value of λ slightly greater than 1.

20. The situation is different in the high-elasticity case, where PCT outperforms $C + T$ for $\lambda \geq 0.4$.

21. If moving to incentive regulation is viewed as an institutional innovation, this empirical result confirms the ambiguity of the relative value of such innovations in LDCs compared to developed countries discussed in Laffont and Meleu (1999).

Chapter 8

1. Competition between those incumbents and entrants has by now been organized.

2. Another option under consideration in the United States consists of simultaneously introducing competition in low-cost areas and organizing universal service auctions for the subsidies needed in high-cost areas in order to obtain affordable prices. However, such auctions can be quite complex, and thus their good performance requires a great deal of regulatory expertise and depends crucially on how genuinely competitive the participants' behavior is.

3. In the case of duopoly, which will be the main focus of our analysis, q_{ij} will designate the output of firm j in area i as discussed below.

4. Although the focus of this chapter is to compare the performance of alternative competitive scenarios, for clarity of exposition it is useful to start from a monopoly framework. At this point the reader might find it useful to glance at figure 8.1 which depicts the generic market structures that we consider in the empirical analysis.

5. Since in our analysis the urban and rural subscribers' populations N_1 and N_2 are held constant, they appear as arguments of the various cost functions only when necessary.

6. Unless indicated otherwise, we assume that the entrant has the same technological efficiency parameter β as the incumbent.

7. For reference, the top panel of figure 8.1 shows a monopolistic situation.

8. Optimal effort equates marginal disutility and marginal cost saving.

9. Note that in the urban sector, it is the marginal cost of the entrant (firm 2) that imposes the price.

10. This interpretation of universal service may be oversimplifying to some extent the policy initiatives in developed and developing countries. For example, in the United States universal service is currently interpreted as the right to purchase a set of services (voice grade plus access to advanced services) at a benchmark price that does not necessarily equal the price of the low-cost urban area. However, in many countries universal service entails uniform pricing.

11. We designate by "balanced-budget" regulation a situation where the firm's participation constraint is binding without transfers from the regulator. Such a constraint means that revenues must recover production costs as well as the disutility of effort.

12. Our empirical analysis shows that in this case the (residual) average-cost function is actually consistently above the inverse demand function.

13. The subscript ac indicates that average-cost pricing is used.

14. An optimization is needed when (8.17) has several solutions in q_1.

15. Excise taxes on telecommunications services have been imposed in the United States at the federal level and by various state and local authorities. In the implementation of the 1996 Telecommunications Act, a universal service fund was funded through surcharges on revenues of all telecommunications carriers as defined in the Act.

16. This price-cap regulatory mechanism is discussed more fully in chapters 4 and 7.

17. Note that here we use a wider range of usage (up to $10\,CCS$ instead of $5.5\,CCS$) than in the previous chapters to account for the higher value of service (than under monopoly) that competition is supposed to bring to subscribers.

18. For all of the simulations we take as the base case a local exchange market consisting of 50,000 urban subscribers and 2,000 rural subscribers in a territory covering about 207 square miles.

19. For entry scenario UT we simulate the cost functions of both the incumbent and the (urban) entrant by adjusting the size of the city and its population to represent the territory served by each. The territory served by the entrant represents one-half of the urban territory formerly served by the monopolist with one-half of the monopolist's urban customers (and hence the same urban population density). The territory served by the incumbent represents the entire territory of the former monopolist, minus one-half of the urban area and therefore, with uniform density, one-half of the urban population. For the TC entry scenario, we assume that each duopolist served a territory having one-half of the area (urban and rural) and one-half of the population (urban and rural) of the former monopolist. All of these simulations were implemented by appropriately modifying the input files "populatn.dat" and "rectangl.dat" as explained in the LECOM documentation (Gabel and Kennet 1991).

20. In section 8.5 we examine the sensitivity of our results to the demand elasticities.

21. See tables A.3 through A.5 in appendix A at the end of the book for the raw data obtained in this empirical analysis.

22. From now on we will consider only scenarios that satisfy the universal service obligation, namely the obligation to serve the urban and rural areas at a uniform price.

23. As mentioned in section 8.2 we have found that a UT scenario in which the incumbent matches the entrant's price in the urban market and sets price equal to average residual cost in the rural market is not viable; that is, there is no rural price that allows the incumbent to break even.

24. We approximate this distortion in the usual fashion, namely as the area of the triangle formed by the demand and supply curves, that measures the "excess burden" of the tax. This is the amount that consumers and producers are willing to pay to avoid the tax.

25. While the phenomenon of corruption is not peculiar to developing countries, its quantitative importance (e.g., in terms of the percentage of GNP concerned by the phenomenon), its generalization to most of the sectors of the economy, and the fact that it is chronic make it a serious impediment to their economic and social development.

26. To be sure, the fact that there are no satisfactory accounting and auditing procedures in developing countries appropriately exacerbates the issue of asymmetric information.

27. We perform this comparison to take account of the fact that the UT solution is likely to be more competitive. It should make the most favorable case for the UT-type scenario in the relevant range of λ, and hence would reinforce the case for cross-subsidies if the TC solution turns out to be still the best. However, we require a rather efficient regulation in the TC solution (optimal price cap), one that might not be feasible in developing countries.

28. Note that because $\underline{UT}_{ac}^{ps}$ dominates UT_{ac}^{ps} in the relevant range of λ and TC_{ac} dominates $TCPC$, we find that as expected, $\lambda^{**} > \lambda^*$. Note also that a comparison of $TCPC$ with UT_{ac}^{ps} rather than $\underline{UT}_{ac}^{ps}$ yields a smaller critical value of λ (between 0.3 and 0.4).

29. In this figure we designate by the "tax-revenues drain factor" the proportion of tax revenues taken away from the universal service funding system.

30. In the case of very high elasticity in the urban market, a somewhat higher value of λ^{**} results that reflects the higher social cost of asymmetric information.

31. Gasmi et al. (2001) find an even more favorable case for cross-subsidies in densely populated developing countries.

Chapter 9

1. Under structural safeguards, local telephone companies are required to maintain a strict separation between the regulated and unregulated sectors of the company (see FCC 1971, 1980, 1999). The separation requirements include separate corporate structures, operating facilities, and physical locations. Information flow among divisions and joint marketing arrangements is also restricted. Accounting safeguards allow the firm to deploy labor and other inputs freely among divisions, but they impose cost allocation rules to separate the costs of the firm into regulated and unregulated sectors.

2. The expression given in (9.2) also allows for disutility to depend on output levels. The implications of this assumption in the context of optimal regulation under incomplete information were discussed in chapters 4 and 6.

3. The higher the fraction of costs born by a firm (i.e., the larger the costs for which it is accountable), the higher its incentives must be to minimize them. This fraction is referred to in the literature as the "power" of the underlying incentive scheme (see chapter 4 for more details).

4. These assumptions would be appropriate in situations where entrants make use of the incumbent's network through the purchase of unbundled network elements. In the United States, network elements are priced according to a TELRIC (total element long-run incremental cost) methodology, which is interpreted as incremental cost augmented by a "reasonable" contribution to common costs. Later in this section we consider an alternative model of facilities-based entry.

5. For any output level this disutility is the result of an implicit level of effort $\bar{e}$ that serves as an indicator of the general level of effort in the industry. For example, effort can be said to be "high," "medium," or "low."

6. Note that a positive Δ suggests that entry could potentially be blockaded.

7. In chapter 5 we analyzed the cost of access lines as a function of overall customer density, where the relative densities of the urban and rural sectors are held constant. In chapter 8 we look at cost functions for the urban and rural sectors individually.

8. With a total subscriber population of 100,000 spread over a city with a total area of about 57.5 square miles, the customer densities in our simulation are 1,006 subscribers per square mile of the residential district, 2,278 per square mile of the mixed district, and 7,260 per square mile of the business district. In the simulations, when the total subscriber population varies, the densities of the districts relative to each other are maintained constant.

9. The actual total numbers of access lines were 6,000, 12,000, 20,000, 40,000, 70,000, and 100,000.

10. More specifically, $PK, PL = 0.6, 0.8, 1.0, 1.2, 1.4$.

11. See below for more on the relationship between the theoretical cost functions and their empirical counterparts. The simulations produced data sets of 900 points. Because some of our cost functions require using zero as an argument, we fit our LECOM cost data to a functional form that is a second-degree polynomial of the appropriate variables rather than their natural logarithms as done in the previous chapters. The expression of the various cost functions used in this chapter is given in appendix A.

12. For clarity of exposition, we adopt here the convention of designating by $\tilde{C}$ the (LECOM-estimated) empirical counterpart of a generic theoretical cost function C.

13. Recall that in our analysis, there is a one-to-one correspondence between the set of values of PL and that of values of e. This correspondence is defined by the relation $e = 1.5 - PL$.

14. The combinations of output levels for these calculations are described in the next subsection.

15. This is true provided that the firm is regulated with a cost-plus type scheme.

16. In the notation of section 9.2 this measure is equal to $[(s(1) - s(0))/C] \times 100$.

17. The relative importance of these access line potential subsidies can be appreciated from table A.12 of appendix A where the values of average costs are provided for different values of outputs.

18. By allocating entirely the common costs to segment 1 ($\delta = 1$), the aim is to obtain the most significant effort allocation cross-subsidization effect.

19. Recall that the function $t(\alpha_2, \delta)$ measures the allocated cost of activity 1 given the common costs allocation parameter δ and the fraction α_2 of the incremental cost of activity 2 born by the incumbent.

20. We should note though that the nonmonotonicity of σ found when q_1 is fixed and q_2 varies does not occur in the case of τ.

21. Note that for the case of activity 1 which is competitive, high-powered regulation is implicit.

22. By perfect regulation we mean regulation with a high-powered scheme.

Chapter 10

1. We addressed these issues briefly in chapter 1 and in somewhat more detail in chapter 3, sections 3.2 and 3.3.

2. For example, relatively crude proxies must be used to account for the effects of technological change. A measure of managerial effort as required in our approach would be equally problematical.

3. LECOM was developed by Gabel and Kennet (1991); the model is described in detail in chapter 2. At that time Mark Kennet was not directly involved in the overall project other than lending valuable assistance in the use of LECOM. Although we were not then aware of it, a number of other computer-based cost proxy models of local telecommunications were simultaneously under development. LECOM, however, was the only publicly available model.

4. In other words, in this case the regulator's desire to minimize rents is not in conflict with the desire to price efficiently. Incomplete information requires a transfer under the optimal mechanism, but the mechanism does not require a distortion in pricing beyond that required by the Ramsey pricing rule.

5. In order to run a large number of simulations over an extended period of time, we created various batch files for automated operation of the model. The actual files used to generate each of the simulations for chapters 5 through 9 are provided in a CD attachment to this book.

6. None of the more recently available models include LECOM's capability of optimizing switch locations.

7. We note that even on the basis of initial cost, fiber is becoming increasingly competitive with copper plant.

8. An exception is our analysis of targeted entry in the universal service application, where we briefly assumed that the entrant possessed a superior technology to the incumbent. In addition in chapter 9 we considered the possibility that the entrant and incumbent might have incentives to choose different levels of effort.

Appendix A

1. In the cost functions presented here, with and without interconnection costs accounted for, most of the parameters are identical due to our rounding to the second decimal. However, in chapter 5, and other chapters of the book, we have carried out the calculations with a much higher precision.

2. Recall from the text our assumption that when the number of subscribers served by a firm varies, those subscribers are kept uniformly distributed over the LECOM density zones constituting a total area of approximately 57 square miles.

3. Again, the reader should keep in mind that the calculations appearing in the main text were carried out with a much higher precision than presented here.

4. The user needs only to quit the Mathematica kernel between chapters in order to eliminate any possibility of conflict.

Appendix B

1. The model platform selected in October 1998 consisted of the HCPM, an internally developed model of the feeder and distribution network, along with a model of the

switching and interoffice transport network developed by HAI Consulting in co-operation with AT&T and MCI. Input prices to calibrate the model were approved by the FCC in October 1999, and support payments were begun under the new mechanism in 2000. The model was approved for use only for large companies with more than 100,000 access lines. Smaller rural companies continue to be supported under an existing program based on embedded costs.

2. "An Analytical Cost Model for the National Core Network" prepared by Wissenschaftliches Institut für Kommunikationsdienste (WIK) Gmbtt. See also "An Analytical Cost Model for the Local Network." These reports are available on the RegTP Web site at *http://www.regtp.de*.

3. Our review of cost modeling approaches is not intended to be comprehensive. In particular, we do not review the so-called top-down modeling approaches that have been used by some regulatory bodies and consulting firms. A top-down model uses aggregate accounting data from incumbent telecommunications providers, with modifications that attempt to ensure that a forward-looking cost estimate is obtained. Such modifications might, for example, exclude accounting costs associated with maintenance of analog switching equipment. In contrast, a bottom-up modeling approach seeks to model all of the individual components of the network. There has been a lively debate among model proponents about the proper modeling technique to use for each intended application. Clearly, top-down models are prone to including costs that are not truly forward-looking, whereas bottom-up models are prone to miss certain hard-to-measure but legitimate costs that firms would encounter on a forward-looking basis.

4. See especially figure 2.2.

5. The Hatfield model was sponsored jointly by AT&T and MCI after MCI defected from the original BCM coalition. An earlier version of the Hatfield model was proposed that did not use the existing boundaries of wire centers, as all of the more recent proxy models other than LECOM have chosen to do.

6. At the equator a resulting grid cell is approximately 3,000 feet square, though the exact dimensions of cells depend on the distance from the equator. In most cases a grid cell is substantially smaller than a CBG.

7. The clustering algorithm used by HAI was rejected primarily because it was done in a preprocessing stage of the model, which raised concerns about the openness and accessibility of the data used. The HCPM loop design approach was chosen on the basis of some statistical analysis by FCC staff demonstrating that the HAI approach systematically underestimated the cost of providing service in very low-density areas and systematically overestimated the cost of providing service in high-density areas. See FCC platform order: Federal-State Joint Board on Universal Service, Fifth Report and Order, CC Docket Nos. 96-45, 97-160, 13 FCC Rcd 21323 (1998).

8. In the universal service adaptation of HCPM, a copper distance limit of 18,000 feet was assumed as a default based on evidence that this amount of copper plant was compatible with traditional voice grade service and an acceptable quality of digital service via modem. Alternative service qualities, such as the provision of ADSL services using copper plant, would require significantly shorter copper distance.

9. A minimum distance spanning tree algorithm minimizes the distance of the overall network. Since the costs of a telecommunications network depend both on distance

and the number of access lines carried on each link in the network (which affects cable and electronics costs), the HCPM algorithms take account of both distance and line related costs.

10. The HCPM incorporates a feature, first introduced by the BCM model, in which terrain factors are identified with the Census block in which each customer resides, and penalty weights are assigned for cost computations associated with difficult conditions. The terrain factors include minimum and maximum slope measurements, depth to bedrock, soil properties, and water table depth.

11. The group included Martin Rodriguez Pardina, Marcelo Celani, Daniel Benitez, and Christian Ruzzier.

12. The Portuguese team was under the leadership of Administrator Professor João Confraria and included Professor José Soares, Ana Margarida Amante, Rita Vala, and Luis Oliveira. Soares (1998) has also done independent research with LECOM in an effort to explore economies of scope and evaluate the magnitude of cross-subsidies between services in Portugal Telecom, comparing stand-alone costs of services with receipts obtained. Soares (1998) created a LECOM-style map of Lisboa by hand for his modeling work, and was able to utilize actual Portugal Telecom input values for LECOM cost parameters. Soares found that joint production of switched and leased lines in Lisboa is not a natural monopoly: It would be more efficient if leased lines were produced by one or two firms and switched by another. Furthermore leased lines produced jointly subsidize switched lines at then-current prices.

13. Although the fundamental design of the HCPM is set up to handle individual customer locations, there may exist trade-offs between accuracy and openness and/or availability of data. The model is capable of handling customer location data at almost any level of aggregation.

References

Armstrong, M. 1998. Network interconnection. *Economic Journal* 108: 545–64.

Averch, H., and L. L. Johnson. 1962. Behavior of the firm under regulatory constraint. *American Economic Review* 52: 1053–69.

Ballard, C., J. Shoven, and J. Whalley. 1985. General equilibrium computations of the marginal welfare costs of taxes in the United States. *American Economic Review* 75: 128–38.

Baron, D. 1989. Design of regulatory mechanisms and institutions. In R. Schmalensee and R. Willig, eds., *The Handbook of Industrial Organization*, vol. 2, Amsterdam: North Holland, pp. 1349–1447.

Baron, D., and R. Myerson. 1992. Regulating a monopolist with unknown costs. *Econometrica* 50: 911–30.

Baumol, W. J. 1977. On the proper cost tests for natural monopoly in a multiproduct industry. *American Economic Review* 67: 809–22.

Benitez, D. A., M. Celani, O. O. Chisari, M. A. Rodriguez Pardina, and C. A. Ruzzier. 1999. Minimizando los costos de las obligaciones de servicio universal en el sector de telecomunicaciones de Argentina a trarés de un modelo de costos. XII World Congress of the International Economic Association, August 1999, Buenos Aires, Argentina.

Benitez, D. A., A. Estache, D. M. Kennet, and C. Ruzzier. 2000. Are cost models useful for regulators in developing countries? World Bank mimeo.

Blackwell, D. 1951. Comparison of experiments. *Proceedings of the Second Berkeley Symposium on Mathematics, Statistics and Probability*. Berkeley: University of California Press, pp. 93–102.

Brock, G. W. 1981. *The Telecommunications Industry: The Dynamics of Market Structure*. Cambridge: Harvard University Press.

Bush, C. A., V. Gupta, D. M. Kennet, J. Prisbrey, and W. W. Sharkey. 1999. Computer modeling of the local telephone network. Federal Communications Commission Report, Washington, DC.

Charnes, A., W. W. Cooper, and T. Sueyoshi. 1988. A goal programming-constrained regression review of the Bell System breakup. *Management Science* 34: 1–26.

Chenery, H. B. 1949. Engineering production functions. *Quarterly Journal of Economics* 63: 507–31.

Christensen, L. R., D. W. Jorgenson, and L. J. Lau. 1973. Transcendental logarithmic production frontiers. *Review of Economics and Statistics* 55(1): 28–45.

Christensen, L. R., D. Cummings, and P. E. Schoech. 1981. Total factor productivity in the Bell System: 1947–79. Christensen Associates.

Christensen, L. R., D. Cummings, and P. E. Schoech. 1983. Econometric estimation of scale economies in telecommunications. In L. Courville, A. de Fontenay, and R. Dobell, eds., *Economic Analysis of Telecommunications: Theory and Applications*. Amsterdam: North Holland, pp. 27–53.

Crandall, R. W., and L. Waverman. 2000. Who pays for universal service? When telephone subsidies become transparent. Washington, DC: Brookings Institution Press.

Evans, D. S., and J. J. Heckman. 1983. Multiproduct cost function estimates and natural monopoly tests for the Bell System. In D. S. Evans, ed., *Breaking up Bell*. Amsterdam: North Holland, pp. 253–82.

Evans, D. S., and J. J. Heckman. 1984. A test for subadditivity of the cost function with an application to the Bell System. *American Economic Review* 74: 615–23.

Federal Communications Commission. *Statistics of the Communications Industry in the United States*. Washington, DC: Government Printing Office.

Federal Communications Commission. 1971. Regulatory and policy problems presented by the interdependence of computer and communications services and facilities. Final Decision and Order. 28 F.C.C. 2d 267 (Computer I).

Federal Communications Commission. 1980. Amendment of section 64.702 of the commission's rules and regulations (Second Computer Inquiry). Final Decision. 77 F.C.C. 2d 384 (Computer II).

Federal Communications Commission. 1999. Computer III remand proceedings: Bell Operating Company provision of enhanced services. CC Docket No. 95-20, CC Docket No. 98-10. Report and Order, 7 (Computer III).

Feinstein, J. S., and F. A. Wolak. 1991. The econometric implications of incentive compatible regulation. In G. Rhodes and T. Fomby, eds., *Advances in Econometrics: Econometric Methods and Models for Industrial Organization*. Greenwich, CT: JAI Press, pp. 225–54.

Flamm, K. 1989. Technological advance and costs: Computers versus communications. *Changing the Rules: Technological Change, International Competition, and Regulation in Communications*. Washington, DC: Brookings Institution.

Førsund, F. R. 1995. Engineering productions functions: Chocolate production revisited. Mimeo, Department of Economics, University of Oslo.

Freidenfelds, J. 1978. A simple model for studying feeder capacity expansion. *Bell System Technical Journal* 57: 807–24.

Frisch, R. 1935. The principle of substitution: An example of its application in the chocolate industry. *Nordisk Tidsskrift for Teknisk Okonomi* 1:1, 12–27.

Fuss, M., and L. Waverman. 1978. Multi-product, multi-input cost functions for a regulated utility: The case of telecommunications in Canada. Working Paper 7810. Institute for Policy Analysis, University of Toronto.

Gabel, D., and D. M. Kennet. 1991. Estimating the cost structure of the local telephone exchange network. Report 91-16. National Regulatory Research Institute, Colombus, OH.

Gabel, D., and D. M. Kennet. 1994. Economies of scope in the local exchange market. *Journal of Regulatory Economics* 6: 381–98.

Gasmi, F., M. Ivaldi, and J. J. Laffont. 1994. Rent extraction and incentives for efficiency in recent regulatory proposals. *Journal of Regulatory Economics* 6: 151–76.

Gasmi, F., J. J. Laffont, and W. W. Sharkey. 1997. Incentive regulation and the cost structure of the local telephone exchange network. *Journal of Regulatory Economics* 12: 5–25.

Gasmi, F., J. J. Laffont, and W. W. Sharkey. 1999a. Empirical evaluation of regulatory regimes in local telecommunications markets. *Journal of Economics and Management Strategy* 8: 61–93.

Gasmi, F., J. J. Laffont, and W. W. Sharkey. 1999b. Competition, universal service and telecommunications policy in developing countries. *Information Economics and Policy* 12(3): 221–48.

Gasmi, F., J. J. Laffont, and W. W. Sharkey. 1999c. The natural monopoly test reconsidered: An engineering process-based approach to empirical analysis in telecommunications. *International Journal of Industrial Organization* 20(4): 435–59.

Gasmi, F., J. J. Laffont, and W. W. Sharkey. 2001. Provision of universal service for telecommunications in densely populated developing countries. In *Telecommunications Reform in India*. Greenwood.

Gasmi, F., J. J. Laffont, and Q. Vuong. 1992. Econometric analysis of collusive behavior in a soft-drink market. *Journal of Economics and Management Strategy* 1(2): 277–311.

Gibbard, A. 1973. Manipulation of voting schemes: A general result. *Econometrica* 41: 587–601.

Green, J., and J. J. Laffont. 1977. Characterization of satisfactory mechanisms for the revelation of preferences for public goods. *Econometrica* 45: 427–38.

Green, J., and J. J. Laffont. 1979. *Incentives in Public Decision Making*. Amsterdam: North-Holland.

Greene, W. H. 2000. *Econometric Analysis*. Paramus, NJ: Prentice-Hall.

Griffin, J. M. 1972. The process analysis alternative to statistical cost functions. *American Economic Review* 62: 46–56.

Griffin, J. M. 1977. The econometrics of joint production: Another approach. *Bell Journal of Economics* 8: 112–27.

Griffin, J. M. 1977. Long-run production modeling with pseudo data: Electric power generation. *Bell Journal of Economics* 8: 112–27.

Hausman, J., and J. Poterba. 1987. Household behavior and the Tax Reform Act of 1986. *Journal of Economic Perspectives* 1: 101–19.

Hurwicz, L. 1960. Optimality and informational efficiency in resource allocation process. In K. J. Arrow, S. Karlin, and P. Suppes, eds., *Mathematical Methods in the Social Sciences*, Stanford University Press.

Kahn, A. E. 1970. *The Economics of Regulation: Principles and Institutions*, vols. 1 and 2. New York: Wiley.

Laffont, J. J. 1994. The new economics of regulation ten years after. *Econometrica* 62: 507–37.

Laffont, J. J. 1996. Industrial policy and politics. *International Journal of Industrial Organization* 14: 1–27.

Laffont, J. J., and M. Matoussi. 1995. Moral hazard, financial constraints and sharecropping in El Oulja. *Review of Economic Studies* 62: 381–99.

Laffont, J. J., and M. Meleu. 1999. Separation of powers and development. *Journal of Economic Development* 64: 129–45.

Laffont, J. J., H. Ossard, and Q. Vuong. 1995. Econometrics of first-price auctions. *Econometrica* 63: 953–80.

Laffont, J. J., P. Rey, and J. Tirole. 1998a. Network competition: I. Overview and non-discrimination pricing. *Rand Journal of Economics* 29: 1–37.

Laffont, J. J., P. Rey, and J. Tirole. 1998b. Network competition: II. Price discrimination. *Rand Journal of Economics* 29: 38–56.

Laffont, J. J., and J. Tirole. 1986. Using cost information to regulate firms. *Journal of Political Economy* 94: 1–49.

Laffont, J. J., and J. Tirole. 1993. *A Theory of Incentives in Procurement and Regulation*. Cambridge: MIT Press.

Laffont, J. J., and J. Tirole. 2000. *Competition in Telecommunications*. Cambridge: MIT Press.

Legette III, J. A. 1985. Natural monopoly in the telecommunication industry: The case of local service. Unpublished Ph.D. dissertation, University of South Carolina.

Littlechild, S. C. 1983. Regulation of British Telecom's profitability. Report to the Secretary of State, Department of Industry, London.

Loeb, M., and W. Magat. 1979. A decentralized method of utility regulation. *Journal of Law and Economics* 22: 399–404.

Maher, M. E. 1999. Access costs and entry in the local telecommunications network: A case for de-averaged rates. *International Journal of Industrial Organization* 17: 593–609.

Manne, A. 1958. A linear programming model of the U.S. petroleum refining industry. *Econometrica* 26: 67–106.

Mitchell, B. M. 1990. Incremental costs of telephone access and local use. Rand Report R-3909–ICTF. Rand Corp., Santa Monica, CA.

Mundlak, Y. 1978. On the pooling of time series and cross section data. *Econometrica* 46: 69–85.

Myerson, R. 1979. Incentive compatibility and the bargaining problem. *Econometrica* 47: 61–74.

Myerson, R. 1981. Optimal auction design. *Mathematics of Operations Research* 6: 58–73.

National Telecommunication and Information Administration, 1988. *NTIA Telecom 2000: Charting the Course for A New Century*. Washington, DC: US Department of Commerce.

Nelder, J., A. and R. Mead. 1965. A simplex method for function minimization. *Computer Journal* 7: 308–13.

New England Telephone. 1986. Massachusetts Incremental Cost Study. Massachusetts Department of Public Utilities Docket, 86-33.

Palmer, K. 1992. A test for cross subsidies in local telephone rates: Do business customers subsidize residential customers? *Rand Journal of Economics* 23(3): 415–30.

Panzar, J. C. 1989. Technological determinants of firm and industry structure. In R. Schmalensee and R. Willig, eds., *Handbook of Industrial Organization*, vol. 1. Amsterdam: Elsevier Science, pp. 3–59.

Press, W. H., B. P. Flannery, S. A. Jeukolsky, and W. T. Vetterling. 1986. *Numerical Recipes: The Art of Scientific Computing*. Cambridge: Cambridge University Press.

Rey, R. F., ed., 1984. *Engineering and Operations in the Bell System*. AT&T Bell Laboratories, Murray Hill, NJ.

Schmalensee, R. 1989. Good regulatory regimes. *Rand Journal of Economics* 20: 417–36.

Sharkey, W. W. 1982. *The Theory of Natural Monopoly*. Cambridge: Cambridge University Press.

Sharkey, W. W. 2001. Representation of technology and production. In M. Cave, S. Majumdar, and I. Vogelsang, eds., *Handbook of Telecommunications Economics*. Amsterdam: Elsevier Science, ch. 6.

Shin, R. T., and J. S. Ying. 1992. Unnatural monopolies in local telephone. *Rand Journal of Economics* 23(2): 171–83.

Shleifer, A. 1985. A theory of yardstick competition. *Rand Journal of Economics* 16: 319–27.

Smith, V. L. 1957. Engineering data and statistical techniques in the analysis of production and technological change: Fuel requirements in the trucking industry. *Econometrica* 25: 281–301.

Soares, J. F. 1998. *Teoria e práctica de subsidião cruzada—Aplicação a uma rede local de telecomunicaes Portuguesa* (Theory and practice of cross-subsidy—Application to a Portuguese local telecommunications network). Unpublished Ph.D. dissertation. Instituto Superior de Economia e Gesto da Universidade Técnica de Lisboa.

Taylor, L. D. 1994. *Telecommunications Demand in Theory and Practice*. Norwood, MA: Kluwer Academic.

Temin, P. 1990. Cross-subsidies in the telephone network after divestiture. *Journal of Regulatory Economics* 2: 349–62.

Varian, H. 1992. *Microeconomic Analysis*. New York: Norton.

von Weizsäcker, C. C. 1980. A welfare analysis of barriers to entry. *Bell Journal of Economics* 11(2): 399–420.

Wimmer, B., and G. L. Rosston. 2000. The "State" of universal service. *Information Economics and Policy* 12(3): 261–83.

Wimmer, B., and G. L. Rosston. 2000. Winners and losers from the universal service subsidy battle. In B. Compaine and I. Vogelsang, eds., *The Internet Upheaval, Raising Questions, Seeking Answers in Communications Policy: Selected Papers from the Telecommunications Policy Research Conference*. Cambridge: MIT Press, pp. 387–412.

Wimmer, B., and G. L. Rosston. 2000. From C-to-shining-C: Competition and cross subsidy in telecommunications. In B. Compaine and S. Greenstein, eds., *Selected Papers from the Telecommunications Policy Research Conference*. Cambridge: MIT Press.

Wolak, F. A. 1994. An econometric analysis of the asymmetric information, regulator-utility interaction. *Annales d'Economie et de Statistique* 34: 13–69.

Wilson, R. 1989. Efficient and competitive rationing. *Econometrica* 57: 1–40.

Wunsch, P. 1994. Estimating menus of linear contracts for mass transit firms. Mimeo. CORE, Louvain-La-Neuve, Belgium.

Index